# THE HANOVERIANS

# DYNASTIES

*General Editor: Nigel Saul*

# The Hanoverians

## *The History of a Dynasty*

Jeremy Black

Hambledon and London
London and New York

Hambledon and London

102 Gloucester Avenue
London, NW1 8HX

175 Fifth Avenue
New York, NY 10010
USA

First Published 2004

ISBN 1 85285 446 4

A description of this book is available from the
British Library and from the Library of Congress.

Typeset by Carnegie Publishing, Lancaster,
And printed in Great Britain by Cambridge University Press.

Distributed in the United States and Canada
exclusively by Palgrave Macmillan,
A division of St Martin's Press.

# Contents

# Illustrations

*For*
*Kenneth Baker*

# *Preface*

'Human beings caught in exceptional circumstances', J. H. Plumb's description of the first four Georges is a good point of departure for a statement of intent. The danger of any book on a royal dynasty is that it degenerates into little more than a narrative of the period centred on the Kings and Queens. That is not my intention, not least because I have already published a history of eighteenth-century Britain. Instead, I want to evaluate the monarchy in this period. To do so entails focusing on the monarchs, and, for that, I offer no apology. Far from being a series of odd, marginal figures, they were centrally located in British and European history. Although the recent re-evaluation of royal consorts in this period is welcome, and there is interesting work on royal children, my stress is on the Kings.

The impact on the British monarchy of the house of Hanover is a subject that requires emphasis, not least because of the importance of the practice of political compromise that developed. In addition, the history of the Hanoverians indicates the importance of foreign policy, the area that interested certainly Georges I and George II most strongly. It is no accident that the best biography of a member of this dynasty, Ragnhild Hatton's *George I* (1978), was both by an expert on foreign policy and by a scholar with a continental background. There is no comparable work on George II, and, indeed, the King has been generally neglected, and still lacks a scholarly biography. While Mijndert Bertram's *Georg II. König und Kurfürst* (Göttingen, 2003) is very useful, especially for his life before he came to Britain in 1714, it is short and entirely based on published material. The longest reigning of the monarchs, George III, lacks a good recent biography, although Grayson Ditchfield's *George III: An Essay in Monarchy* (2002) has much to offer. In contrast, E. A. Smith's *George IV* (1999) eminently fits the bill as a biography. Peter Jupp is working on a major life of William IV.

If this helps to explain the balance of this book, it does not address the central issue, which is a consideration of the political position of the monarch. This shows how the dynamic interaction of monarchy and country changed. It is also important to consider why the Hanoverian personal union of Britain and Hanover from 1714 until 1837 was more successful than the earlier Stuart one of England and Scotland. Seeing the strengths and weaknesses of the dynasty as a whole provides a real addition to the general understanding of the period. At the same time, it is important not to treat the Kings as bloodless political agents, nor to forget the uneasy coexistence of royal majesty and a public world that was far from the self-image of politeness for which we so often remember the age. The coronation of George II, on 11 October (os) 1727, saw the soaring drama of Handel's *Coronation Anthems* but also, at the close, the confusion noted by César de Saussure that suggested an unruliness just kept at bay:

> the big doors were thrown open and the crowd allowed to enter and take possession of the remains of the feast, of the table linen, of the plates and dishes, and of everything that was on the table. The pillage was most diverting; people threw themselves with extraordinary avidity on everything that hall contained; blows were given and returned, and I cannot give you any idea of the noise and confusion that reigned. In less than half an hour everything had disappeared, even the boards of which the table and seats had been made.[1]

The court itself was far from the literary ideal of politeness, and indeed, among the monarchs, only George III really matched this standard. Thus, in 1717, George I felt able to use the standard pun of mounting women and horses when 'Mr de Johnston' presented his much younger wife.[2] George told him that if he 'connoissoit aussi bien en cheveaux qu'en femmes il ne pourroit manquer d'etre bien monté'.[3]

I have a number of debts that I am happy to acknowledge. The British Academy, the German Academic Exchange Scheme and the Wolfson Foundation provided valuable support on archival research trips. Material from the Royal Archives is cited by permission of Her Majesty Queen Elizabeth. I would like to thank the Duke of Bedford, the Marquess of Bute, Earl Fitzwilliam and the Wentworth Woodhouse Trustees, the late Earl of Harrowby and the Trustees of the Harrowby

MSS Trust, the Earl of Elgin, the Earl of Malmesbury, the late Earl Waldegrave, Lady Lucas and John Weston-Underwood for permission to consult their collections of manuscripts. I am grateful to the National Portrait Gallery for permission to reproduce the illustrations. I would also like to record my thanks for the hospitality of Hilmar Brückner, Gerhard Menk and Armin Reese on German archival trips, as well as to Leopold Auer for assistance in Vienna, and to note the inspiration of Tim Blanning's special subject many years ago.

I am most grateful to Bill Gibson and Grayson Ditchfield for their comments on an earlier draft. Although not widely known to the general history-reading public, they are two of the finest scholars working on the period and I am fortunate to have their advice and encouragement. Neither is responsible for any errors that remain. Mijndert Bertram also provided a useful reading of the text, while John Derry, David Flaten and Richard Gaunt made helpful comments on particular chapters and David Baldwin and Peter Wilson on specific points. Martin Sheppard proved an exemplary editor, improving the text by a close reading and offering valuable advice.

It is a great pleasure to dedicate this book to Kenneth Baker. He and I worked together for many years on a fascinating, albeit unsuccessful, attempt to launch a Museum of British History. During and since that period, I have much enjoyed Kenneth's company, and his jovial and generous hospitality, have been grateful for his encouragement of my work, and have greatly admired his commitment to making British history accessible, not least through his support for the history of British caricatures. Kenneth has a particular interest in, and knowledge of, the Hanoverians, and I am delighted that he is happy to accept this dedication.

# Abbreviations

| | |
|---|---|
| 152M | Exeter, Devon Record Office, Addington (Sidmouth) papers |
| Add | Additional Manuscripts |
| AE. | Paris, Ministère des Relations Extérieures |
| Ang. | Angleterre |
| Aspinall, George III | A. Aspinall (ed.), *The Later Correspondence of George III* |
| AST. LM. Ing. | Turin, Archivio di Stato, Lettere Ministri, Inghilterra |
| BL | London, British Library |
| Bod | Oxford, Bodleian Library, Department of Western Manuscripts |
| Cobbett | W. Cobbett (ed.), *Cobbett's Parliamentary History of England ... 1066 to ... 1803* (36 vols, 1806–20) |
| CP | Correspondance Politique |
| CRO | County Record Office |
| Darmstadt | Darmstadt, Staatsarchiv, Gräflich Görtzisches Archiv, F23 |
| EK | Englische Korrespondenz |
| Hanover | Hanover, Niedersachsisches Hauptstaatsarchiv |
| HL | San Marino, California, Huntington Library |
| HHStA | Vienna, Haus-, Hof-, und Staatsarchiv, Staatskanzlei |
| HMC | Historical Manuscripts Commission |
| HP | London, History of Parliament, Transcripts |
| MD | Mémoires et Documents |

Munich        Munich, Bayerisches Haupststaatsarchiv, Gesandtschaf-
              ten

NAS           Edinburgh, National Archives of Scotland

*Polit. Corr.*  R. Köser (ed.), *Politische Correspondenz Friedrichs des
              Grossen* (46 vols, Berlin, 1879–1939)

PRO           London, Public Record Office, now known as National
              Archives

RA            Windsor Castle, Royal Archives

SP            State Papers

WW            Sheffield, Archives, Wentworth Woodhouse muniments

Unless otherwise stated, all dates are new style. Old style dates are marked (os). Dates after monarchs are their regnal dates rather than their dates of birth and death. Unless otherwise stated, all books are published in London.

# 1

# The House of Hanover

'I never saw anybody in such glee as the King was this day at the Levee which was much crowded; he complimented the Duke of Argyll upon the behaviour of the Argyllshire men.'

John Maule MP, 24 April (os) 1746, on the response at court to the battle of Culloden.[1]

The accession of a new dynasty to the British throne in 1714 was the product of three Stuart failures. First, there was a failure of politics. In 1688–89, in what, to its supporters, was known as the Glorious Revolution (but, to its opponents, was a usurpation), James II of England and VII of Scotland (1685–88) had lost his kingdoms and crowns to his nephew and son-in-law, William III of Orange. The second failure was dynastic. William, who ruled from 1689 until 1701, and his wife and co-ruler, Mary II (James's elder daughter by his first and Protestant marriage), who died in 1694, had no children. Their successor, James's younger daughter by his first and Protestant marriage, Anne (1702–14), had many children from her marriage to Prince George of Denmark, but none survived to adulthood. The most long-lived, William, Duke of Gloucester, died in 1701. Thirdly, the Jacobites, followers of the exiled Stuarts, were unable to seize control of events when Anne died in 1714.

As a result of the death of Gloucester in 1701, the issue of the succession, which had been pushed to the fore when James II and VII was driven from the throne, became even more acute. To exclude from the throne both his son, known variously as the 'warming pan baby' or James III and VIII, another Catholic, who, in 1701, succeeded to the Jacobite claim, and a large number of individuals with better claims than the Hanoverians, but all of whom were Catholic, the Westminster Parliament in 1701 passed the Act of Settlement, which, instead, provided for the succession of the Electoral house of Hanover. The house of Hanover's claim to the English and Scottish thrones derived from James VI and I's daughter, Elizabeth (1596–1662), who had in 1613 married Frederick V (1596–1632), Elector Palatine, a Calvinist stalwart of the Protestant cause in Germany, and the short-lived King of Bohemia in the early stages of the Thirty Years War, as a result of which Elizabeth was known as the 'Winter Queen'. Elizabeth's youngest daughter, Sophia (1630–1714), had married Ernst August of the North German Protestant princely house of Brunswick-Lüneburg (1629–98) in 1658. The future King George I was the eldest of their large family of six boys and one girl.

Ernst August and his brothers, whose joint inheritance shaped the duchy of Hanover, which in 1692 became one of the electorates of the Holy Roman Empire (the Princes of the Empire who elected the Emperor), did not know much about Britain. Nor did many of their British subjects like them, an attitude that did not change for many after the accession of the new dynasty; although their new subjects did care what they did. Much modern scholarship is indifferent to the Hanoverians; in part because these Kings did not dominate their age, as their Stuart and Tudor predecessors had done. Yet, although this scarcely fits with our general image of them, the Hanoverian Kings were among the most successful monarchs in British history, and certainly an obvious, if not a shining, contrast to the failed Stuarts.

There is no denying that at times, under all four Georges (although not William IV) the Hanoverians were extremely unpopular. They were also not the most competent of monarchs. The British monarchy lost a significant portion of its subjects thanks to the War of American Independence (1775–83), the cause of which owed much to George III's unpopular and unsuccessful role as the last King of the North American colonies. Under the same ruler, Hanover was conquered and lost to French control from 1803 until 1813.

Yet these Kings were also successful. First, they were so in a dynastic sense. The succession was maintained in the Hanoverian line, and there was no repetition in Britain either of the republican episode of 1649–60 that followed the execution of Charles I, or of the monarchical coup of 1688–89. Indeed, republicanism was only successful in North America, and then it was entered into reluctantly in 1776, only being achieved after a war that was as much the First American Civil War as a war of independence against Britain. Compared to the political world of 1678–89 – when Charles II and then James II and VII had faced the Popish Plot, the Exclusion Crisis, the Monmouth Rising and the Glorious Revolution – the situation, at least in England, after the defeat of the Jacobite rising in 1715 and the consolidation, with George I's support, of Whig hegemony between 1716 and 1722, was less volatile. Yet, the fundamental stability of the system was still challenged by the existence of a Stuart claim to the throne; as indeed was Britain's international position.

Hanoverian dynastic success in Britain was a major achievement, but not due to the strength of any threat from republicanism. Instead, it was because the Glorious Revolution of 1688–89 had created a fundamental schism of loyalty in Britain, with the Jacobite movement becoming a legitimist threat to Protestant parliamentary monarchy. This threat revived from 1714, after George I succeeded Anne, the last of the Stuarts to reign, and remained serious until crushed on the battlefield at Culloden in 1746. The extent of Jacobite support is a controversial topic among historians, but numerical support had not decided matters in 1688 or 1714.

A dynastic history of Britain should include the Stuart claimants: James II and VII from 1689; his son by his second marriage, 'James III and VIII', from 1701; and the latter's sons, Charles Edward Stuart ('Charles III' from 1766), and Cardinal Henry, Duke of York ('Henry IX', from 1788). It was a sign of the resolution of the crisis that George III, who was referred to by Henry as the Elector of Hanover, took steps both to support Henry, who had been hit hard by the French invasion of Italy, with a pension from 1800 until his death in 1807, and to purchase the Stuart papers. In addition, George IV in part supported the cost of the monument in St Peter's by Antonio Canova to 'James III and VIII', 'Charles III' and 'Henry IX' commissioned by Pope Pius VII. This was also an aspect of the closer relations between the British Crown and the Catholic Church that was a result of the French Revolution.[2]

Earlier, in a very different world, two rival Princes had competed on Culloden Moor in 1746: Charles Edward Stuart, Bonnie Prince Charlie, the heir to the Jacobite cause, and George II's second and favourite son, William, Duke of Cumberland (1721–1765). Thus, in the crisis of the Hanoverian state and monarchy, the royal family played a vital role.

The major new fort at Arderseer Point near Inverness, built after Culloden in order to help prevent an invasion of Scotland via the Moray
Firth, was appropriately named Fort George. Cumberland was an active
general, more akin (although less successful) among the royal generals
of the 1740s to his first cousin, Frederick II (the Great) of Prussia
(1740–86), than to another royal military leader, Louis XV of France
(1715–74).

The remainder of Charles Edward's life was a disappointment – a
collapse of support in Britain, abandonment by foreign backers, and
increasing drunkenness and purposelessness – that reflected the cost of
defeat. Even Pope Clement XIII refused to recognise him as King after
his father died in 1766, referring to him instead as the Count of Albany.
The Stuarts also failed as a dynasty: Charles Edward's disastrous marriage
in 1772 to Princess Louise of Stolberg-Gedern, who left him in 1780, was
childless, and he left only illegitimate children; while Henry, a cleric,
who succeeded to the Jacobite claim in 1788, did not marry.

In contrast, the Hanoverians, until George IV, maintained a succession
in the direct line, while ensuring sufficient cadet lines. They also were
able to marry well. The need to choose Protestant spouses ensured that
the most prestigious dynastic prizes were outside their range: they could
not marry with the Habsburgs, the Bourbons or the Wittelsbachs, and
the conversion of the Wettins of Saxony to Catholicism further reduced
their options. As a result, the House of Hanover could not repeat its
dynastic success in gaining Britain by advancing claims when the Habsburg dynasty came to an end in the male line in 1740, or when the
Bavarian branch of the Wittelsbachs did the same in 1777. Nor was a
member of the House of Hanover able to stand for election as King of
Poland when the position fell vacant in 1696, 1733 and 1763, for that was
also a Catholic state. Instead, the Wettins held the crown of Poland
from 1697 until 1763.

Nevertheless, within the parameters of Protestant Europe, the house
of Hanover did well. A double marriage scheme with Prussia – the heirs
of Prussia and Britain to marry a princess of the other house, actively
pursued in the 1720s and early 1730s, failed totally, with serious political
results during the reign of Frederick William I of Prussia (1713–40).
However, George II was able to marry three of his five daughters into
European ruling houses. His eldest daughter, Anne, the Princess Royal,

married William IV of Orange in 1734. The House of Orange was the closest the Dutch came to a royal house, and one that the Stuarts had twice been happy to marry royal daughters into. Amelia and Caroline never married, but Mary, the fourth daughter, married Frederick of Hesse-Cassel in 1740. Hesse-Cassel was one of the leading German Protestant states, and Frederick's father was Frederick I of Sweden, so the marriage was a prestigious one. It proved disastrous, however, and the spouses separated. Louisa, the next daughter, married in 1743 the heir to the Danish crown, later Frederick V.

The association of the Stuarts with Catholicism, autocracy and France helped bolster the popularity of the Hanoverian dynasty, especially in 1744–59 when France and Jacobitism were closely linked in a series of invasion schemes during first the War of the Austrian Succession and then the Seven Years War. This led to an upsurge of loyalism, as the royal family was seen as central to the Protestant establishment, and there was a conscious echo, in their defence of it, of William III's role as royal warrior in 1688–90 in securing this establishment by expelling James II and VII from the three kingdoms. In response to the French invasion attempt in March 1744, a scheme thwarted by a serious storm in the Channel, Lancelot Allgood, a Northumberland landowner, wrote to the Lord Lieutenant, the Earl of Tankerville:

> Your Lordship may be assured that the gentlemen, clergy and freeholders in this part of our county retain a just impression in their minds of the fatal consequences of any invasion or rebellion, wherefore His Majesty may be fully satisfied of our inviolable attachment to his sacred person and government.[3]

Richard Tucker reported government propaganda in action in the shape of the charge to the grand inquest in Dorset given by the judge, who dwelt on the dangerous consequences if 'James III and VIII' became King: 'as the family have been supported and bred up at the charity of France and nursed in the politics of that country they will be under such obligations there that this nation must become a province of France'.[4]

The following year there was an even greater upsurge in anxious loyalism, as Charles Edward's success in Scotland led to fears that George II would be overthrown. On 22 October (os) 1745, Richard Finch, a

London tradesman, in a letter that reiterated the theme of loyalty to crown and constitution, claimed that

> A native of London who went abroad before this rebellion began and knew the discontents of the people before would scarce credit the zeal, affection and loyalty, which appears everywhere all over the nation, on behalf of the King, and the Protestant religion; to the degree that smaller matters seen to be cancelled; the newspapers every day full of pathetic incitements to fight for our King and our liberties ... Our most gracious King and our excellent constitution were never so greatly the love and delight of all ranks and orders of men as at this time.[5]

In practice, the response across the country was far more varied, which helped to explain the determination shown by the dynasty's supporters to obtain support. This significantly focused on opposition to 'James III and VIII', particularly to his Catholicism, rather than on the virtues and value of George II. There were also more prosaic reasons for being pro-Hanoverian, not least the fear that a Jacobite restoration would lead to the annulment of the National Debt.

After Culloden in 1746, the Hanoverian monarchy was stronger and its legitimacy largely unchallenged. The crisis with the Thirteen Colonies, which became the kernel of the United States of America, did not lead to comparable problems in Britain, although there was an invasion scare in 1779, the Gordon Riots in 1780, and a serious crisis in Ireland. In contrast, from the early 1790s, the example of Revolutionary France helped to encourage radicalism within the British Isles, most dangerously in Ireland, where there was a rebellion in 1798. Yet, again, this was a challenge that monarchy and state surmounted. Just as parliamentary unions – of England (and Wales) with Scotland in 1707 and with Ireland in 1801 – reflected the crises of those periods but also produced a more unitary state, so, in some measure, the monarchy likewise benefited from challenges.

Even before the French Revolution helped to produce a rallying of the social elite and of much opinion around country, crown, and church in the 1790s, contrasts had already been drawn with France, *Berrow's Worcester Journal* of 14 August 1788 claiming

> While anarchy and confusion pervade the French dominions; and the irritated subjects of Louis seem ripe for rebellion, the King of Great Britain

and his family are enjoying a pleasing relaxation amongst their subjects, all of whom, from the peasant to the peer, give the most ample testimony of their fidelity and attachment.

The monarchy, in the person of George III, served as a potent symbol of national identity and continuity. The execution of Louis XVI of France in January 1793 led to a powerful reiteration of monarchical ideology in Britain, becoming part of the process by which the British were differentiated from the French. As opposed to in the past, Catholicism itself was now on the side of the Hanoverians. In 1791 Cardinal Antonelli, the Prefect of the Congregation for the Propagation of the Faith, who had authority over the Irish Catholic Church, instructed the four archbishops there on the religious duty of obedience to the government of George III, and, in 1792, Pope Pius VI sought British assistance in deterring the threat of French attack. English Catholics also showed strong loyalty to George III.

On 30 January 1793 Samuel Horsley, the Anglican Bishop of St David's, a supporter of the ministry of William Pitt the Younger, gave the annual Martyrdom Day sermon in Westminster Abbey before the House of Lords. This marked the anniversary of the execution in 1649 by a republican regime of Charles I, the individual elevated most closely to sainthood by the Church of England. In the first half of the eighteenth century, 30 January had served to mark the Jacobite challenge to the legitimacy of Hanoverian rule and had often been a focus for discontent and riots, although the Catholicism of the Jacobites made it difficult for them to invoke the cult of Charles I. In 1793, in contrast, the day served to affirm not the Stuart house but the institution of monarchy itself. Horsley delivered a powerful attack on political speculation and revolutionary theory, in which he stressed royal authority. According to Horsley, the existing constitution was the product and safeguard of a 'legal contract' between crown and people, while the obedience of the latter was a religious duty. Horsley's forceful peroration linked the two executions:

> This foul murder, and these barbarities, have filled the measure of the guilt and infamy of France. O my Country! Read the horror of thy own deed in this recent heightened imitation! Lament and weep, that this black French treason should have found its example, in the crime of thy unnatural sons!

The congregation rose to its feet in approval. Indeed, once atheistic

France had been identified with Antichrist, Horsley could see Catholics as allies.[6]

If the fate of religion and monarchy in Britain seemed clearly challenged by developments in France, that, however, did not mean that all rallied to the cause of Kings, for the execution of Louis XVI also helped focus the interest of British radicals on the position of the King.[7] Treasonous plotters in Britain were less interested in killing George than in detaining and re-educating him, in the hopes of some, to act as the King in a revolutionary democracy.[8] This was an aspect of the widespread extent to which allegiance and national identity were still manifested in dynastic terms.[9]

Indeed, between 1788 and 1815, the monarchy played a greater role in political ideology than it had done between 1689 and 1746. In the earlier period, an emphasis on monarchy had been compromised by serious differences over the legitimacy of the dynasty, as well as the contentious nature of constitutional arrangements after 1688. No such problems hindered a stress on monarchy on the part of conservative elements from the 1790s. Whatever the failings and foibles of individual members of the royal family the role of the monarchy was one that conservatives could support.

This was an important part of the success of the Hanoverian monarchy, but the course of the French Revolutionary and Napoleonic Wars was also significant. The royal family did not win personal glory in these conflicts, nor did they take as prominent a role in campaigning as William III had done in Ireland and the Low Countries in the 1690s, or as George II at the battle of Dettingen in 1743 and his son, William, Duke of Cumberland, in Scotland and the Low Countries in 1744–48 had done. As young men, neither Frederick Prince of Wales nor George III were trained for war or given opportunities to serve, although in the early 1770s George chose to have himself painted wearing uniform. He also visited the fleet, in 1773, 1778 and 1789, and during his visit to Weymouth in 1794 spent many happy hours on board warships. In 1774, the addition of a Marine Gallery to Queen's House helped associate George with the country's naval glory.

Other members of the royal family also failed to win personal military glory. George III's brother Edward, Duke of York (1739–67), had begun a military apprenticeship during the Seven Years War, but did not pursue it in peacetime, and died before the War of American Independence. Another brother, William, Duke of Gloucester (1743–1805), was considered for the post of Commander-in-Chief of the army during the latter conflict, but was not appointed. Of another brother, Henry, Duke of Cumberland (1745–1790), it was written 'the country has lost a most able admiral; and the King a most affectionate brother: although there are those who think he was never equal to the command of a canoe; and that he deserted his brother in the hours of misery and misfortune'.[10] The 1799 landing in Holland under George III's second son, Frederick, Duke of York (now best remembered in the nursery rhyme for marching troops up and down a hill), ended in failure. Despite the heroic manner of his portrait by John Hoppner, York's command of the British force in the Low Countries in 1793–94 was also unsuccessful, and ended with the government, against George's wishes, insisting on his recall.

Nevertheless, York played a significant role in modernising the army: a role that should be remembered in considering not only the sons of George III, a group usually dismissed with critical remarks, but also the extent to which members of the royal family could make an impact. Succeeding Jeffrey Amherst as Commander-in-Chief in 1795, York was a more effective administrator than he was a field commander. He faced a formidable challenge: Britain was up against a strong opponent. It was necessary both to manage the major expansion in army strength that had begun in 1793 and to cope with the consequences of the defeat and retreat of the army in 1793–95. In reviving the army, York took particular care to raise the quality of British officers, an objective that would have pleased two previous royal commanders, George II and William, Duke of Cumberland. Although he could not abolish the practice of purchasing commissions, York made it less deleterious, both by raising the number of free commissions and by establishing minimum periods of military service for promotion. His care for merit in the army matched his father's for merit in the church. York was unsuccessful, however, in ending absenteeism among officers.

York also encouraged schemes for military education, especially the plans of Lieutenant-Colonel John Le Marchant for a military college, which was to be the basis of the Royal Military College at Sandhurst. He also addressed the conditions of the ordinary soldiers, including their food, accommodation, medical care and punishment; soldiers were

provided with greatcoats, a practicable step that accorded with the active
philanthropy pushed by his parents. York was also a supporter of the
standardisation of drill; indeed consistency was a standard theme in
York's policies, and this helped to turn a collection of regiments into
an army. He was also a supporter of the cause of light infantry, a cause
associated in particular with Sir John Moore. York was forced to resign
in 1809 when a former mistress, Mary Anne Clarke, falsely accused him
of selling promotions, but he was reappointed Commander-in-Chief by
his brother the Prince Regent in 1811, holding the post (including from
1820 while also heir to the throne) until he died in 1827.[11]

York was no Wellington; but, in his way, he played as crucial a role.
Certainly, he was the sole member of the royal family to stand alongside
Cumberland as a major military figure in Hanoverian Britain. Despite
his naval career, William, Duke of Clarence did not put to sea during
the French Revolutionary and Napoleonic Wars. Other sons of
George III, however, took an active role. Ernest, Duke of Cumberland
(1771–1851), who served against the French with Hanoverian forces
in 1793–94, 1806 and 1813–14, did so without particular success. Given
the forces he was given command over, this was not surprising, and
he gained a justified reputation for bravery. Edward, Duke of Kent
(1767–1820), a Major-General in the British army, took part in the
capture of Martinique and St Lucia in 1794. The youngest brother,
Adolphus, Duke of Cambridge (1774–1850), served as a volunteer with
the British forces in the Low Countries in 1793, and as a colonel, major
general, and, from 1798, lieutenant general in the Hanoverian army.
Transferring with the last rank to the British army in 1803, Adolphus
became commander of the home district the following year. He was
military governor, then governor, of Hanover from 1813. George's
nephew, and later son-in-law, William, Duke of Gloucester (1776–1834),
the son of his brother William, served as a colonel in the campaign in the
Low Countries in 1794, and was held to have behaved well as a brigade
commander and major-general in the campaign in Holland in 1799.

There were no disasters and humiliations for the British crown akin
to those that affected most of the European dynasties. French troops
did not seize London, as they did other major capitals including Berlin,
Lisbon, Madrid, Moscow, Naples, Rome, Turin and Vienna; and, indeed,
Hanover itself in 1803. The royal family was not obliged to accept a

royal marriage with Napoleon, as the Habsburg Francis I had to do for his daughter, Marie Louise, Napoleon's second wife. There was also no forcible abdication to make way for one of Napoleon's relatives, as happened in Spain in 1808. A Napoleonic marshal did not gain the throne, as did Bernadotte in Sweden, and survival was not obtained by humiliating subservience to Napoleon, as in the cases of Bavaria, Prussia and Saxony. The Peace of Amiens of 1802 was far more a truce between equals made necessary by Austria's exit from the war than an abject British surrender to France.

In 1742, 1744 and 1782, the British monarchy had appeared one of the weakest in Europe, its rulers unable to sustain in office ministers who enjoyed royal confidence – Walpole, Carteret, and North respectively; yet, by 1810, it was the strongest in Europe other than the Romanov regime in Russia, or Napoleon's monarchical dictatorship, which lacked comparable legitimacy. Other European rulers, such as Louis XVIII of France, the Kings of Naples, Portugal and Sardinia, and William V of Orange (first cousin of George III), took shelter in Britain, where Louis XVIII was dependent on British financial support. William V was granted a large suite at Hampton Court. Others took cover behind British forces, especially the navy, for example the King of Naples in Sicily. Although British ministers had to consider what would happen if Napoleon invaded – would they have an army in Dover or concentrate forces south of London? – it never happened.

In addition, Britain became *the* world empire in this period. In 1714, Britain was already one of the leading colonial powers, with extensive territories in North America, valuable sugar islands in the West Indies, such as Barbados and Jamaica, and important bases in West Africa, India and the Mediterranean, but Britain was not yet the leading colonial power. While it had gained Gibraltar, Minorca, Newfoundland, Nova Scotia, and recognition of its claim to Rupert's Land to the south of Hudson's Bay at the Peace of Utrecht (1713), which had ended the War of the Spanish Succession, Britain's colonial territories were far less extensive, populous and wealthy then those of Spain, while France was an important colonial rival, and the Dutch still an important colonial force. The British attempt to seize Quebec from the French in 1711 had been unsuccessful, and there was little sign that the British would be able to gain major colonies from other major European powers, as distinct from seizing territory from often weaker non-European peoples, as in North America.

By 1837, the situation was totally transformed. Spain had lost its empire in Latin America (although it retained its Caribbean islands); and France had lost most of its eighteenth-century empire: Canada, Mauritius, St Lucia and the Seychelles conquered by Britain, Haiti independent as the result of a successful rebellion, and Louisiana sold to the United States in 1803. Although Britain had lost its Thirteen Colonies and the Old North West beyond the Appalachians, and had failed in its expeditions to Argentina and Egypt in 1806–7, it was the strongest state in the world and the leading power on the oceans, and had the best system of public finance. By 1837, as far as the Western presence was concerned, Canada and Australia were under British control, the colony of South Australia being founded in 1836. The British, by then, dominated much of India, particularly Bengal and the south, and also, from 1815, ruled Ceylon (Sri Lanka) and, from 1826, parts of Burma. Cape Town had been acquired from the Dutch during the wars with France, with George III very pleased about its capture for the second time in 1806, while other gains acknowledged at the Congress of Vienna (1814–15) included Trinidad, Tobago, St Lucia, Malta, Guyana, Heligoland and the Ionian Islands. Ironically, George had criticised the expeditions to the West Indies as a distraction from the war in Europe and one that lost many men to disease, while he had also been unenthusiastic about the plan for an attack on the French forces in Egypt in 1800.[12] Hanover had also made significant territorial gains in the Vienna settlement and its new royal status as a kingdom was acknowledged. Moreover, aside from territorial gains, in the two decades after the Congress of Vienna, British policy and power played a crucial role in securing Greek independence and that of Latin America.

Britain was so successful in this period, it might fairly be asked how much was due to the monarchs. As individuals, the monarchs could only achieve so much, not least because the amount that any one individual could oversee was limited. The first three Georges were diligent, especially the first and the last. George I inherited from his father a commitment to being an active ruler concerned to govern well and to enhance the interests of his dynasty. His attitudes also reflected a more general culture of government in seventeenth-century northern Europe, one that has been described in terms of a well-ordered police state, in other words a carefully regulated government.[13] George III added another moral dimension to good government with his Anglican piety.

The determination of the first three Georges to fulfil the *métier* of kingship as understood in the period is such that any treatment of their reigns has to focus heavily on their political aspirations and governmental policy. This might appear to contrast with the more recent treatment of the royal family, both the Hanoverians and their successors, in terms of personal life and, frequently, scandal, but this would be misleading. In fact, Elizabeth II and her predecessor, George VI, have been exceptionally hardworking, although their personal political opinions are far less clear than those of their predecessors (bar the Queen's support for the Commonwealth), and appear to have little to do with their diligence.

Aside from the factor of time affecting what the Hanoverian monarchs could do, there was also that of distance. The monarchs did not know their British dominions, and, in response to crises at a distance, did not travel to intervene in person. No monarch crossed the Atlantic, an omission publicly regretted by Prince Charles in 2004. It would have been a lengthy journey, but, in the length of time George II spent in Hanover in 1736, George III could have easily got to Boston, New York or Philadelphia, and back. As a young man in naval service, William IV visited the West Indies, while his brother Edward, Duke of Kent, served in the army both there and in Canada.

Between William III and George IV, no monarch visited Ireland, and William had only gone there to conquer it from James II. Although, during the Jacobite rising known as the '15, 'James III and VIII' was briefly there from 22 December 1715 (os) to 4 February 1716 (os), George IV was also the first of the Hanoverians to visit Scotland, which he reached by sea. The politics and patronage needed to handle Ireland and Scotland were not seen as requiring the royal presence; instead, they were the task of ministers, both in London and in Edinburgh and Dublin. The planned coronation of 'James III and VIII' at Scone was thwarted by the Jacobite defeat in 1716.

None of the Hanoverian monarchs visited northern England and, further south, what they saw was limited. Neither George I nor George II made the progresses rumoured as imminent in the press, and, for both, England essentially meant the royal palaces near London, nearby hunting areas, and the routes to and from ports from which they could sail to and from Hanover: principally Harwich, but, due to a storm on the way back from the 1725 visit to Hanover, including Rye in 1726. George I also visited Newmarket for the races in 1717, while George II visited Cambridge as well as Newmarket in 1728. George III travelled more widely in England (although never outside it), especially to Melcombe Regis near Weymouth, which he visited most years from 1789 to 1805, but also to Portsmouth in 1773 and 1778, Oxford in 1785, Cheltenham and Worcester in 1788, and the Plymouth area (staying at Saltram) in 1789, generally travelling with his wife and daughters; but he did not see most of the country. Indeed, given the fact that he had more time available to travel in Britain, both because he never went abroad and because of his longevity, it is striking how much he stayed close to home. In that respect, he was far more like Louis XVI than Joseph II of Austria or Gustavus III of Sweden, or indeed George I as a young man.

None of the Hanoverian monarchs visited Liverpool, Manchester, Leeds, York, Newcastle or Norwich, an omission that contrasted with George's brother-in-law Christian VII of Denmark, who visited northern England in 1768, traveling along the Bridgewater canal and also visiting the industries of Leeds, and George's brothers, Edward, Duke of York, who visited Yorkshire in 1761 and 1766, and Henry, Duke of Cumberland who visited Berwick in 1771. Nevertheless, whereas George I had taken the waters in Germany, George III took those at Cheltenham in 1788, and at Worcester that year he visited a carpet works and a china factory. On an outing from Cheltenham, George also visited the area round Stroud which was 'deservedly distinguished for industry and manufactures' and was shown 'in regular gradation, the whole process of making cloth'. The following year, George visited the carpet works at Axminster.[14]

Aside from not knowing most of his dominions, there were also restrictions on what the monarch could do arising from the nature of the constitution and the political system. An anonymous memorandum of 1765 noted 'the method practised in the nomination of governors in the plantations was for the First Lord of Trade to deliver to one of the Secretaries of State a list of *three* persons to be laid before the King for His Majesty's *option*, whereupon the Secretary of State made out the warrant accordingly'.[15] Whatever the King's power in appointments, the role of Parliament was an important constraint, as its management was not directly handled by the monarch. When, in response to Virginia's rejection in 1765 of Parliament's right to levy Stamp Duty, George III was advised that this was a matter 'of too high a nature for the determination of your Majesty in your Privy Council; and is proper only for the consideration of Parliament', he responded by giving directions that the issue be laid before it.[16]

Nevertheless, the small size of government (by modern, and by some contemporary European, standards), and the non-executive role of Parliament, still left many opportunities for royal scrutiny and initiative. The limited authority of government institutions in a system where court favour was very important, power not necessarily based upon tenure of a formal office, and only the monarch could arbitrate effectually in disputes, led Kings to act. A continued display of royal favour seemed necessary for the maintenance of the authority of ministers, institutions and edicts, and, indeed, was also important to members of the royal family. Angered by William, Duke of Cumberland's failure to protect Hanover from the French in 1757, and by his agreeing to the disbandment of his army, George II treated his son in a humiliating fashion when he returned to London, leading the latter to resign all his military posts. George also criticised the Duke to the Duke of 'Newcastle, telling him 'a scoundrel in England *one day* may be thought a good man *another*. In Germany, it is otherwise. I think like a German'.[17]

While most royal intervention in government and politics was reactive, it could be combined with a more active drive, that could affect both policy and power. Posts could become influential because favourites filled them, royal favour could qualify the autonomy of institutions, and the procedures for appointment and promotion, and those close to the ruler could enjoy considerable influence. Those who played cards with George II in the evening generally then supped late with him, and this gave them a valuable entrée, although not necessarily any real policy impact. The role of those close to the monarch was particularly apparent in George I's early years, as the King was dependent on advice about British politics, and was especially feared in the early 1760s, when George III relied on John, 3rd Earl of Bute.

At these moments, the general tension between the regularisation of power, through the establishment of agreed administrative procedures, and the personal intervention of the monarch reached a highpoint. The

British Kings had less freedom in this direction than many of their continental counterparts, although the opportunities and problems posed by Hanover and the British colonies offered chances to alter this by increasing their power and giving them opportunities to influence the situation in Britain. At the same time, there was in fact no *secret du roi* or secret royal policy focused on enhancing royal power within Britain. Even had there been such a policy (and the closest to a *secret du roi* was the undoubted attempt to use British resources to achieve Hanoverian goals), it was difficult to ensure continuity in policy between reigns. This was symbolized by the dissolution of Parliament on the death of a monarch. The calibre and interests of individual monarchs varied and were unpredictable, and the Kings could not readily institutionalise change.

The importance of the attitude of individual rulers represented a powerful element of discontinuity that encouraged those unhappy about patronage and policies, for example the Whigs in the mid and late 1780s, to look forward to the accession of the heir to the throne – the reversionary interest. This, in turn, enhanced potential discontinuity, as was seen in particular when George III's insanity led to the Regency Crisis of 1788–89.

Nevertheless, the absence of a programme to strengthen monarchy did not mean that the Kings were without considerable significance. Because the British government was the King's, there was, at the least, a formal need for the royal assent recorded in royal signatures for instructions and appointments. Thus, on 27 October 1760, on the third day of his reign, George III was having to sign such lowly appointments as a cornet in the army.[18] Such signings focused the King's power in patronage, and also gave the King the opportunity to discuss matters with ministers. The role of George I is apparent in a letter of 1726 from Richard Arundell, MP for Knaresborough, when the post of Surveyor General of Works became vacant:

> upon which Sir Robert Walpole recommended me to the King who has consented to give me the employment. Great endeavours have been used to make [William] Kent Comptroller, though with no effect, and he [Walpole] told me yesterday that he was obliged to make Ripley Comptroller to obviate the Duke of Devonshire's recommendation, and remove Howard from the Board, who is to have Dartiquenave's place, and Dartiquenave

the Gardens and that he had spoke to the King to put Kent into Ripley's employment which was agreed to.[19]

Ripley, who worked for Sir Robert Walpole on his new seat at Houghton, indeed held the post of Comptroller of the Board of Works from 1726 until 1738, while Charles Dartiquenave was a Whig socialite who, in 1726, exchanged the Paymastership of the Royal Works he had held since 1706 for the Surveyor-Generalship of the King's Gardens. The merry-go-round of posts, here involving appointments concerned with palaces and their gardens, reflected the Whig spoils system, with its emphasis on loyalty and connection, but the merry-go-round required the assent of the crown, and could not take place without the King's approval.

The King played a more important role in foreign policy. Diplomats were appointed,[20] and paid, by him, and foreign envoys were accredited to the King. This was no mere formality. Monarchs frequently talked with these envoys, and these conversations provided clues about government policy, as in 1747 when George II told the envoy of Charles Emmanuel III, King of Sardinia, that the success of Allied operations in Provence would permit the dictation of peace terms to France.[21]

Due to the nature of the sources, discussion with ministers, whether over patronage or policy, and other royal interventions in government, are particularly apparent with George III. Richard, Earl of Mornington, who became Governor General in India in 1797 (where, thanks in part to the generalship of his brother, the future Duke of Wellington, in 1803, he was to expand British power greatly) for instance was made aware of George's interest:

> from the King, I have received the most gracious declaration of approbation, and especially of the manner in which I had withstood the temptation of carrying out a train of followers, and filling my hands with engagements from Europe.[22]

Many letters from the King survive for his reign, and they indicate how active he was. As an example, in 1791, George III took a keen interest in the government parliamentary majorities during the Ochakov Crisis as he hoped they would give energy to government policy and have an impact abroad.[23] For George III, sources are far more plentiful than for his two predecessors (which encourages scepticism about claims that he was much more 'active' than they were), but it is nevertheless difficult to ascertain the source of George's opinions,[24] while there are problems in assessing the impact of royal views and those of concerns about Hanover. It is also still necessary, for George's reign, to employ scepticism when approaching contemporary claims about these views and concerns. Thus, in 1766, George, 3rd Earl of Albemarle, a former protégé of William, Duke of Cumberland, blamed the replacement of the Rockingham ministry by that of William Pitt the Elder, 1st Earl of Chatham, on George's concern for Hanover:

> You will stare and perhaps shake your head when I tell you it was by the advice of his German ministers. The King of Prussia [Frederick II], tired of soliciting England for the arrears due to him, informed the Hanoverian ministers that unless he was paid (or indemnified by some part of America), and immediately, that he would seize upon the Duchy of Lunenbourg and immediately. This so alarmed Munchhausen that he sent an express to the King [George III] with his alarms, and saying at the same time that no man could deal with the King of Prussia but Mr Pitt, that he had a confidence in him, and a diffidence in all his Majesty's ministers. This determined the King so suddenly, and so unexpectedly to send for Mr Pitt.

Albemarle's account is indicative of beliefs about the influence of Hanover on royal views, but the Duke of Newcastle, the politician with the greatest experience of government, was rightly sceptical about the claim.[25] Indeed, it is the caution of the Kings in pushing their prerogatives that emerges most clearly, and sufficiently so for outrage to be expressed when this caution had apparently been abandoned, especially by George III. The comparative dimension was readily offered by the male Stuarts. Their expulsion and exclusion in 1688–89 had created what was seen as, at least implicitly, a compact, if not a contract, between crown and people. The *London Chronicle* of 7 May 1757 declared

> The notions of the Divine Right of Kings to do wrong; of their hereditary indefeasible right to the crown, as an unalienable patrimony; of the unbounded extent of the prerogative above law; these and the like high flying notions, have been abdicated with that unfortunate family which acted upon them, and since the Revolution [1688], they are not popular even at court, where these flattering doctrines might expect most favour.

The newspaper was correct. The Hanoverians did not share Stuart views on the royal prerogative, and their departure from Stuart sacral monarchy was also seen by the fact that Anne was the last British ruler to touch for scrofula, the 'King's Evil'. Begun in 1058, by Edward the Confessor, and used to make explicit the divine sanction of royalty, the practice had been deliberately abandoned by William III. Anne revived it, touching thousands, including the young Samuel Johnson.[26] George I, who regarded touching as a superstitious relic, stopped it, and was not encouraged to revive it by its continuation by the exiled Stuarts. This was a major change in the symbolisation of British monarchy, away from the sacred and magical. Thereafter, royal philanthropy was to be very different in its character. Support for institutional provision and patronage was to be the basis of the modern position and established multiple contacts between the royal family and the public.[27]

Views of the Hanoverians have often been critical, resting on a mixture of suspicion about their political intentions and disquiet about their private lives. The latter have been presented as, at best, unfortunate, and, more commonly, amoral or immoral, and this certainly influenced the views of Queen Victoria on her predecessors, including George I and George II. Contemporaries shared these views to a degree, but it is necessary to appreciate the particular political and personal view of the critics in order to evaluate their comments. The oft-repeated gripes of individuals, such as Lord Hervey and Horace Walpole for the reign of George II, need to be treated more as evidence of the criticism that was inseparable from royal courts and British politics than as the basis for a modern objective judgment. The early historiographical legacy is fraught with excessive condemnation and only now can it be redressed systematically. The reality is less lurid and more impressive than the caricature. In place of possible incest, stupidity, madness, untrammelled lust, and plain oddness, comes shrewdness and, in most cases, diligence. The Hanoverians were politically calculating men of ability, usually with the qualities necessary for the task.

# 2

# Britain and Hanover

As it was obvious that the regency of Hanover ought neither to form laws nor enter into any treaties which might prove injurious to Great Britain, consequently it behoved the ministers of this country to have prevented their entering into any alliances which might involve serious consequences to the interests of England.

Charles James Fox, 1786 [1]

The Hanoverians were part of the sequence of dynasties that ruled Britain and the British empire, but it would be foolish to neglect the extent to which the monarchs were also rulers of Hanover and concerned about its interests.[2] Indeed, in 1745, when Charles Edward Stuart's landing in the Western Isles launched the greatest crisis to the Hanoverian dynasty, George II was not in London but in Hanover. Furthermore, he was less speedy in deciding to return to Britain than the Lord Justices, the ministers left in control in London, would have liked, while his second son, William, Duke of Cumberland, then in command of British forces opposed to France in the Low Countries, was reluctant to send troops to Britain. Cumberland replied to the Duke of Newcastle's letter pressing him to do so: 'I am surprised to see this romantic expedition revived again. But I don't doubt but that Sir John Cope will be able to put a stop immediately to this affair'. In fact, Cope, the commander of the forces in Scotland, was defeated at Prestonpans, opening the way to England for Charles Edward. Cumberland also persuaded George to defer sending British troops back from the Low Countries; again a mistake.[3]

Both Britain and Hanover were in part shaped by the dynastic personal union (rulership of different states by the single monarch) of the Hanoverian monarchy. Looked at differently, the latter also created a polity that interacted with these two states: George I, who had become

Elector of Hanover in 1698, essentially created a new state from 1714, just as James VI of Scotland had done when he also became James I of England in 1603. Although, in common with the general European trend at the time, George's rule of Hanover and Britain did not lead to novel constitutional, political or administrative arrangements, the personal union, and the resulting territorial agglomeration, was given common purpose at the international level by the dynastic concerns of the ruler.

Personal unions were scarcely new in British history. From 1066, England had been linked to parts of France under the Norman and then the Plantagenet dynasties. The accession of James VI to the English throne began a personal union that was not extended to a parliamentary union until 1707, while, under William III (1689–1702), the position of the house of Orange in Dutch politics was linked to Britain. Personal unions were also common on the Continent: for the eighteenth century, the list would include those of Poland and Saxony, Sweden and Hesse-Cassel, Russia and Holstein-Gottorp, and Denmark and Oldenburg.

These personal unions have received insufficient attention for a number of reasons, among which teleology plays a major role: the place of personal unions within the typology of European states is unclear, and they can seem anachronistic. Instead, most relevant historical work has addressed the pre-history and subsequent development of unitary states, and little attention has been devoted to the discussion of personal unions in the eighteenth century, not least because, unlike, say, the earlier union of Aragon and Castile (the basis of Spanish unity), they did not lead to modern states.

The role of personal unions in international diplomacy has been far more extensively considered for the sixteenth century, and this contrast with the eighteenth raises the issue of how best to define and to analyse apparent modernity in state formation, and focuses attention on the nature of political progress. Underlying the relative neglect of personal unions, such as that of Britain and Hanover, and the modern concentration on unitary states in the eighteenth century, or on what are presented as such, is a teleology, as these states apparently represented not only the future, but also the present, understood as the states best able to survive in the highly competitive international relations of the period.

This is questionable. In the nineteenth century nation states, such as France, Germany, Italy and the USA, were not obviously more successful than multi-ethnic states, such as Austria, Russia or Britain (which then included Ireland, as well as India and the Dominions), and it is mistaken to assume that the more or less centralised national state was superior to the composite monarchy. The acme of the latter, the Habsburg monarchy, in fact survived until 1918, and its demise was perhaps not as much of a foregone conclusion as has often been assumed in the past. Moreover, the Habsburg monarchy did not fare worse in the Napoleonic era (1799–1815) than smaller, more homogeneous states in defending itself against France. In addition, a different form of composite organisation, federalism, was effective, both at the small scale of Switzerland and at the larger scale of the United States. The latter, alongside the British empire, was, in an involuntary fashion, the major political creation of the English-speaking world, and of the age of George III.

The contemporary test of political effectiveness focused on international competition, and the Hanoverian monarchs were actively involved in this sphere. The defence of a monarch's inheritance and people in peace and war was foremost among his duties and, by the eighteenth century, this role was generally more pressing than the defence of the faith; although, thanks to the end of the Seven Years War in 1763, this emphasis was far less true for George III, at least for his first fifteen years on the throne, than it had been for his two predecessors. Foreign policy was a sphere in which the British crown had considerable power: diplomats were appointed, paid, answerable to, and dismissed by the King. However much the waging of war depended on parliamentary support, in the shape of the voting of subsidies, the role of Parliament in peacetime diplomacy was limited.

Prior to the Union of 1707, England and Scotland had acted as one in foreign policy, although there had been tensions between the two Parliaments, and one reason for their union was to prevent the Edinburgh Parliament from making separate arrangements for the succession after Anne died. The relationship between England and Scotland under the Hanoverian dynasty tends to be ignored, certainly in contrast to that of Britain and Hanover. Only one of the Hanoverian rulers ever visited Scotland – George IV in 1822; and, although that visit was of considerable symbolic value, and looked toward the frequent trips there of his niece, Victoria, it was not a journey that had any particular political significance. Nevertheless, the relationship between dynasty and Scotland was important, not least in the negative sense that part of Scotland remained a Jacobite hotbed until the imposition of central governmental control in Highland Scotland after Culloden. Punitive expeditions were dispatched then, with instructions to kill the Jacobites and destroy their property. Some of these expeditions, particularly those sent into remoter sections of the western Highlands, were especially cruel, characterised by killings, rapes, and systematic devastation that did not exempt loyal Highlanders. There was subsequently a major legislative programme that extended royal powers. Thus, in 1746, an Act regulating nonjuring meeting houses specified that the ministers should pray for the King by name, thus making it clear that the Pretender, 'James III and VIII', was not intended. In 1747, the principal hereditable jurisdictions were abolished. Thomas Sherlock, the influential Bishop of Salisbury, had urged 'the main thing to be provided for is we secure an execution of the *king's* laws in the country; which is at present under the absolute *will* of the lairds'.[4] The Act abolished regalities – their jurisdictions were assumed by the royal courts, while heritable sheriffdoms were similarly abrogated and their powers transferred to the crown.

This was the basis, however, not of a social transformation but of a new relationship between crown and Scottish elite. The willing cooption of powerful Scots through patronage continued, but now with no alternative Jacobite focus for loyalty. Sir Charles Hanbury-Williams, a loyal Whig, was shocked to hear in 1753 that six English regiments had been given to Scots, but George II, who controlled army patronage, felt this a safe course of action. Scottish officers gave him, and his successors, good service. If Alexander Murray of Elibank played a central role in the Jacobite 'Elibank Plot' of 1751–53, with its schemes for the murder or capture of George II, his brother James played a key role in the battle outside Quebec that led to the fall of the city in 1759, while Lord John Murray, half-brother of the Jacobite commander Lord George Murray, was an aide-de-camp to George II, and eventually the senior general in the army.

This reconciliation gathered pace as Jacobitism and nonjuring faded, and as a new order focused on the economic and military benefits of the expanding British empire came to dominate Scotland, an order that lasted until the imperial withdrawal and economic decline of the late 1950s to 1970s. The role of the monarchy in encouraging this reconciliation, in large part through military patronage and through not challenging the management of Scottish politics, was more important to Britain's long-term political history than the Hanoverian connection, although this encouragement was also modest, and played a smaller role than the monarchs' interest in the Electorate.

The constitutional position and political problems involved in the Hanoverian connection were more complex than the post-1707 relationship with Scotland, in part due to the international consequences, and they created one of the leading political difficulties of the reigns of George I and George II, and a difficulty that threw the role of the monarch into prominence. During their reigns, the contentious nature of the Hanoverian connection indeed meant that it was, and is, impracticable to separate the issue of royal influence in the formulation of foreign policy from that of Hanoverian concerns, for the latter gave force and direction to royal concerns and initiatives.

The Electorate of Hanover was geographically part of the north west of modern Germany. In 1714, it was constitutionally one of the nine Electorates in the Holy Roman Empire, the loosely united assemblage of territories that comprised modern Germany and Austria and some bordering areas, and in 1714 was presided over by an elected Emperor, Charles VI (1711–40), the Habsburg ruler of Austria, Bohemia, Hungary, the Austrian Netherlands (Belgium), and much of Italy. As with most German principalities, Hanover's frontiers were established by feudal, not geographical, considerations, but most of the Electorate was between the Elbe and the Weser rivers, the North Sea and the Harz mountains. However, there were also important sections between the Elbe, Mecklenburg, Holstein and the Baltic, and also west of the Weser.

Hanover's frontiers lacked strong natural defences, and had not been supplemented by any system of fortifications. As a result, the Electorate was regarded as vulnerable to attack, and was dependent for its defence on the size of its army. This was, like that of most German principalities, modest in size. The army was established in 1665 around a core of troops from Osnabrück and totalled 5000 men. It was increased with the Dutch War (1672–78) and thereafter averaged 10–16,000 men, with a peak of 22,000 during the War of the Spanish Succession (1702–14).

The establishment was reduced in 1715 to a size of 14,500–15,000, but increased again after 1727 to reach about 19,000 which was maintained until 1741, although the British diplomat Thomas Villiers reported it 21,000 strong in December 1739.19,442 strong in 1740, the army rose, as a result of wartime expansion, to 24,982 in 1741, 26,400 in April 1742, 25,564 in 1744 and 26,471 in 1748.

As a result of peacetime reduction, the average strength then fell to 21,000, before war led to an increase to 27,146 in 1756 and 37,146 in 1763. The peacetime strength was then an average of 14,218 until war again led to a rise from 15,503 in 1775 to 23,197 in 1783. The peacetime average was then 21,000, although this included two regiments serving the British East India Company in 1781–92. Including replacement recruits sent out, these totalled 170 officers and 2800 men. Due largely to disease, sixty-nine of the officers failed to return, only four of whom were killed in action, while only about half the men returned fit for further service. The army numbered 17,836 in 1789.

From 1793 until 1802 the army was usually about 18,000 men strong but with a maximum of about 25,000. This small size was explained by Hanover's involvement in the Prussian-controlled north German neutrality zone following the peace of Basel in 1795. After French occupation ended, the field strength in 1813–15 averaged 15,000. The army was reorganised in 1815 to total 29,363 men, but 18,000 of the infantry consisted of militia. This was changed in 1820 when the army was to total 20,812, a complement maintained until 1833 when, as a result of reorganisation, the infantry was to total 15,168 and the cavalry 3,340, while there were around a thousand artillery and support troops: these numbers excluding unmobilised militia.

Given that the population at least doubled and the territory increased significantly the proportion under arms declined significantly over the period, but then it did in most German territories.[5] Such a force did not place too heavy a burden on Hanover's primarily agrarian economy, which was not particularly advanced by the standards of the age, and it was sufficient for pursuing small-scale quarrels with weak neighbours, such as the Duke of Mecklenburg-Schwerin or the Prince Bishop of Hildesheim.

Other, and more powerful, rulers could intervene in such quarrels, however, and Hanover suffered from its military weakness, which was particularly marked in comparison with neighbouring Prussia. In January 1751 Frederick II, the Great, of Prussia told the French envoy in Berlin that, if war broke out, he would invade Hanover in order to capture the Electoral treasury, and that, if he failed to seize it, he would impose, under threat of burning everything, a massive daily levy until the treasury was delivered. Two months later, the Prussian Foreign Minister said that, in the event of war, Prussia would use a conquered Hanover as a source of supplies.[6] When Hanover was actually attacked – first by the French in 1757 – it was rapidly conquered; William, Duke of Cumberland being defeated at Hastenbeck on 26 July. In 1762, the Hanoverian minister in London, Baron Behr, suggested to the Bavarian envoy that a German league, of the leading Electors, should be formed, so that the participants were not always at risk of being invaded on the slightest pretext,[7] but nothing was done. It is also necessary to appreciate that Hanover was by no means independent and sovereign. As Elector of Hanover, the British King was the Emperor's liegeman. This, in itself, made the connection between Britain and Hanover problematic, although Britain's indirect position as a *Reichsstand* gave it a certain degree of influence in Germany.

The Hanoverian army offered no real protection against attack by powerful rulers, while Hanover's geographical and international position made it liable to pressure. The Electorate's trans-Elbean territory, the Duchy of Saxe-Lauenburg, occupied in 1689, made Hanover particularly sensitive to developments around the Baltic, especially in Mecklenburg and the Schleswig-Holstein isthmus, while its western possessions made it concerned about events in the Westphalian Circle. Hanover lay astride any Russian advance into northern Germany, a major threat from the reign of Peter the Great (1689–1725), under whom, and against George I's wishes, Russian troops had wintered in neighbouring Mecklenburg in 1716–17, as well as astride any Danish moves south into Lower Saxony, any French advance toward the western frontier of Brandenburg (Prussia), and any attempt by the Electors of Brandenburg (Kings in Prussia) to amalgamate or otherwise link up their widely separated territories in Westphalia and the Lower Rhineland with Brandenburg. There were Prussian territories to the east and west of Hanover, just as there were Danish possessions to the north and west.

Hanoverian security, therefore, dictated a search for allies and supporters,[8] of which Britain was the most prominent, and Hesse-Cassel,
its aid purchased with British subsidies, the most immediately useful
militarily. In 1729, when Hanover was threatened with Prussian attack,
George II was particularly grateful for Hessian assistance. Generally, it
is difficult to distinguish royal from ministerial views, but, when Townshend, with George in Hanover, wrote to Newcastle, it was clear what
the King thought:

> I am by the King's express command to acquaint your Grace that H.M.
> thinks himself in a very particular manner obliged to the Landgrave of
> Hesse Cassel upon this occasion, who by his great fidelity and readiness
> in executing engagements, has extremely contributed to the happy turn
> which this affair seems now to have taken; his Prussian Majesty's present
> peaceable disposition being, in the King's opinion in great measure owing
> to the early motion of the Hessian troops, and to the apprehensions of a
> strong diversion on that side in favour of H.M.[9]

Yet, Hanover was also threatened as a consequence of the dynastic, and
thus political, link with Britain. The European perception was that
Britain and Hanover were part of a much closer union than was in fact
the case: it was hard to believe that George I and George II could act
in a separate capacity as King and as Elector. An attack on, or threat
to, the Electorate appeared an obvious pre-emption of, or response to,
unwelcome British moves. More specifically, it offered an apparently
low-risk way to influence the conduct of Britain by intimidating the
King-Elector, although most schemes of this type were impractical. In
January 1726, for example, George Lockhart advanced a scheme for the
Jacobites to seize Hanover with the assistance of Austrian troops and
hold it until George I abandoned Britain, while, in December 1741,
Horace Walpole reported from Florence that the Jacobites were claiming
that the French would not evacuate Hanover 'but on conditions very
advantageous to the Pretender's family ... which they interpret to be
the dismembering Scotland from England, and settling themselves there'.

Conversely, the dynastic link provided a drive to British-Hanoverian
policy that posed both opportunities and threats. Throughout the union
(1714–1837), there were always two distinct international realities, and it
was always clear, when a formal treaty was signed with other powers,
which country was committed by its King or Elector; separate treaties

were signed even on occasions when the head of state committed both countries at the same time. The administration of the two units was also separate, and it is wrong to see the designation of the successive Georges as His Royal and Electoral Majesty as mere etiquette.[10] Nevertheless, too much can be made of these distinctions. Although British ministers struggled to maintain these distinctions, both in discussion with foreign envoys, and when faced with domestic criticism,[11] it is not surprising that their arguments were greeted with general scepticism; and such issues as marital links with other ruling families eroded the distinction. In addition, Hanoverian ministers were aware that their views were judged abroad in the light of responses to British policy and interests.

At times, British ministers sought to stress the common interests and bonds of Britain and Hanover. In 1751, when Newcastle, then Secretary of State for the Northern Department, complained of Prussian conduct, he wrote 'one sees the affectation of distinguishing the King from the Elector'. The previous year, Newcastle had rejected the Dutch proposal that, instead of George II paying half of the intended joint subsidy to the Elector of Cologne, he pay two-thirds – one-third as King and one-third as Elector, claiming that it was

> contrary to all practice, for His Majesty, in the same act, to enter into any engagements in two different capacities; and in the instructions the King has been pleased to give to Baron Steinberg, there is not, as I apprehend, any particular description of the capacity, in which His Majesty proposed to be engaged.[12]

In 1722, the Holy Roman Empress, Elisabeth Christine, niece of Duke August Wilhelm of Brunswick-Wolfenbüttel, told George I's envoy in Vienna that George needed to distinguish between his character as King and as Elector. Foreign royalty, ministers and diplomats, however, were also impatient with the attempts of their British counterparts to differentiate between the two dominions. In January 1742, Hardenberg, the Hanoverian envoy in Paris, assured Cardinal Fleury, the leading French minister, of the Elector of Hanover's good intentions, but refused to answer questions about the King of Britain. Jean-Jacques Amelot, the French Foreign Minister, commented, in a letter intercepted and deciphered by the excellent British deciphering department (which was linked to its first-rate Hanoverian counterpart), that pushing the idea of one person having two roles had given Fleury an impression of bad faith. Four years earlier, faced by hostile Austro-Hanoverian moves, Frederick II asked his envoy in London whether he should regard the King of England as one or two people,[13] in short whether Britain was not, through the King, a party to Hanoverian moves.

At root the common bond was Protestantism – a theme much vaunted in Hanoverian marriages, such as those of George II with Caroline of Ansbach and of his daughter Anne to William IV of Orange. The personal union of Britain and Hanover was a long-lasting one that was only brought to an end when William IV died in 1837, as the inheritance in the female line that took Victoria to the throne in Britain did not exist in Hanover; instead her uncle, Ernest, Duke of Cumberland, succeeded there. Victoria was the daughter of George III's fourth son, Edward, Duke of Kent, while Ernest was the fifth son. In contrast, the Saxon-Polish union lasted from 1697 to 1704 and from 1709 to 1763, while that of Sweden and the Landgravate of Hesse-Cassel between 1730 and 1751. The Britain-Hanover union lasted for five reigns, while the other two lasted for only two and one respectively.

In his will, George I had stipulated an eventual division of Britain and Hanover after the death of his then sole grandson, Frederick, later Prince of Wales, the Electorate going to Frederick's second son, if he had one, and, failing that, to the Brunswick-Wolfenbüttel branch of the house of Brunswick, but the will was suppressed by George II.[14] Had the will stood, then William, Duke of Cumberland would have become ruler of Hanover, and this might have led him to marry and have an heir, which he did not do. Had he not married, Hanover could have become a secondgeniture, as the Grand Duchy of Tuscany became for the Habsburgs from 1765, so that, on Cumberland's death in 1765, it would have passed to Frederick's second son, Edward, Duke of York, and, on his death without heir, to George III's second son, Frederick, Duke of York. As Frederick died in 1827 and George IV had no sons, Hanover would then have gone to the next brother, William, Duke of Clarence and, when the childless William became King in 1830, to his brother, Ernest, Duke of Cumberland, who, in fact, succeeded there seven years later.

The suppression of George I's will involved George II not reading his father's will when it was presented to him at a meeting of the Privy

Council and his getting hold of the copies held by August Wilhelm of Brunswick-Wolfenbüttel and the Emperor Charles VI. British resources were used to this end: the Treaty of Westminster of 25 November (os) 1727 with August Wilhelm included not only a mutual guarantee but also a British subsidy. The will was not mentioned in the treaty, but George's ratification was dependent on its delivery. The government proclaimed the treaty as a triumph of foreign policy, but was less keen on advertising the amount of money promised to Brunswick-Wolfen-büttel.[15] Frederick, Prince of Wales, in turn, considered a division of the inheritance, with his second son, Edward, becoming Elector, but neither he nor George II made any arrangements to that effect.[16] George II took the idea seriously, as he feared the anti-Hanoverian attitudes of George III as Prince of Wales, but he tended to think Hanover's integrity best served by the maintenance of the British connection, and in 1744 received this advice from the Hanoverian Privy Counsellors when he consulted them.[17] In 1759, however, George II was driven by anger at what he saw as the neglect of Hanover to advocate a division. The occasion was Newcastle's response to the King's question about the prospect of Hanover gaining territory as a result of the Seven Years War. The Duke argued that there would be a return to the pre-war territorial status quo in Europe in the eventual peace, upon which George let vent:

after expressing great dissatisfaction with us, our ingratitude in doing nothing for him, who had suffered so much for this ungrateful country. To which I took the liberty to reply that this war had been most expensive to this nation; that it would increase our national debt 30 millions; that it would be impossible for us to retain all our conquests at a peace; and that whatever advantages the Electorate should gain, would be thought, by everybody, to be so far a diminution of what might have been retained for this country; and that *that* was the *point*; and the apprehension of all his servants. His Majesty then said, since you will do nothing for me, I hope you will agree to separate my Electorate from this country ... pass a short Act of Parliament, that whoever possesses this Crown, shall not have the *Electorate* ... *George* will be King; and his brother Elector.

Philip, Lord Hardwicke, the Lord Chancellor, replied:

As to the question of *separation of the Electorate*, your Grace knows it has been seriously talked of before, but nobody could see their way through it either *here* or *in Germany*. There can be no other way, but passing an

Act of Parliament laying disabilities upon that *branch*, which should be in possession of the Electorate, unless they should renounce and abdicate it; and there recurred the danger of creating *Pretenders* even in the family of Hanover itself. Consent of parties now in being would not help this in future. But I perfectly agree the thing is extremely to be wished.[18]

This was not taken further under George II, while George III did not pursue the idea of dividing the inheritance; instead, the will he drew up in 1765 stated that his eldest son would inherit both crown and Electorate.

The Hanoverian inheritance, which, in the case of the Electorate was itself the recent product of the fusion of the inheritances of several branches of the house of Brunswick, as a result of the maintenance of the primogeniture introduced by George's father, Ernst August, did not divide until 1837, as it could readily have done given the number of sons that Ernst August (six to adulthood), George II (two to adulthood), Frederick, Prince of Wales (four to adulthood), and George III (seven to adulthood) all had. Instead, culminating with the gain of the British throne in 1714, the inheritance showed anew that dynastic accretion was the classic route to growth in the early modern period, as the history of Spain, Austria, and seventeenth-century Prussia, or rather of the Habsburg and Hohenzollern families, also demonstrated. After 1714, however, territory was to be gained by the Hanoverians by conquest, negotiation and settlement, and not by marriage.

Territorial amalgamation through dynastic means posed serious political problems in terms of management as much as policy. The monarchs appreciated the consequences of personal union, but the bulk of the British political nation understandably did not, and they did not understand that their Kings had duties to the Electorate. This provided a basis for political discord. The rule of the Hanoverians posed not simply the question of dynastic legitimacy, but also one of political intention. Intended to secure and stabilise the Protestant Succession after the failure of William III and Anne to produce direct heirs, Hanoverian dynasticism was in fact a destabilising force in British politics, although, unlike in the case of Philip V of Spain (1700–46), there was no attempt to gain principalities for younger sons, as he successfully sought to do in Italy.

As the *modus operandi* of Hanoverian dynasticism was foreign policy, it is scarcely surprising that the latter constituted a major topic of political debate. The royal role in the formulation and conduct of foreign policy, a characteristic of all monarchical states in this period, and a longstanding source of controversy in Britain, was thus made more controversial by the diplomatic and domestic consequences of royal intervention arising from the interests of the personal union. It is this that dynasticism really denoted, but, in British political debate, it was commonly misunderstood as Hanoverianism. Furthermore, the charge of Hanoverian counsels failed to do justice to the divisions within the government of the Electorate, and neglected the extent to which dynastic interests were often different from those of the Electorate as understood by Hanoverian ministers, who, in 1757, debated the continued value of the link with Britain.

British visitors to Hanover during the reign of George III, who never visited the Electorate, picked up a sense of neglect, and travel accounts communicated this to the wider public. In his *A Tour from London to Petersburg* (1780), John Richard noted:

> The absence of the Elector renders the court of Hanover exceeding gloomy ... Party matters formerly carried some Englishmen so far as to treat Hanover with the greatest contempt, and the Hanoverians do not mention England with any marks of cordial friendship. They seem to consider the absence of their Elector as a disadvantage to them, and this is probably true.

Alexander Thomson added in his *Letters of a Traveller* (1798),

> The towns in these dominions are not without trade and manufactures; but the whole of the Electorate has suffered much by the accession of the house of Hanover to the crown of Great Britain; notwithstanding a respectable civil and military establishment is constantly maintained, out of the revenues of the country.

Others sought to present a more benign account, John Moore by stressing the Englishness of Hanover:

> Hanover is a neat, thriving, and agreeable city. It has more the air of an English town than any other I have seen in Germany, and the English manners and customs gain ground every day among the inhabitants. The genial influence of freedom has extended from England to this place.

Tyranny is not felt, and ease and satisfaction appear in the countenances of the citizens.[19]

Prior to 1760, the presentation of Hanover and the image of German politics was far bleaker. Indeed, Elizabeth Montagu noted a change in 1763 when she wrote from London about Charles William, who had recently married George III's eldest sister, Augusta:

> The mob are much vexed at the departure of the Prince of Brunswick for whom they had conceived a violent liking ... I never thought I should live to see German Princes the favourites of the mob, but Mr Pitt could make the Grand Seigneur or Sophi of Persia so.[20]

Under George II, it had been different, and the pursuit of interests and acceptance of commitments that did not accord with traditional British ones, and that, however misleadingly, could be presented as Hanoverian, aroused disquiet among British ministers, and also provided their critics, such as William Pitt the Elder in the winter of 1755–56, with an opportunity for arguing that ministers were betraying both national interests and their supposed role as balancers of royal power. Thus, on 15 October 1757, the *Monitor*, then the most influential London newspaper, declared:

> The country which supplies the crown with the sinews of war, has a right to inspect into the conduct, and to demand satisfaction, of those who dare to give him bad advice: by which the blood and treasure of the nation shall be misapplied or squandered away; and the glory and interest of the crown and kingdom be diminished and injured.

This criticism has to be considered because it conditioned the assessment, both by contemporaries and subsequently, of George I and George II, and indeed of the dynasty. Both George I and George II sought to maintain the dynamism of Hanoverian expansion, but by 1721 it was clear that George I's high ambitions could not be realised. George II also failed to acquire East Friesland, Hildesheim and Osnabrück (in the last case seeking unsuccessfully to replace the situation whereby a Hanoverian Prince was the alternative ruler of the prince bishopric). There has, however, been a failure on the part of most scholars to understand, let alone appreciate, the nature, dimensions and validity of contemporary criticisms of Hanoverianism made by those formally in opposition and by many of those in government circles. All too often, historians of domestic politics have underrated foreign policy, while many scholars of the latter have failed to understand domestic politics, in part because they have treated criticism as unfounded or inconsequential.

In response to criticism of Hanoverianism, there is the counter-argument that the British had perforce to accept a European role, whatever their rulership; that, in short, the Hanoverian connection was not the cause of interventionism. In addition, although compared to alliances with, and strategic concerns about the Low Countries, the Hanoverian connection was not central to British interventionism, it was, and still is, argued that the connection might have been useful to such a project, possibly greatly so, for diplomatic and military reasons. Pro-Hanoverian interventionism has also been defended on the basis that America was conquered in Germany; that the commitment of forces and money in Germany during the Seven Years War (1756–63) ensured that French efforts were distracted from the defence of New France (Canada).

This defence of foreign policy and, in practice, of the Hanoverian link is flawed. The French could not readily switch resources between land and sea, while the need by Britain in 1748 and 1802 (the Treaties of Aix la Chapelle and Amiens) to return important colonial gains in order to compensate for the deterioration of Britain's position in Europe under-lines the degree to which the relationship could work in an opposite direction. Indeed, in 1755 the French Foreign Minister presented an attack on Hanover as a way to counter French naval weakness compared to Britain,[21] while the *Monitor* fruitlessly warned on 23 September 1758:

> As the crown is, by the Act of Settlement, restrained from making war in favour of a foreign state without consent of Parliament: by parity of reason no part of a British conquest or dominion ought to be given back to an enemy, upon any other consideration than in exchange for some place or privileges to be restored to the British crown.

In 1806, the future of Hanover – whether it should be left under Prussian occupation, seized by Napoleon or returned to George III, became an important issue in negotiations involving the three, leading to concern that British goals might be affected by Electoral interests, and vice versa. Thus, after a British expeditionary force defeated the French at Maida in Calabria on 4 July 1806, the Prussian envoy in France reported that

August that Napoleon had offered to ensure the return of Hanover if the British withdrew from their base in Sicily.[22] Seven years later, British subsidy treaties with Prussia and Russia included a stipulation for the return of Hanover from French control. Count Munster, the Hanoverian minister in London, also succeeded in getting the British to press Prussia for the cession of Hildesheim, Ravensburg and Minden to Hanover, although only the first was conceded.[23]

The Hanoverian connection was sometimes defended on the grounds that the Electorate was an ally in time of need, but there was also criticism of the deployment of Hanoverian troops in Britain. On 29 March 1756, William Pitt the Elder opposed an address to George II to send for Hanoverian troops to prevent a threatened French invasion of England, arguing that the danger should be met by raising new units in Britain, but the government won the divisions in the House of Commons. The resulting deployment led, however, to a well-publicised scandal when a Hanoverian soldier arrested at Maidstone on suspicion of theft was released from the custody of the civil authorities by the order of the Earl of Holdernesse, a Secretary of State. When Pitt became Secretary of State later in the year he ensured that the King's speech opening the parliamentary session that December included the promise that the Hanoverian troops would be sent back to the Electorate.

These points need to be borne in mind when considering the role and impact of individual monarchs and of the dynasty as a whole. It is also crucial to note how the situation changed with time, undercutting any stress on a similar experience throughout the dynasty. As far as the reigns of the first two Georges were concerned, the Hanoverian link weakened Britain as an international force because, due in large part to the Jacobite claim, the link was unpopular with many in the British Isles and challenged the crown-elite co-operation on which successful politics depended. The existence of a Jacobite claimant also directed attention to the character of the two Georges; although, in turn, their supporters focused on the Kings' Protestantism, which was their strongest political card.

The situation was made more serous because of support for Jacobitism from Britain's opponents. As a result, there was a serious threat to the British state in periods of war and international crisis from 1689 until 1759. Conversely, the defeat of Jacobitism at Culloden in 1746, and of

French schemes for a pro-Jacobite invasion in 1759, with the British naval victories of Lagos and Quiberon Bay, greatly strengthened the British state and monarchy, and, with them, the Hanoverian dynasty. The domestic situation was transformed, as the identity and ability of the monarch became less central, and the Hanoverian issue less serious. George III's sons did not have to defend the dynasty on the moors of Scotland, as William, Duke of Cumberland did in 1746, while, had Frederick, Duke of York commanded against the Irish rising in 1798, he would not have been fighting a resistance motivated by Jacobitism. A stress on change draws attention to the very different challenges that the monarchs had to face.

# 3

# *Father and Son*

The same violent and corrupt measures taken by the father will be pursued by the son, who is passionate, proud and peevish, and though he talks of ruling himself, he will be just as governed as his father was.

Thomas, 3rd Earl of Strafford, a Jacobite, on the
first two Georges, 1727 [1]

The first two Hanoverians, George I (1714–27) and his son George II (1727–60), have not had a terribly good press. Unpopular with their contemporaries and each other, they have not subsequently been seen as great rulers. George I is chiefly remembered for his personal life, not least the thirty-two-year incarceration of his adulterous wife, Sophia Dorothea (1666–1726), the disappearance (and presumable murder) of her lover, Philipp Christoph von Königsmarck in 1694, and George's subsequent attachment to Melusine von der Schulenberg, whom he made Duchess of Kendal. George II is generally seen as a headstrong, blinkered boor, manipulated in his early years as King by his wife, Queen Caroline (1683–1737), and by his chief minister, Sir Robert Walpole (1676–1745). Neither King has left much correspondence to provide his own point of view, nor to offer sympathetic insights on character and goals. Indeed, the contrast with the correspondence left by George III is striking: dropped from a modest height, the published volumes of the latter could well be fatal to those below.

Yet both Kings played a major role in the development of the British monarchy. Their reigns were crucial to the solid establishment of the constitutional and political conventions and practices that are known as the Revolution Settlement, after James II and VII's replacement by William III in the 'Glorious Revolution' of 1688–89. The legislation that made it up (which included the 1701 Act of Settlement enshrining the claim to the British throne of Sophia of Hanover, mother of the future George I) was passed from 1689, but much of the political settlement was not solidified until after 1714. In particular, the defeat of the Jacobite uprising of 1715–16, the '15, by George I's troops marked a triumph over the forces opposed to the new order. This triumph was repeated in a clash of dynasties in 1746 when the army that crushed Charles Edward Stuart at Culloden, significantly, was led by George II's second and favourite son, William, Duke of Cumberland.

The clash of dynasties was also a struggle over national identity that reflected part of the working out of the Glorious Revolution. This could be seen as providential blessing or usurpation, and the contrast challenged anew the practice of compromise that, throughout, had been the victim of the politics of Stuart Britain and the Stuart failure to compromise. Furthermore, the Williamite victory over James II and VII ensured that the political ideas associated with the victors of the 'Glorious Revolution' were widely disseminated, and, as a consequence, the notion of the monarch as answerable for his conduct was in the background throughout the reigns of George I and George II.

The reigns were also important because they determined the character of the Anglo-Hanoverian monarchy. Although the consequences of this new polity were less dramatic than those stemming from the personal union of England and Scotland under James VI and I in 1603, this had been by no means clear when the new dynastic personal union was created. Britain-Hanover was similar to Poland-Saxony. In each case, a state with a degree of public participatory politics (Britain and Poland) found itself linked to one that was more clearly the expression of a ruling house (Hanover and Saxony). This led both to serious problems of adjustment at the domestic level, and to an attempt to create a degree of unity at the international level that aroused controversy.

Both George I and George II were interested in the details of foreign policy and sought to use British resources to help secure gains for Hanover.[2] Compared to most of their British ministers, both men were very knowledgeable in European affairs and military matters, well travelled and competent in languages, and this made them better able to give effect to their policies. In foreign policy, British ministers tried to take advantage of the skill, contacts and commitment of the Kings;

what Newcastle termed the 'figure our King makes abroad'. In 1719 James Craggs, Secretary of State for the Southern Department, wrote to his fellow Secretary of State, James Stanhope, that it would be good if George I could spend two or three days at The Hague on his return from Hanover: 'I hope his presence will remove all the doubts and difficulties that remain on the part of the States [Dutch government], establish an entire good correspondence between us and them, and be very popular in that country'.³ Aside from receiving foreign diplomats, the King could also send letters directly to foreign sovereigns, as when George I wrote to Charles VI opposing the plan of Victor Amadeus II, ruler of Savoy and Piedmont and then King of Sicily, for the marriage of his heir to one of Charles's daughters.⁴

As Elector, George I sought to win territories from the partition of the Swedish empire and to place a westward limit on the expansion of Russian power under Peter the Great. In turn, George II pursued Hanoverian territorial interests in neighbouring principalities, especially in Mecklenburg, East Friesland and Osnabrück. As a leading Protestant power, Hanover was also involved in the defence of confessional interests, especially during the reign of George I, complaining, for example, about the brutal treatment of Polish Protestants in Thorn (Torun) in 1724. Both rulers also sought to counter Hanoverian vulnerability to attack from France or Prussia. The ambitions and interests of George I and George II maintained the dynamism of Hanoverian policy: one, however, that was unwise and, in large part, unsuccessful in itself, and a source of concern and anger to numerous British ministers and diplomats. Unwilling to share a monarch with an obscure German state, the British seldom appreciated that the Electorate deserved the attention of the Hanoverians. Public criticism of the lengthy royal visits to Hanover was intense, and was shared by ministers. On occasion, as in 1721, the latter pressed the King against going to Hanover.⁵

The consistent and readily apparent Hanoverian ambitions of both Kings made their British ministries vulnerable to domestic criticism and Hanover to foreign attack, and George I and George II learned, however reluctantly, to accept the limitations of their position. By 1721, it was abundantly clear that the high ambitions of George I had been disappointed, and the same was apparent of George II by 1748, when he had to accept that Hanover would make no gains from the War of the

Austrian Succession, whereas his hated nephew, Frederick the Great of Prussia, had seized Silesia in 1740–41 and East Friesland in 1744, thus ensuring that Prussia clearly became the major North German power.

Within Britain, there was a similar learned, if reluctant, willingness to work within bounds in domestic politics. The crown was important politically, and indeed the court remained a crucial sphere in which careers were advanced and policies formulated.[6] As the monarch remained the ultimate political authority and his favour was the first step to power, his court remained the political centre, since it provided access to him. It was in his court that a ruler displayed clearly who was in favour and who was not. George II, who was not one to change his opinion of individuals easily, did not hesitate to snub William Pitt the Elder in public, Henry Harris writing in December 1750, 'Saturday was a devilish dull day at court ... Not seven persons in the circle ... The Paymaster General not spoke to, scarce looked at, upon this thin occasion'.[7]

In contrast, once the Newcastle-Pitt ministry had been established, Newcastle was pleased by relations between George and Pitt in 1757, seeing them as crucial to the stability of the ministry: 'The King is quite civil, and behaves very well to him, and indeed he deserves it, and His Majesty is satisfied. I have laboured all I can do to produce the good humour, and I have succeeded, and I must do them justice they have done their parts well'.[8] The importance of the demonstration of royal favour was shown in 1759, when, after initially refusing, George allowed himself to be bullied by Pitt into awarding the knighthood of the Garter to the latter's brother-in-law, Earl Temple, a reluctant but necessary step.[9]

As a side-effect of the tendency to underrate royalty, Whig historiography sidelined the pre-1760 Georgian court; instead, Parliament was seen as the crown's dominant partner after the Glorious Revolution. While it is true that George II's Closet was not Henry VIII's Privy Chamber, the insignificance of the early Hanoverian court has been overdone. This was true not only of the relations between King and ministers, but also of those with more intimate favourites. Thus Amalia Sophie Marianne von Walmoden, George II's mistress, who became his acknowledged mistress after the death of Queen Caroline in 1737, being made Countess of Yarmouth, was an influential political figure because of her access to George, whose favours to her were not ignored by the populace. In 1736, William Pulteney reported,

> One Mrs Mopp, a famous bone-setter and mountebank, coming to town in a coach with six horses on the Kentish Road, was met by a rabble of people, who, seeing her very oddly and tawdrily dressed, took her for a foreigner, and concluded she must be a certain great person's mistress. Upon this they followed the coach, bawling out, 'No Hanover Whore, No Hanover Whore'. The lady within the coach was much offended, let down the glass, and screamed louder than any of them, that she was no Hanover whore, she was an English one, upon which they all cried out, 'God bless your Ladyship', quitted the pursuit and wished her a good journey.[10]

Thus Mrs Mopp reprised Nell Gwynn's patriotic claim under Charles II not to be French; a sentence that can be variously reordered without losing the meaning.

At the same time, George II was careful not to allow his women to compromise his political position. When he was Prince of Wales, his mistress, Henrietta Howard, Countess of Suffolk, had links with the opposition to Walpole. After George came to the throne in 1727, she enjoyed little power, but this had not been predicted, and George's earlier favour for her had been seen as a sign that Walpole would not survive the change of monarch. Walpole, however, did not make the mistake of some ministers and courtiers of assuming that Henrietta was the power behind the Prince. Instead, close to George's wife, he claimed to have 'the right sow by the ear'.[11] Johann Daniel Schöpflin, who was in Britain from September 1727 until the end of January 1728, writing a report about its politics for the French government, claimed that Queen Caroline was important to George II's popularity. He also wrote:

> The King is much more popular than George I. As much as he can, he tries to make himself popular. His father did not know English and hated the people. George II likes the English and knows the language. The Germans do not take a role in the government of England as they did under George I ... it appears that George II is more firmly on the throne than his father was.[12]

The Kings were not autocrats, and they had to learn the limits to their power and authority, especially as the consequences of the party conflict constrained the crown's freedom of political manoeuvre. This constraint had made it very difficult for William III and Anne to create and sustain the mixed ministries of Whigs and Tories they sought, for the growth of party loyalty led party leaders to resign from or refuse to accept office because the monarch also employed men of another party.

The constraints became even clearer under George I and George II. Although it has been claimed that the Tories were keen to serve the crown, and that George I and II were willing to turn to the Tories [13] (which would have enlarged the crown's ability to manoeuvre), there is little evidence after 1715 for the second contention, and the first probably underrates the role of Jacobite sympathies. George I and George II both detested the Tories as the party whose ministry had negotiated the Peace of Utrecht in 1713, ensuring Britain's exit from the War of the Spanish Succession (in which the young George II had fought) and abandoning Britain's allies, including Hanover. George I and George II suspected the Tories of Jacobite inclinations and were alienated by Tory opposition to their commitments to continental power politics, and by Tory hostility to continental Protestantism. In these areas, Tory opinions and ideology, as well as Tory politics, conflicted with royal interests; although much depended on the importance attached to Hanoverian Toryism. In 1714 the French envoy reported that George II, then Prince of Wales, would not suffer the sight of any Tories, regarding them all as Jacobites.[14] George II's instruction to the Lord Chancellor, Lord King, in 1727 to increase the number of Tories on the commissions of the peace included the injunction to 'still keep a majority of those who were known to be most firmly in his interest', which George ordered King to keep secret, suggesting that he was really seeking with the increase to curry popularity.[15]

At times of political tension, as in 1717 and the mid 1740s, when the monarchs risked the defeat of their favourite ministers, James Stanhope and John, Lord Carteret respectively, they were prepared to threaten that they would turn to the Tories for support, but there was little substance to these threats. When George I and George II sought Tory help (more on an individual than an entire party basis), they did so only in order to serve Whig ministries and measures. The inability and unwillingness of Tory leaders to offer their support helped to make discussion of such schemes abortive, as in 1717–18. When, in 1717, Lord Trevor was granted an audience with George I, the King was made to listen to a defence of the Utrecht settlement, not a way to endear the Tories to George.[16]

The Kings had to rely on the Whigs, severely limiting their ability to break with the latter in the event of a dispute. As a consequence, they had to make concessions in ministerial and policy choice. George I fell out with Walpole and his brother-in-law and political ally, Viscount Townshend, in 1717, when these ministers opposed his Baltic policy and supported his son, George, Prince of Wales, in the first of those hardy perennials of Hanoverian royal politics: clashes with the heir. The political significance of the clashes was a testimony to the continued role of crown and court in politics. In 1717, George I lent full support to a rival ministerial group, which led to Townshend's dismissal and Walpole's resignation; but, with financial confidence hit by the South Sea Crash in 1720, he had to accept a multi-stage reconstitution of the ministry in 1720–22 that left Walpole dominant, a process taken further with additional ministerial changes in 1724 and 1725.

After Walpole's fall in 1742, which George II had very much opposed, he backed Lord Carteret, only to be forced to part with him twice: in 1744 and 1746. Carteret lacked sufficient support in the Commons. In 1757, George II was obliged to accept that the sole ministry that could fight the Seven Years War was one led by William Pitt the Elder and the Duke of Newcastle. This brought to a close his long and repeated efforts to keep from power Pitt, whose public criticism of pro-Hanoverian measures he loathed. The King, earlier, had showed no hesitation in indicating his views, not least in pressing Newcastle not to cooperate with Pitt,

> I pray you to consider my promise to Fox. If Pitt will come in with a great number of followers, it is impossible you can direct the administration, and I know that by inclination he will distress my affairs abroad, which are so enough already. I shall be glad to see you on Monday, and with a resolution to come in and support my affairs.[17]

Both Georges also had to accept that an inability to determine the composition of the ministry had consequences in legislative and policy terms. In other words, the attitude of the Kings was crucial if parliamentary monarchy was to work, for an incompetent and unyielding monarch might well have led to the collapse of the Revolution Settlement. Instead, much of the credit for Britain's modern constitutional monarchy rests with those who redefined the royal position between 1689 and 1707, and then made it work over the following half century. The parliamentary monarchy that was a product of the 'Glorious Revolution' was successful because it could respond to changes in the political world, not least in the interests and abilities of individual monarchs.

The somewhat uncertain use of royal authority under William III gave way to a 'managed' approach under Anne, George I and George II. Neither crown nor ministry possessed sufficient strength to dominate the other, and the constitutional guidelines that sought to define their relationship, such as the Act of Settlement of 1701, were vague, providing scant guidance for most political eventualities, and dependent upon mutual goodwill. There was as yet no received understanding of such central issues as the collective responsibility of the Cabinet, the particular responsibility of the departmental head, the special role of the first minister, and the notion that the King should choose his ministers from those who had the confidence of Parliament.[18]

Conventions by which Parliament could participate in policy formation, nevertheless, developed. This was not so much a product of Parliament, or, more particularly, politicians able to manage it, seizing the initiative, as in conventional Whig interpretations of British political development, but, rather, a new stage in the longstanding relationship between crown and Parliament. It was one in which the crown was seen, certainly by foreign commentators aware of continental comparisons, as respecting the nation's liberty and liberties.[19] Parliamentary monarchy required a monarch willing to work with Parliament, and thus focused attention on the intentions of the ruler. Walpole managed to show the crown that a parliamentary monarchy could help it to achieve most of its aims, and the political nation that it could provide stability, continuity, peace and lower taxes. He also helped ensure that the political and governmental system worked despite frequent and lengthy absences by George I and George II in Hanover (not that these visits were viewed in the Electorate as absences). The ability to make the system work in the absence of the rulers gave the ministers in both London and Hanover more independence, but also posed the problem of developing attitudes and practices to minimise disagreement, both within the ministries and between them and the distant monarch. Recent experience was not helpful. Anne had never left England as Queen, and, although William III had spent much of his reign abroad, either on campaign or tending to his Dutch interests, this had contributed in 1698–1701 to a serious breakdown in relations between the King and a Parliament that felt ignored.

The situation was generally less troubled under the Hanoverians than it had been under William, although he had faced particularly difficult circumstances. Under the first two Georges, ministers whom the crown favoured, largely for their views on foreign policy, fell because they did not enjoy the support of Walpole, and because their policies were not likely to gain parliamentary approval. Carteret was demoted in 1724 and Townshend resigned six years later. The very fact that two Secretaries of State, the ministers concerned with foreign policy, should depart in accordance with the wishes of the First Lord of the Treasury indicated the willingness of the crown to accept the implications of parliamentary monarchy, although, in each case, Walpole only obtained his goal with considerable difficulty.

For similar reasons, George II maintained Walpole in power in 1727, and did not appoint his 'favourite', Spencer Compton, in his place. George accepted that Walpole's command of a parliamentary majority made him indispensable to the crown. Walpole's success in meeting the crown's financial needs through obtaining parliamentary support for a generous Civil List was of great importance for the avaricious George II. In 1733, when there was pressure at court to remove Walpole after his failure to push through the changes in taxation known as the Excise Scheme, George chose to support him rather than the Earls of Chesterfield and Scarborough, courtiers to whom he had been close as Prince of Wales. George was mindful not only of the need to have Parliament managed, but, also, of parliamentary views: in December 1753, Henry Fox found him 'too full of yesterday's debates to say anything to me on Lord Kildare's subject this morning'.[20]

Despite the importance of Parliament, the role of the crown was still central. However constrained and affected by political exigencies, monarchs chose ministers. General Thomas Erle, a long-standing MP, wrote in 1717,

> The King is certainly master of choosing who he thinks fit to employ ...
> No honest man will come into measures to compel the King to employ
> anyone, let his capacity be what it will, nor to distress those employed,

out of peevishness to the person. But if the Public is apparently in danger by evil counsels the cry will then be general; and there are many instances how fatal it has been to our Kings when they have been tenacious of a favourite, who has justly incurred the odium of his subjects.[21]

In 1742, a prominent Tory, and sometime Jacobite was kept out of the Admiralty Board:

> A List was drawn up; amongst them Sir John Hynde Cotton was put down; upon the scheme, as was before said, of placing the administration upon the broad bottom. This list was presented to the King. He struck out Sir J. H. Cotton with his own hand. This alarmed all people to a high degree. The seeds of a vehement and formidable opposition were sowed anew.[22]

The role of George II's eldest son, Frederick, Prince of Wales, in the political crisis of 1741–42 reflected a very different aspect of the influence of the royal family, because, as Duke of Cornwall, the Prince controlled many boroughs in a county that was heavily over-represented in Parliament. Frederick was very much in the hands of superior political intelligences and personalities, but the attitude of the heir to the throne was in this case a decided advantage to the opposition.

Frederick, Lord North, First Lord of the Treasury from 1770 until 1782, told the Commons on 27 February 1782:

> the King had a right to admit and dismiss from his councils whomever he pleased: and he might, without assigning any cause, or without fixing any guilt upon the person, recall that confidence which he had been graciously pleased to bestow upon any one of his servants.

This right, however, had to bow to the winds of necessity, as George III and North discovered in 1782. North, who was defeated on 27 February on an address against continuing the American war, announced the government's resignation to the Commons on 20 March, but George was unable to secure the new ministry he wanted. Nevertheless, many of the possibilities of entrenching greater parliamentary power were never pursued in this period. Parliamentary inquiries into government accounts lapsed after 1714, estimates of annual military expenditure were generally passed without detailed scrutiny, successive ministries ignored appropriation clauses, and Parliament did not develop executive powers, unlike the Estates of Bohemia and Württemberg.

If monarchs needed to appoint and, if necessary, sustain a ministry that could get government business through Parliament, this was a shifting compromise, and one subject to contingency and the play of personality. Conventions developed but were subject to strain and debate. Compromise was a two-way process. If George I had to accommodate himself to Walpole, it is also clear that Walpole had to adapt to George. This involved political skills and a sense of responsibility on the part of both men. The way in which Walpole had to respond to George also throws light on royal preferences. Support for Hanover included a subsidy treaty with Hesse-Cassel in 1726, by which Hessian troops destined for the defence of Hanover were paid by Britain, not Hanover. Walpole was also expected to find money for George's female German connections,[23] and to spend time as a courtier, attending on the royal family, as on 3 July (os) 1724, when he was present at George I's review of the Foot Guards in Hyde Park.

George II was no different: in 1738, the Earl of Malton was informed that, although Walpole had pressed the King, 'he had the misfortune and concern to find that he could not prevail'.[24] Similarly, Newcastle and even Pitt had, at least in part, to respond to George II's interests and views. This was seen in particular in the dispatch of a substantial force to Germany in 1758 in order to protect Hanover from French attack and permit George to heed ministerial pressure to keep Hanover in the war. Three years earlier, Newcastle had written to Holdernesse, the Secretary of State with George in Hanover, 'I am sure you will take a lucky moment, when *we* are in good humour, to lay the letters before the King ... His Majesty must see the regard we have had to His German dominions'.[25]

German first by birth, training, loyalty and inclination, both Kings were pragmatists who did not have agenda for Britain, other than helping Hanover; a situation that contrasted with George III. In part, with George I and George II, this was a sensible response to circumstances; in part it was the consequence of a complacency that arose from diffidence, honesty and a measure of dullness. In addition, by the standards of the age, George I, born in 1660, was old when he came to the throne, while George II, born in 1683, was no youngster, although neither was troubled by sustained ill-health. If George II was advised by his doctor not to go to close the parliamentary session in 1749, that

was a rare occurrence.[26] Neither man sought governmental changes akin
to those introduced by Peter the Great (1689–1725) or by Frederick
William I of Prussia (1713–40). At times, however, they showed at least
aspects of an autocratic temperament, although this was taken no further
than complaints. In 1752 Newcastle wrote to his ally Hardwicke, in his
own hand, from Hanover, where he was accompanying George II:

> I know the King still very uneasy about our juries, and our laws. He this
> day talked much against the late Jury Bill, said the crown had lost a great
> deal by it, that formerly they depended on the Sheriffs, who were all (except
> those of London) appointed by the crown. That my Lord Townshend had
> told him that he was much against it, but as he was then just going out,
> he was not to oppose it.

Arguing that the measure should have been thrown out by the House of
Lords, George added, 'It is a terrible thing, that legacies from ministers
who are going out, and have nothing to answer for, and are only *to please*
at the expense of those who remain in have such lasting effects'. Newcastle
noted George II's more general disquiet at signs of popular independence: 'the spirit of the City [of London], and the acquittal of the printer
are bad symptoms, and give the King just cause of uneasiness'.[27] Concern
about another aspect of law and order was shown in the royal speech
opening Parliament on 15 November 1753, in which George said that he
was appalled by the rise in murders and robberies. The speech was been
written by the ministers, but George had to accept it.

George II also expected high standards from the central government.
In 1758, Newcastle noted about money for Hanover, 'His Majesty wanted
this money to be sent away in twenty-four hours. I told him this holiday
time nobody was in town, no office open, that caused very severe
reflections'.[28]

Neither George had pretensions to mimic the lifestyle of Louis XIV
(1643–1715) or the Emperor Charles VI (1711–40). Instead, they presented
themselves in a relatively modest fashion. Also, although both men
were prepared to be prodded into levées, ceremonies and other public
appearances, they preferred privacy. George I, whose mother had had
to defend him from accusations that he was insensitive and cold,
held neither morning levées nor evening drawing rooms attended by
visitors, and it was a sign of the growing political crisis in 1717 that he

made a major effort to win support by entertaining extensively at Hampton Court.[29] This entertaining continued, so that on Twelfth Night – 6 January (os) 1718 – there was a great ball at court, in which George played cards with a large group of aristocrats, including Sarah, Duchess of Marlborough, the Dukes of Kent, Kingston and Newcastle, and the Earl of Halifax. This was at once an instance of the use of the court as a focus of aristocratic society, and a public gesture, as the ball was widely reported in the press.[30] The following month, George was reported as losing 3000 guineas when he played ombre at court with the Duchess of Monmouth and the Countess of Lincoln.[31]

George II was less reclusive and more outgoing, in part thanks to the prompting of his wife, but he did not master the arts of popularity and was regarded as being very rude to British aristocratic visitors to Hanover in 1750. He, however, could converse in English, even if it was accented, whereas his father could not. George I had made little effort to learn English, and this was readily apparent. After a short sentence in English at the start of his speeches to Parliament, the King gave them to the Lord Chancellor to read out. The large Hanoverian household he brought with him further helped to insulate him from British society.

Both Kings were keen on the army, enjoyed the company of military men, and were proud of their own martial experiences, which, in George II's case, included participation in the victories of Oudenaarde (1708) and Dettingen (1743). In Sir John Thornhill's depiction of the royal family in the Painted Hall at Greenwich, George I and George II as Prince of Wales are shown wearing armour. George II had the Guards' regimental reports and returns sent to him personally every week, and, when he reviewed his troops, he did so with great attention to detail. This is recorded, for a review of the Hanoverian troops held in 1735, in a large painting by J. F. Lüders.[32]

Yet, although the Kings had an impact on policy and politics, the political system could accommodate the interests and choleric attitudes of both men with relatively little difficulty. Despite periodic rows about Hanoverian interests, neither King swamped Britain with German ministers, nor a Germanic system of government; had they wished, their ability to do so would have been very greatly limited by the Act of Settlement. Indeed they showed less interest in German models of government than Queen Victoria's husband, Prince Albert, was to do a

century later. Strong Lutherans, George I and George II were still ready
to conform to the Church of England. A Lutheran chapel had been
established at St James's Palace for those brought over by Anne's husband, George of Denmark, but George I and George II used the Chapel
Royal.[33] Such compliance was also more generally seen. Thus Augusta
of Saxe-Gotha, who, in 1736, married Frederick, Prince of Wales, initially
refused to take communion in the Church of England and, instead,
attended a Lutheran chapel, but she then began to attend services at the
Chapel Royal and, eventually, to become a devout Anglican. George II
was depicted, in a painting attributed to J. Valentin Haidt, with figures
associated with the Moravian Brethren, a German Protestant community
that established a presence in England, but the majority of Anglican
bishops were not hostile to them, and, in 1749, supported the passage
of the Moravian Act which recognised the Moravian Church.[34] Friedrich
Michael Ziegenhagen, who served as royal Lutheran chaplain at
St James's Palace from 1722 until his death in 1776, was very interested
in assimilating Pennsylvania Germans into the empire.

George I and George II sponsored a number of bishops whose beliefs
were generally regarded as heterodox, George I's name appearing on
the title-page of the prominent latitudinarian Benjamin Hoadly's controversial sermon on the text of 'My Kingdom is not of this world'; and
the sermon was published with George's stated and publicly proclaimed
approval. Hoadly also enjoyed promotion under George, becoming both
a royal chaplain and Bishop of Bangor in 1715, and being translated to
Hereford in 1721 and to Salisbury in 1723. Charles Trimnel, Bishop of
Norwich, who was made Clerk of the Closet to George and was his
confessor, had been a prominent opponent of High Church views and
a critic of their most vocal proponent, Dr Henry Sacheverell. In 1721 he
was translated to the lucrative and prominent see of Winchester. The
noted Huguenot preacher Jacques Saurin received a royal pension from
George I, who was impressed by his sermons: a volume of them were
dedicated to George.[35] In addition, George II's wife, Caroline, had
extensive and radical religious views and patronised controversial
clerics.[36] In contrast, George II was quietly non-controversial.

The Hanoverians were not seen as threats to the Church of England
comparable to that presented by the Catholic Stuarts. In March 1714,
when attempts were made to probe the possibility of his succeeding the

ailing Anne, 'James III and VIII' had refused to abandon his Catholicism, the basic requirement for support, although he did agree to grant religious freedom.

This is a rather unheroic account of the development of a measure of political stability, but it is one that captures the character of a limited monarchy that lacked a rigid constitution, and was thus particularly dependent on circumstances, especially the attitude and role of individual monarchs. Neither George I nor his son did much to win popularity for the new order (certainly far less than George III was to do), but, far more crucially, the extent to which their attitudes or policies actively sapped consent was limited. This was crucial when there was a rival dynasty in the shape of the Stuarts, with 'James III and VIII', falsely described as the 'warming pan baby', the claimant throughout both reigns.

Stability also had to be fought for. The value of counterfactual (what if?) speculation is clearly pertinent for both 1715 and 1745 when Jacobite success seemed a serious prospect. In 1745–46, there was the additional hazard of an invasion for which the French were making serious preparations; as in 1744, they were largely thwarted by the weather, although British naval strength was also a major factor. George I and George II ultimately survived these crises because they displayed more level-headedness, and less panic in a crisis, than James II and VII had shown in 1688. Had George II fled to Hanover when the Jacobites, advancing on London, reached Derby on 4 December (os) 1745, then the coherence and morale of the Whig ministry would probably have collapsed; while Cumberland's eventually successful generalship serves as a reminder of the extent to which Britain had to be fought for between 1688 and 1746, just as continental dynasties, such as the Bourbons in Spain in 1704–15, had to fight to establish themselves in succession wars. In these conflicts, the image of rival claimants was as much at issue as their ability: George I and George II benefited from the degree to which, while not popular, they were at least acceptable, in particular thanks to their Protestantism. This could also be a strongly positive pro-Hanoverian factor. There was strong Dissenting support for the Hanoverians in the crises of 1715 and 1745, with Samuel Chandler's *Great Britain's Memorial against the Pretender and Popery* (1745) going through many editions.

Stability was therefore achieved as a result of victory. It was followed by empire. George II presented himself as a necessary part of the process, making compromises, such as his acceptance of Pitt, in order to secure goals. In 1757 he told Baron Haslang, the long-serving Bavarian envoy, that the reference to religion which might offend Catholic envoys, that he had made in the royal speech to Parliament, had to be seen in the context of his domestic position: that he had to say what would please the 'people' in order to get them to pay more readily for the measures of the government.[37] This was a shrewd response to the circumstances he found himself in: George was able to see the dichotomy that faced him and to act as necessary for domestic politics, as well as in the interests of foreign policy.

There was no attempt to increase royal authority, as there was in Sweden with the bringing to a close of the 'Age of Liberty' by Gustavus III in 1772. Instead, the British system can be seen as a successful compromise that reflected the strengths and weaknesses of hereditary monarchy. Such an approach may seem complacent, indeed Whiggish, and it risks smoothing over crises, such as those in 1742 and 1746, in favour of a more schematic approach. Nevertheless, the flexibility of the system allowed for changes in the ability and activity of monarchs, while it also prevented the development of a system of powerful personal monarchy.

Hereditary monarchy lacked the emphasis on individual ability of its 'meritocratic' counterpart, whether electoral (Kings of Poland, Popes) or dictatorial (Cromwell, Napoleon), but it had an important advantage, certainly over dictatorial monarchy, in the form of the greater continuity that stemmed from an assured succession and, therefore, stability. None of the Georges possessed the drive or military ability of Napoleon, but there was no need for the British state to be directed by such a figure, with all the unpredictable dangers and personal whims that he would have entailed. Ultimately, the eighteenth-century British world produced another model of monarchy, in the shape of the American president, an elected limited monarch. This form was to be a durable one. It provided a means to choose, an agreed method of succession, and a way to produce individuals of apparent merit. Such a system, however, had only been devised in response to the unwanted breakdown of rule by the British crown. Within Britain, no such expedient was necessary nor appeared so. The early and mid eighteenth century was a period in which ardent republicanism found little favour in Britain.

# 4

## *George I*

The King has not a thought with relation to his affairs either at home or abroad, that is not entirely agreeable to the sentiments of your friends ... he has certainly done more towards declaring his inclinations than the most sanguine man among us could ever hope for ... it was our misfortune last summer that His Majesty was apt to think he did everything that we could in reason expect from him, when in reality there was nothing essential done that could convince the world with whom he placed his credit and confidence.

Thomas, Duke of Newcastle to Horatio Walpole, 1724[1]

To British contemporaries, George, who was crowned on 20 October (os) 1714, seemed a distant figure. Unlike William III, who had seized power in 1688–89, and who was familiar with English politics and politicians from earlier visits, marriage into the English royal family and extensive intervention in English domestic politics, George knew relatively little of the country. He had only visited it once – in the winter of 1680–81, when a marriage with the future Queen Anne was in consideration, and being pressed by his mother Sophia's brother, Prince Rupert of the Rhine, although support from other quarters was limited. In the event, Anne married Prince George of Denmark.

George was also a relatively old man when he came to Britain's shores again. Born on 28 May 1660, he was already fifty-four, the oldest occupant of the throne upon his accession, although the current Prince of Wales may challenge that. Relatively short, he was physically fit, and his 'china-blue' Brunswick eyes were an impressive feature. George had had a happy childhood. His mother, Sophia, was devoted and was keen to ensure that her children grew up in a happy environment. As a result, she was careful to keep those she saw as overly religious, and thus inflexible, from her children. In 1661 George's father, Ernst August, had become ruler of the prince bishopric of Osnabrück, a territory that, after the Peace of Westphalia of 1648, alternated between a Catholic Prince Bishop and a Protestant member of the house of Hanover, ensuring that he and his wife were financially independent and could bring up their children as they deemed fit.

His parents offered George very different leads. Ernst August was interested in hunting and riding, although in Osnabrück he also set the pattern of a conscientious administrator. George was to emulate his father in this, working hard at the *métier* of rulership. In contrast, among his brothers, Maximilian and Christian Heinrich were lazy, a contrast that was to be repeated with George III and his three brothers. In each case, the death of the elder son might have led to a very different monarch, although younger sons given the prospect and responsibility of power could mature into the role, as George VI was to show. Sophia was more bookish than Ernst August, and George sought to please her by being a conscientious pupil. He also took after Sophia by becoming, in her eyes, a rationalist in religious matters, an approach that his son, George II, with his interest in ghosts and werewolves, did not share. At the same time, it is important to note George I's piety.

The apprenticeship of power demanded that the future George I acquire military experience. His uncle and, later, father-in-law, Georg Wilhelm, Duke of Celle, arranged for George to drill a company composed of the sons of his courtiers, a surprise George enjoyed; and in 1675, aged only fifteen, he accompanied his father on campaign, bringing his formal education to a close. Western Europe was then convulsed by the Dutch War (1672–78), with the expansionism of Louis XIV of France opposed by the Dutch, the Holy Roman Emperor Leopold I, most of the German princes, and Charles II of Spain. The risks involved in campaigning were shown the following year when Friedrich August (1657–76), the eldest nephew and likely eventual heir to Rudolf August, Duke of Brunswick-Wolfenbüttel, died on campaign. George, who in 1675 showed courage in the military operations he was engaged in, was more fortunate. His father took pride in his conduct, especially at the battle of Conzbrücke. The value of George's earlier upbringing was shown on campaign, not least his skill as a rider. The following year, he took part in the siege of French-held

Maastricht, while in 1677 and 1678 he came out from the shadow of the previous generation and was given independent command.

George's education also advanced in other ways. In 1676 he made the under-governess of his sister pregnant. Despite his parents' attempts to claim that the child was not his, the boy looked like George. He was not acknowledged, and he and his mother departed from the historical record, a fate like that of many of those who have fallen for the charm of princes. Ernst August then appears to have arranged for Maria Katharine von Meysenburg (1655–1723), the younger sister of his own mistress, Klara Elisabeth von Platen, to become the mistress of the younger George; a way for the father to influence his son's situation, although the psychological consequences were less clear.

George's position also became more important when Ernst August, who had become Duke of Hanover in 1679, introduced primogeniture (undivided inheritance by the eldest son) as a means to enhance the family's position. This was to isolate George from his brothers bar the youngest, another Ernst August, as the others were alienated by the loss of their prospects. The introduction of primogeniture followed George's marriage in 1682 to his first cousin, Sophia Dorothea (1666–1726), the heiress to Georg Wilhelm, Duke of Celle (1624–1705), a marriage that was a crucial step in the consolidation of the family's interests. The future George II was born from this union in 1683.

The marriage, however, was a failure. A combination of the young Sophia Dorothea's immature and flighty nature and of George's absence on campaign ensured that relations between the two were cold by 1686. First George and then Sophia Dorothea took lovers. Sophia Dorothea's, Philipp Christoph von Königsmarck, a Swedish count and Hanoverian colonel, was more charismatic, glamorous and sensual than George. Sophia Dorothea and Königsmarck met in 1689 and became lovers in 1692, but the affair did not remain a secret for long, and Sophia Dorothea ignored hints that she should be prudent. Her wish to end her marriage threatened Ernst August's plans to link the Hanover and Celle inheritances and, in July 1694, Königsmarck was intercepted in the Leineschloss palace on a nocturnal visit to Sophia Dorothea, murdered, and probably thrown into the river in a weighted sack, prefiguring the plan made by Rigoletto for the lecherous Duke of Mantua in Verdi's opera, as well as the fate of Rasputin. As George at the time was in Berlin, Ernst August was most likely the key controller of the killing.

Sophia Dorothea was then detained and the marriage dissolved, with Sophia Dorothea regarded as the guilty party and thus denied remarriage. Georg Wilhelm agreed that his daughter should be confined under his care at the manor house of Ahlden, where she remained until her death, while George was given care of their two children. The entire episode scarred George; in part because of the humiliation it entailed. The double standards involved, given his own adultery and that of Ernst August, were of course commonplace, and an aspect of male *gloire*; they were also important if the integrity of the succession, in the shape of the legitimacy of children, was to be preserved.

Ernst August became increasingly ill from early 1695, ensuring that George had to take a major role in the government of the Electorate. Indeed from 1688 George, in a successful attempt to educate him to the demands of statecraft, had been admitted to the audiences Ernst August held daily with his leading ministers.

After he succeeded his father in 1698, George was interested in ensuring that Georg Wilhelm kept his promise to detain Sophia Dorothea, but was also increasingly looking further afield, toward the English succession (it was assumed that arrangements for the English throne would be followed by those for that of Scotland). In 1698, he pressed William III on his position in the line of succession. The Act of Settlement of 1701 placed George's mother Sophia and her issue above the fifty-four Catholics who had a better hereditary claim, particularly the house of Savoy, whose claim ran through Charles I's daughter Henrietta, and the Wittelsbach and Modenese houses, whose claims ran through Sophia's elder brothers. This carried George most of the way toward his succession to the throne in 1714. Queen Anne understandably did not want either Sophia or George in London: she claimed it would make her 'look at her coffin every day that remained of her life'. Nevertheless, Regency and Naturalization Acts further secured the position of the Hanoverian dynasty; and, in 1706, the future George II gained both the Garter and the titles Duke of Cambridge, Earl of Milford Haven, Viscount Tallerton and Lord Tewkesbury.[2] There was to be no Queen Sophia, as she died on 8 June (ns) 1714, before the much younger Anne, who died on 1/12 August 1714. Had Anne, born in 1665, who died aged forty-nine, lived as long as Sophia, born in 1630, then George I, while Elector, thanks to the absence of female succession in Hanover, would not have become King; instead, George II would have been the first of the Hanoverian monarchs.

On the day of Anne's death George I's proclamation rapidly followed, and he was crowned on 20/31 October. As King, however, George suffered from the difficulty of learning to adjust to his new role. The nature of politics in Britain was very different from that in Hanover, and the conduct politicians judged appropriate was not that understood by George. In particular, he found it difficult to appreciate the legitimacy of opposition. George's failure to learn English – all documents from ministers were translated into French for him, and the ceremonial of his coronation had to be explained in Latin – and his obvious preference for Hanover, which extended to a low opinion of British doctors and the preference for a German one,[3] further contributed to this sense of alien rule, causing complaint, among Whigs as well as Tories. Lady Anne Paulet was ready to believe a report that George would not return to Britain from Hanover for the winter of 1716–17, 'for I fancy he is so much easier where he is that he will like to be from us as long as he can'.[4]

In contrast, George and his Hanoverian advisers literally thought that his journeys to Germany were important for his health. In 1719 he travelled to the German spa of Pyrmont to take the waters, doing so again in 1720, 1723 and 1725. In 1718 George's thwarted wish to go to Germany was motivated in part by concern about his health.[5] That year Friedrich Bonet, the Prussian envoy, reported that George disliked England, for its language, constitution, political parties and continual importunities for royal favour, whereas he was master of all of those in Hanover. He also noted that, in contrast, the Prince and Princess of Wales, then linked to the opposition, conspicuously always spoke English, and that the Prince spoke it well and correctly.[6]

Concern about George's goals was exacerbated by a sense that his preference for Hanover entailed an abandonment of British national in-terests, as resources were expended for the aggrandisement of Hanover, and as the entire direction of British foreign policy was set accordingly. In particular, there was a clash over Baltic policy that indicated the complex issues that British politicians had to address after the accession of the Hanoverians. Alongside Peter the Great of Russia and Augustus II of Saxony-Poland, Frederick IV of Denmark had attacked Charles XII of Sweden in 1700, launching the Great Northern War (1700–21). The Danes had sought to seize Sweden's territories in northern Germany, occupying the duchy of Bremen (between the Elbe and the Weser) in August 1712, but this was an area of interest to neighbouring Hanover. To pre-empt another Danish invasion, George, as Elector, in collusion with the Swedes, in 1712 occupied another Swedish territory, the duchy of Verden (between the duchy of Bremen and that of Celle). In turn, in response to the shifting international situation, in October 1715, George, as Elector, declared war on Sweden in response to Danish and Prussian pressure: only thus, as agreed in their treaty of June 1715, would the Danes vacate Bremen for his forces,[7] and the Prussians suspend boundary disputes. In addition, in return for Russian recognition of Hanover's *de facto* possession of Bremen and Verden, George, as Elector recognised Russia's conquests from Sweden other than Livonia.

George's wish to use British naval and financial resources to advance his interests against Sweden clashed, however, with British assumptions, not least that of playing an even hand in Baltic power politics. The issue helped divide the ministry. More generally, there appeared to be an abandonment of national interests. A reasonable critique of policy was advanced on this basis: within five years of his accession, George was at war with Spain, and close to war with Russia (once concern about Peter the Great's expansionism had replaced hostility to Charles XII of Sweden, who was shot during a siege in 1718). Having proscribed the Tories and divided the Whigs, he was also seeking to implement a controversial legislative programme. The continental interventionism of the reigns of William III and Anne, although costly, lengthy and of mixed success, had at least been directed against an unpopular power, France, that many found threatening. In contrast, George, from 1716 allied with France, an alliance he worked to preserve,[8] pursued a foreign policy that struck scant resonance with the political experiences and xenophobic traditions of his British subjects.

Jacobite propaganda made much of the Germanic nature of the Hanoverian regime. While Whig publicists presented the Stuart cause as foreign because Catholic, their Jacobite counterparts had no hesitation in proclaiming the alien nature of the Hanoverians, despite their Protestantism. In many senses, it was easier to attack them as usurpers than William III, who was both son and husband to Stuart Princesses, was careful not to proscribe the Tories, and, by the admittedly uncharismatic standards of both George I and George II, was not without qualities. The alliance with France also undercut one of the principal criticisms directed against the Stuarts, that they were pro-French.

As a result of George's interests, politicians were forced to define their attitudes towards states they knew little about, in the context of a rapidly-changing international situation. Hanover's close involvement in the Great Northern War of 1700–21, which led to Sweden ceding Bremen and Verden in 1719, meant that George expected from his British ministers a greater commitment to Hanoverian interests than he was subsequently to require or receive in the early 1720s. Differences of opinion over foreign policy were treated as tests of loyalty. The commitments necessary to gain Bremen were even regarded as excessive by such a leading Hanoverian courtier as Friedrich von der Schulenburg.[9]

On the other hand, George's reign was not so much the wholesale Hanoverian takeover that some feared as an implicit aspect of the Hanoverian succession. It was more like the dual monarchy of nineteenth-century Austria-Hungary. George I adapted to British institutions, conforming to the Church of England, despite his strong Lutheranism. In response to the opposition from much of the lower clergy to the toleration of Dissenters (Protestant Nonconformists), Convocation, the clerical assembly, of which there was one for each archdiocese, was prorogued continually from 1717, with the exception of a brief session in 1741–42, as was the Convocation of the Church of Ireland. This was, however, not the result of an independent decision by George, but rather one by the government. Royal support for the Dissenters led, from 1722, to a small *regium donum* (king's gift) given annually to trustees from the Baptist, Independent and Presbyterian churches, the funds used to supplement the incomes of their indigent clerics. In addition, from 1726, Sir Robert Walpole obtained Indemnity Acts, protecting the Dissenters from malicious prosecution, especially office-holders who had failed to take communion. These and other measures were very unwelcome to many supporters of the Church of England, but they were not akin to Stuart support for Catholicism. Indeed, in 1723 and from 1725, the crown also gave an annual grant of £1000 to the General Assembly of the Church of Scotland (an Established Presbyterian Church) to assist in the struggle against Catholicism: royal bounty was used to support catechists and missionary ministers. Furthermore, George's ecclesiastical policies were scarcely new. It was under Queen Anne in 1709 that Dr Henry Sacheverell had felt able to argue that the church was in danger under the Revolution Settlement, as interpreted by the Whigs.

Other aspects of the reign also did not represent a radical departure. George I's dispute with his son, the future George II, fitted into a parliamentary framework, with court and Leicester House (where the Prince's court was based) parties at Westminster. The failure of the Jacobite rising of 'James III and VIII' in 1715–16, another stage in a series of Jacobite failures, indicated early in the reign that the establishment on which George depended was determined, in turn, to maintain his rule and able to do so. George's place in British politics was not of his choosing but a consequence of the limitations in royal authority and power that stemmed from the 'Glorious Revolution' and subsequent changes. George was sensible enough to adapt and survive; unlike James II and VII and 'James III and VIII', he was a pragmatist. Lacking the decisiveness, charisma and wiliness of Louis XIV of France and Peter the Great of Russia, George did not have an impact or win a reputation comparable to either, but their ambitions were out of keeping with his position.

The major domestic issues of the reign involving George were his antipathy towards the Tories and his clash with his son. In July 1721, the Duke of Newcastle, a firm Whig, wrote that

> the report of the Tories coming in having reached the king's ears, he has been so good as to declare to me and many other of his servants the concern he has at the report, and has assured us that he neither has or ever had any such thoughts, and is determined to stand by the Whigs, and not take in any one single Tory. He is very sensible the Whig party is the only security he has to depend on, in which he is most certainly right.[10]

The opposition of Hanover to the Peace of Utrecht, the peace with France negotiated by the Tory ministry in 1713, had led George at his accession to look to the Whigs. This leaning was reinforced by his suspicion of Tory Jacobitism and by advice from both his envoy in London and the Dutch government. In contrast, both Whigs and Tories had enjoyed favour during Anne's reign, and her last leading minister, Robert Harley, Earl of Oxford, had sought to head a mixed ministry, albeit one that centred heavily on the Tories, because of the commitment of most Whigs to the continuation of the War of the Spanish Succession. There had been hopes, once he came to the throne, that George would also preside over a mixed ministry. William Bromley, a prominent Tory, wrote on 3 August (os) 1714, two days after the death of Anne, whom he had served as Secretary of State, about the absence of Jacobite action: 'everything has been carried on with the greatest unanimity, all ranks of people expressing their duty to the king, and their satisfaction in our present settlement, so that we have just ground to hope the enemies of our constitution will be discouraged from making any attempts to disturb us'.[11] Tory hopes were to be dashed. George did not reappoint Bromley Secretary of State, and the latter was soon speaking in the Commons against the ministry, as well as collecting money for the plot to restore the Stuarts with the help of Sweden.

George did not want a coalition government. If individual Tories, such as Viscount Harcourt in 1720 and Lord Trevor in 1726, were accommodated, it was only at the price of abandoning their colleagues and principles. In 1723 Newcastle noted that Carteret, the Secretary of State for the Southern Department, who was seeking to supplant Walpole, had broken off with the Tories, 'thinking to carry his point with the Whigs, which he knows agreeable to the king'.[12] After George came to the throne in 1714, Tories were dismissed from a range of posts, including in the armed forces – a course of action that pressed hard on a landed society that had been suffering from the dangerous combination of high wartime taxation and an agrarian depression. This party preference exacerbated the normal problems of diminished and altered opportunities that accompanied both demobilisation and the accession of a new monarch. The Tories were treated far more harshly than had been the case under William III. Parliamentary business was also resolutely partisan. George informed his first Privy Council that he wished for the repeal of the Occasional Conformity and Schism Acts, while Tory ministers were impeached on the charges of having betrayed national interests by the negotiation of the Peace of Utrecht and in an attempt to tar the party as Jacobite.

The attack on Tory leaders was seen as very partisan. *An Address to the Peers of England*, a Jacobite pamphlet, condemned George I for send-ing British money to Hanover, decried Dutch, German and Huguenot influences, and added:

> see how your cruel German king thirsts after English blood. He resolved to cement the foundations of his reign by the blood of English nobles, to make room for German barons, and before he set foot on English soil sold the life of noble Ormonde to the Dutch States, contrary to the example and policy of English kings who begun their reigns with acts of clemency and amnesty, as if he would vie with the example of heathen Rome.[13]

Similar themes were to be repeated, and provide an undercurrent of criticism against which George had to operate. Thus, a Jacobite pamphlet of 1721 set out to contrast 'James III and VIII' and George. It claimed that at dinner James ate only English dishes – 'roast-beef, and … Devonshire pie', liked English beer, and was offended by the load of the British national debt

> and the severest hardships contracted and imposed to support foreign interests. He lamented the ill treatment, and disregard of the ancient nobility, and said, it gave him great trouble to see the interest of the nation abandoned to the direction of a new set of people, who must at any rate enrich themselves by the spoil of their country.[14]

By turning against the Tories, George encouraged support for Jacobite plans. In 1715, the Jacobites planned three risings. 'James III and VIII' was to copy the Duke of Monmouth in 1685 and William III in 1688 by landing in the south-west of England, which was seen as the centre of a rebellion that was to lead to a march on London. There were also to be risings in the Scottish Highlands and the Borders. The rising in the south-west was nipped in the bud due to poor leadership, indecision, and effective government intelligence that led to the arrest of the leading conspirators. In Scotland, in contrast, the rising was initially successful and both Perth and Aberdeen were captured. The leader, the Earl of Mar, lacked, however, the necessary dynamism. He failed to exploit initial successes and at the battle of Sheriffmuir on 13 November (os) 1715 was unable to exploit his numerical superiority. The rising in the Borders was not coordinated with that in the Highlands. The Jacobite force advanced into Cumbria, eventually capturing Preston where they were outnumbered and, on 14 November (os) 1715, forced to surrender.

The government forces then focused on the Jacobites in Scotland. James 'III and VIII' had landed at Peterhead and moved on to Scone where his coronation was planned, but, in the face of the Duke of Argyll's advance, the Jacobites retreated, James sailed back to France, and his force dispersed. The Hanoverian dynasty had survived its baptism of fire. Jacobite support in Scotland was at a higher pitch then during the rising in 1745–6, but that had not compensated for poor leadership.

Support for 'James III and VIII' from many Tories encouraged George I to rely on the Whigs, but this reliance also limited his political options. Concern about the impact of Hanover on British foreign policy contributed powerfully to the 'Whig Split', a deep division among the Whigs in 1717–20, that led a section under Robert Walpole, the most prominent Whig in the House of Commons, to seek tactical cooperation with the Tories in order to achieve the overthrow of the Whig government. This was a serious problem for George, one provoked by his foreign policy and his handling of the struggle for influence between the leading Whigs. It was one that he could not counter, however, by turning to the Tories. In addition, George was suspicious of links between Walpole and George, Prince of Wales.

George's personal vulnerability flowed from family disputes. His choleric quarrel with his son and heir, which interacted with and seriously worsened the political disputes, was a classic feature of dynastic politics: the tension between ruler and heir, and between those who looked to one or the other. Such disputes look modest in comparison with what happened elsewhere at this time. Among George's contemporaries, Peter the Great had his son and heir, Alexis, killed in 1718. Victor Amadeus II of Sardinia (1675–1730) was imprisoned until he died by his heir, Charles Emmanuel III, when he tried to retract his abdication. Yet these family disputes had the capacity seriously to disrupt British politics, and thus to affect the stability of the crown.

To note problems shared with other dynasties is not the same as to deny responsibility or blame. If the Hanoverians faced tensions in their family, and divisions among their ministers, then part of the art of royal politics was the ability to tackle such problems. The assertion of royal will, without the creation or worsening of serious political divisions, was crucial, whatever the formal constitutional powers of the sovereign. In 1717 George I proved unable to assert himself in this manner, helping

to precipitate a crisis. Differences between George and his son gathered
pace in 1716, when George forced the dismissal of his son's Groom of
the Stole, the Duke of Argyll, a rival in the army of William Cadogan,
who enjoyed the King's favour, and limited the Prince's rights as Regent
during the King's first visit back to Hanover. Despite Argyll's dismissal,
the Prince continued to show favour both to him and to his brother,
the Earl of Ilay, angering the King by so doing. Efforts to effect a
reconciliation between father and son after the 1717 session failed.

   Difficulties climaxed in November 1717, in a dispute over the christening of Prince George's second son, George William (1717–18): George I
had wanted the baby named George, while the Princess, who was worried
by a prediction about the name, favoured William, a name she thought
would also be more agreeable to the British nation.[15] The Prince and
Princess wanted the Prince's uncle, George I's youngest brother, Ernst
August, Prince-Bishop of Osnabrück, and from 1716 Duke of York and
Albany and Earl of Ulster, as a godfather, but the King insisted on the
choice of the Lord Chamberlain, Newcastle, whom the Prince detested.[16]
After the christening on 28 November (os) 1717, the easily-flustered
Newcastle was convinced that the Prince had threatened him, and the
King took the matter in hand, in part for political reasons. The dispute
rapidly led to the expulsion of the Prince from St James's, and his
establishment of a rival court at Leicester House. George I took charge
of the Prince's children, whom, he insisted, must remain at St James's,
an insistence for which he gained legal support. The dispute earned the
King much criticism, especially when the young George William
died,[17] although, according to the Austrian diplomat Johann, Freiherr
von Pentenriedter, the nobility, unused to the sort of treatment
Newcastle had received, favoured the King.[18] George also insisted that
no one could hold offices in his own and his son's households or be
received in both.

   Ministers found it essential to win the public support of the monarch
in order to underline their own influence and hold on power, but the
degree to which the King would allow a minister or group of ministers
in effect to deploy royal power or influence itself posed problems. In
the Whig Split of 1717, George lost the support of Walpole and his
brother-in-law, Viscount Townshend, because he was too closely associated with their rivals, James Stanhope and the Earl of Sunderland.

Townshend and Walpole were reluctant to support the fiscal, political and diplomatic consequences of George's Baltic policy, and the King reconstituted the ministry in December 1716. He promoted Stanhope, an ex-army officer whom he felt he could deal with, to the crucial Secretaryship of the Northern Department, which was responsible for relations with northern Europe, and demoted Townshend from that post to the Lord Lieutenancy of Ireland. Townshend had made the mistake of not accompanying George to Hanover in 1716. As so often with ministers who stayed behind, he found it difficult to retain royal confidence.

The promotion of Stanhope, failed, however, to produce either ministerial harmony or a smooth parliamentary session in 1717. A political crisis ensued that April. The ministry had exposed the Gyllenborg Plot, a conspiracy that committed Charles XII of Sweden to help the Jacobites in return for Jacobite money, and were determined to use it to secure a definite parliamentary commitment to support George's anti-Swedish policy. The conspiracy itself indicated the risks posed by George's aggressive foreign policy: the Jacobite rising in 1715–16 had failed, but it had also revealed that the Jacobites could raise substantial forces within Britain. As a result, after war with Britain broke out in 1718, the Spanish government sought to mount an invasion in 1719, only for most of the fleet to be dispersed by a violent storm off Cape Finisterre. The small force that landed met with some Highland support but was defeated at Glensheil.

In 1717 Walpole and Townshend split openly with Stanhope and Sunderland over the demand for support against Sweden. In parliamentary terms, this was a sensible decision, as support there for a war against Sweden was weak and suspicion of Hanoverian designs behind British foreign policy acute. It was, however, hardly the issue to divide over if the purpose was to increase George's favour towards Walpole and Townshend. The brothers-in-law probably hoped to force George to recognise that parliamentary support for his foreign policy could only be obtained by coming to terms with them, and by making concessions over foreign policy. Stanhope thought that they might even have intended to make George abdicate in favour of his son.

Instead, the net result was to drive George further into the arms of Stanhope and Sunderland. One of the striking aspects of the Whig Split was George's unequivocal support for his ministers and his determination to use all royal patronage to this end. When, in April 1717, Parliament was asked for funds to enable George to concert measures with his allies against hostile Swedish designs, the opposition countered by accusing George's Hanoverian ministers of using British money to support Hanoverian territorial aggrandisement. Townshend's dismissal for voting against the measure in the Lords was followed by the resignation of Walpole. George was very sorry to lose Walpole and tried to persuade him to stay.

Sunderland wrote in 1717 'upon the whole, I don't doubt, but the King's steadiness will carry it'.[19] Once the King was committed, however, it was difficult for him to avoid the consequences of criticism and opposition from those opposed to the ministers, and, more particularly, to escape damage if those ministers were weakened. Equally, the political crisis added to the existing one inside the royal family. John, Lord Perceval noted that the 'Walpolites' were increasingly seen as 'the Prince's party'.[20] In 1718 an attempt at a reconciliation between George I and the Prince failed: the Prince's letter contained no assurance of better conduct. When the King asked for one, the Prince was angry.[21] There was also dissension over the Prince's Civil List and over whom the Prince could employ.[22] The King's terms for a reconciliation were reported:

> Provided the Prince would dismiss such of his servants as were disagreeable to the King, and that for the future he would take none but such as should be approved of by His Majesty. That he should give up his children and such a sum for their education as His Majesty should appoint. That he should neither see nor keep correspondence with any but such as His Majesty should approve of, and lastly that he should beg the Dukes of Roxburgh and Newcastle's pardon.[23]

The strong interest shown in the rift from the outset by British and foreign commentators is an instructive guide to their belief in its importance. Reports of a possible reconciliation were eagerly recounted or debated,[24] and led to speculation about their likely consequences. There were also reports about more extreme solutions, including that George would oblige his son to return to Hanover. This indeed led Frederick William I of Prussia, George's son-in-law, to instruct his envoy Bonet to open links with the Prince.[25]

The dispute was also reported extensively in the press, much to the fury of the King, who was livid that letters between him and his son were printed.[26] Nevertheless, the government felt it important to explain its views. The pro-government *Weekly Journal* of 18 January (os) 1718 sought to counter critical reports:

> Several false reports, being spread about, concerning the unhappy difference betwixt the King and the Prince of Wales, we shall give an account of it, according to the copy of a letter transmitted by the Secretary of State to foreign courts.

The paper urged the Prince to follow the contrite example of Prince Hal, later Henry V. The dispute with his son ensured that George I did not go to Hanover in 1717 or 1718. Instead, he spent much of the two parliamentary recesses at Hampton Court, entertaining far more lavishly than was his wont. George also wooed support during his trip to Cambridge and Newmarket in October 1717. The King's preferences were shown in his visit to the Earl of Orkney's seat at Cliveden. Orkney (1666–1737), whom George had made a Lord of the Bedchamber in 1714, shared the King's military background, and had fought in the Nine Years War and the War of the Spanish Succession. The rift between father and son continued, with no ball held at court on the Prince's birthday in 1718. The importance of royal support to the ministry was dramatised by the distribution of patronage to its supporters. On 31 March (os) 1718, the Dukes of Newcastle, Montagu and St Albans and the Earl of Berkeley were elected knights of the Garter. In April Stanhope and Cadogan were made earls, and Cobham and Charles Fane viscounts.

Foreign policy remained a major cause of disagreement in Parliament, with the opposition claiming in 1718 that support for the Holy Roman Emperor in Italy, which led to war with Spain in 1718–20, was not in the national interest, but rather designed to ensure Austrian backing for Hanover, a reasonable assertion. Concern about George's views also extended to the government's religious policy. George was a Lutheran, although he conformed to Anglican liturgy in the Chapel Royal. From 1717, in concert with Stanhope and Sunderland, George backed a policy designed to limit the position of the Established Church. They supported the repeal of the Occasional Conformity, Schism and Test Acts, and the passage of an Act to limit the independence of the universities of Oxford and Cambridge, where most of the clergy of the Established Church were trained. This attempt to win the support of the Dissenters led to widespread alarm about the future of the Established Church under George. The Occasional Conformity and Schism Acts were both repealed in 1719. The first, passed in 1711, had been designed to prevent the circumvention of communion requirements for office-holding by Dissenters communicating once a year; the second, passed in 1714, had been designed to make separate education for them illegal.

The Peerage Bill, initially proposed in 1718, only to be withdrawn and then pushed the following year, caused much anxiety. A product of George's feud with the Prince of Wales, this was an attempt to restrict the membership of the House of Lords, preventing the future George II from creating fresh peers when he came to the throne in order to buttress a new ministry that he might appoint. Newcastle had been confident that a clear demonstration of royal favour for the ministry would help secure the passage of the legislation:

> I think it appears very plain that our master places his confidence, where all honest men must wish it, which in my opinion will go a great way towards making every thing easy and when once people come to see that somebody at present will think himself as ill used if the Bill does not pass ... I should hope they would be afraid of acting as they did the last year.[27]

Stanhope, himself, was in no doubt of the importance of George's backing:

> nobody can be so mad as to think of proposing any fixed resolution to the King upon matters of this consequence without knowing previously the sense of our friends in England. They must govern us, and especially our friends of the house of Commons ... When your Grace shall see our good master you will learn from himself how much he has at heart not to be baffled a second time in this matter.[28]

In the event, in December 1719, Walpole's opposition, which exploited concern among MPs about closing the door to their upward social mobility, helped kill the Bill in the Commons, but there are also indi-cations that George I was less in favour of the limitation of the royal prerogative than his ministers, although, as so often with Georges I and II, 'the problem is the lack of direct evidence and the conflicting nature of the circumstantial evidence'.[29] George's name was certainly used extensively by supporters of the Bill. Thus, Earl Cadogan wrote

> The King has the matter so very much at heart, and believes it so highly important for his service, that his Majesty cannot doubt of the concurrence and assistance of all those who are his real friends, and who either have received, or expect to receive, any mark of his favour. I can assure you these are the King's own thoughts, and not the insinuations of his ministers.[30]

Had the Bill passed, then William IV would have been unable to threaten creations in order to secure the passage of the First Reform Act in 1832.[31]

In 1720 Walpole returned to government. This reflected both the political weaknesses of the latter, and Walpole's own desire to play a major role in a Whig ministry. Walpole and Townshend benefited from tension between Stanhope and Sunderland, on the one hand, and George's German confidants, Bernstorff and Bothmer, on the other. This was linked to differences within the government over Baltic policy, as well as to anxiety over how best to support the cost of military and diplomatic preparations. These differences were not new. Throughout the period of the Whig Split, ministers had expressed concern about the German advisers. In May 1718, James Craggs, the Secretary of State for the Southern Department, had noted governmental concern that Charles VI would not agree to British diplomatic demands 'because from our German quarter here I suspect he is assured that he need not'.[32] In October 1719, however, Stanhope was able to promise that Bernstorff's influence had been overcome, with George again playing the crucial role:

> I cannot promise that the old man will be left behind [in Hanover] but I may safely assure your Grace that though he should come [to Britain] the King will do whatever shall be proposed to him to make everybody sensible that he is not to meddle in English business. He is exceedingly piqued and mortified at his declining credit.[33]

The following month, Newcastle repeated the account, adding 'This the King has ordered us to tell everybody', and, somewhat implausibly, 'the fact is, the Germans have no more interest with him than the subjects of any other nation'.[34]

The wish to end the rift between King and heir also was important in Walpole's return to office. The end of the crisis was also related to the state of the Civil List, the parliamentary grant to the crown; ending the Whig Split would help ensure that the accumulated debt of the Civil List would be paid off. Walpole played a part in arranging, through the offices of Caroline, Princess of Wales, the reconciliation between George and his son. On 23 April (os) 1720, the Prince of Wales made his submission to his father and, next day, the opposition Whigs followed. Walpole soon steered the Bill for tackling the Civil List debt through the Commons.

A financial scandal, however, swiftly hit both government and crown. Involvement with the ministry had helped lead George into the serious scandal of the South Sea Company, the crash of what had basically become a fraudulent financial conspiracy on a massive scale. This was correctly seen as a crisis that reflected the corruption of the governing order,[35] and one that required ministerial change. George, had been elected Governor of the company by the Court of Directors in February 1718, replacing the Prince of Wales. He had not paid for the shares he held. Like other prominent people, George I had taken them as bribes to promote the company. Its crash in September 1720 ensured that he lost his prospects of massive winnings, but he still made a gain of £45,304.

The search for guilty men was focused on the ministry, and the situation appeared propitious for the Jacobites. John Menzies wrote from Paris in October 1720, 'it wants but kindling the train of powder by some strong hand, and a right conduct in placing the train'. As 'James III and VIII' observed in December 'matters seem at present to be very ripe in England'.[36] The crisis led to pressure for George to return early from Hanover, and gave Walpole a central role in restoring public finances and in shielding the King from the South Sea Scandal. In August 1721 Carteret, a protégé of Sunderland, noted, 'The King is resolved that Walpole shall not govern, but it is hard to be prevented'.[37] George had eventually not only to reconcile himself to Walpole, but also to accept the latter's position as leading minister.

Walpole's active role in thwarting and exposing the Jacobite Atterbury Plot in 1722 underlined his zeal for the Hanoverian Succession and commended him greatly to George. The King's support helped Walpole supplant his rivals, a process helped by the death of Stanhope from a cerebral haemorrhage in February 1721, and of Sunderland from pleurisy in April 1722. Bernstorff had already left England in 1720. Sunderland had been involved in Jacobite plotting, although the extent of his complicity remains controversial. After his death, his former adherents were removed from power, Carteret being demoted in 1724 from Secretary of State for the Southern Department to Lord Lieutenant in Ireland.

Walpole's continued ability to dominate the House of Commons and to manage the public finances successfully commended him to George. In 1722 Archibald Hutcheson, a successful opposition candidate, hoped that ministerial failure to win the two Westminster seats in the general election would

> open the King's eye, and give him a different view of things, than that in which sycophants and flatterers, and I may say traitors to him and to their country, have set the same. This might occasion an alteration of some in employments; who, although they deal pretty much with the Devil, would appear to His Majesty not to be such conjurers as they pretend to.[38]

In fact, Walpole had the two candidates elected for Westminster unseated by the House of Commons on petition on 6 November (os), and, on 3 December (os), two government candidates were returned. Both electoral and parliamentary politics showed Walpole as a master politician.

Walpole also benefited from the resolution of the complex interaction of court and ministerial politics with foreign policy and with divisions in the French and Hanoverian ministries. Townshend, then closely allied to Walpole, accompanied George to Hanover for the first time in 1723, and Walpole was able to persuade George that Carteret and his protégé, Sir Luke Schaub, the envoy in Paris, were harming the Anglo-French alliance. Other ministerial changes made George's favour towards Walpole clear. In 1725, the Duke of Roxburgh, Secretary of State for Scotland, and the Earl of Macclesfield, the Lord Chancellor, both fell. The maverick Tory Viscount Bolingbroke was foolish to believe in 1727 that George was going to dismiss Walpole.

The South Sea Company was not the sole fraudulent company with which George was involved. An active supporter of improved commercial links between Britain and Hanover, George also backed the development of the port of Harburg, and his grandson, Frederick, became Governor of the Harburg Company, which was granted a charter in 1720 in order to develop trade between Britain and Hanover. However, the company's attempt, in 1722, to raise funds in Britain by means of a lottery was judged fraudulent by the House of Commons, and the Sub-Governor, John Barrington, was expelled from his seat in the House for his role in promoting and carrying on a fraudulent undertaking. His support for Hanoverian goals had earlier led Barrington to speak in the Commons in 1721 for a subsidy to Sweden, and he had gained an Irish peerage in 1720.

Aside from frauds, there were other direct pressures on British ministers to provide benefits for the Hanoverian elite, including favours at the Customs and profits from government patronage. A failure to note or understand the impact of such controversies and pressures leads to an inability to grasp the real basis to hostility to the Hanoverian connection. British ministers linked to George were also seen as corrupt. A House of Commons' motion in June 1717 to charge Cadogan, a favourite of George, and, characteristically, a military man, with embezzling the funds entrusted him for bringing over Dutch troops to help suppress the '15 was defeated by only ten votes.

Nevertheless, George I's return to London from Hanover in 1719 was greeted with acclamations in Pall Mall, with windows not illuminated in the King's honour being broken by the public, while César de Saussure, a Swiss visitor, recorded that the London mob cheered George in 1725 and subsequently mourned him in 1727, while also celebrating George II's accession.[39] It is unclear whether this was simply the fickle mob using any opportunity for an 'event', or a popularity particular to London, or evidence that the general unpopularity of George I and George II has been overstated. They were, after all, the Whigs' monarchs, although it is unclear how much personal popularity this brought them.

As an individual, George I was a figure of suspicion because of the incarceration of his adulterous wife, Sophia Dorothea and the disappearance of her lover Königsmarck, and also because of rumours about his own personal life. The divorced Sophia Dorothea never came to Britain. Scurrilous ballads made much of the theme of the royal cuckold. *Sir James King's Key to Sir George Horn's Padlock* dwelled on the theme, while an *Address to Britannia* included 'Pray let no cuckold be still ruler over thee / Nor any German bastard begot in privity'. Another manuscript verse that circulated satirised George and his alleged mistresses, condemning their influence on him and their competition for his attention by contrasting them with the goddesses vying for the attention of

Paris.[40] It was claimed that Ernst August's mistress had played a key role in the disappearance, and presumed killing, of Königsmarck because he had allegedly deserted her for Sophia Dorothea; but there is no real basis for these reports, although their repetition was an indication of the lurid conspiracy reports to which the disappearance gave rise.

The estrangement from Sophia Dorothea, the extra-marital relationship and the illegitimate children were an established feature of George's life when he became King, and made an enduring stick with which his British subjects could beat their ruler. The estrangement of King and wife had not been matched under Charles II and James II and VII. Part of the criticism was unjustified. It was widely reported that Sophia Charlotte, created Countess of Leinster in the Irish peerage in 1721, after she had 'plagued all mankind about her title',[41] and Countess of Darlington in the British peerage in 1722, was George's mistress. In fact, she was his half-sister and loved her husband, while no one close to the royal circle suggested that George had incestuous relationships.

George, instead, seems to have been faithful to Melusine von der Schulenburg (1667–1743), who in 1690 was appointed a lady-in-waiting to George's mother, becoming George's lover from at least 1691: their first daughter was born in 1692. She was the thin 'Maypole' contrasted with Darlington's plump 'Elephant': they frequently travelled in the same coach, which may have been responsible for the claim that they were both George's mistresses. In fact, Sophia Charlotte was envious of Melusine, not least because she gained a superior social rank. Melusine, who was kind, well educated and from a prominent family, provided George with the calmness he did not find in his excitable and angry wife. Melusine and George were very close and had three daughters – born in 1692, 1693 and 1701, and passed off as the children of Melusine's sisters, to whom George showed much affection. Indeed, he took much pleasure in this second family, not least when it was supplemented by grandchildren: two grandsons born in 1722 and 1724. George often took late suppers with Melusine and her daughters. His first family meanwhile had grown. The marriage of the future George II in 1705 was followed, in 1707, by the birth of George's first grandson, Frederick. A first granddaughter, Anne, followed in 1709. When George became King, Melusine and their daughters came to Britain, and were installed at St James's Palace, as was George, Prince of Wales, and his family bar

Frederick, who was left in Hanover as a pledge of the dynasty's continued interest in the Electorate.

Melusine herself was naturalised as British in 1716. She became Duchess of Munster in the Irish peerage that year, and Duchess of Kendal in the British peerage three years later, while she also benefited from the spoils system that Britain offered the Hanoverians. She received £15,000 worth of South Sea Company stock as a secret present, in the hope that she would strengthen the King's support for the company; Sophia Charlotte received the same present, while Melusine's two younger daughters were given £5000 each.[42] Melusine was also reported to have received money from British peers as rewards for their receiving the Garter and other benefits, while the demotion of Carteret in 1724 was attributed, in part, to her influence.

Politically, far more problems were created in 1722 when George granted Melusine the patent for the Irish coinage. This she subsequently sold, at a profit of £10,000, to William Wood, whose exploitation of the patent was to cause a political storm in Ireland. Although Walpole, whose advice on share dealings was sought by Melusine,[43] referred to her as as much 'Queen of England as anyone ever was', she was at most a morganatic wife, certainly not a Queen Consort. The absence of the latter helped lead to rumours about George. It also left the position of Queen uneasily between Melusine, Sophia Dorothea, and Princess Caroline, who wore the Hanoverian royal jewels at George's coronation. The terms of his divorce allowed George to remarry but, under English church law, he could not do so while his divorced wife was alive, as she was until 1726.

George's relationship with Melusine created less of a stir than the rumours about the Königsmarck affair. Amours on the part of kings were scarcely new. At George's coronation, the Duchess of Portsmouth, one of Charles II's mistresses, found herself with the Countess of Dorchester, his brother James II and VII's mistress, and the Countess of Orkney, the mistress of William III, leading Dorchester to remark 'who would have thought that we three whores should find ourselves together here'.[44]

As later with radical pornography in the 1790s and 1800s, humiliation was a powerful political weapon: to demystify the monarch and subject him to ridicule and abuse was part of a determined attempt to weaken his position. Jacobite protestors seriously damaged the equestrian statue of George set up in London in Grosvenor Square in 1726.[45] The scurrilous ballads and verse that circulated about George's personal life, nevertheless, also provided an opportunity for popular expression about George that helped to secure his position. Such expression was partly tolerated, in marked contrast to the more repressive censorship in continental Europe. Satire also provided George with an identity that was not Hanoverian. It was far better for him to be lampooned for human weaknesses than to be perceived as an obvious alien – criticism that was also advanced.

Governmental sensitivity over George's life continued after his death. In 1732, the British diplomatic service was used in an attempt to suppress the sale of the *Histoire secrète de la duchesse d'Hanover*, an anonymous work written by Karl Ludwig von Pöllnitz.[46] Aside from rumours concerning George's relations with women, there were also unfounded suggestions that his relationship with Mustapha and Mehmet, the two Turkish grooms of the chamber, the latter of whom was in charge of George's private accounts, was improper.

Assessments of George as King have focused on the period 1714–21. This is understandable, given that these were the years in which George worked through the consequences of gaining the throne, that international relations were particularly complex and important in this period, and that the years 1722–27 are more obscure, in domestic politics, court life and foreign policy. This chronological emphasis on the first half of the reign is unfortunate, however, since the way in which George worked with the Walpole-Townshend group after 1721 is also of considerable interest: the King showed then both political skills and a sense of responsibility. An incompetent and unyielding monarch might well have led to the end of Hanoverian rule in Britain, just as James II and VII had brought about the end of the power of the male line of the Stuarts.

George was still active in the latter years of the reign. Indeed, of the Hanoverians, he was the most active as King in his last years. This is made particularly clear by references in the ministerial correspondence covering George's visit to Hanover in 1725, which show the King playing an active role in scrutinising documents and mediating governmental decisions.[47] George's visits to Hanover in 1723 and 1725 also saw bouts of diplomatic activity in which George played a major part, especially in trying to secure better relations with his son-in-law and nephew, Frederick William I of Prussia. This was necessary not only for dynastic reasons, as George looked for Prussian marriages for his grandchildren, but also for diplomatic protection for Hanover. In 1723, concern focused on Peter the Great and, in particular, on Russian threats against Denmark, whose possession of Schleswig had been guaranteed by Britain and France. To both ends, George travelled to Prussia in 1723, confirming, in a treaty signed at Charlottenburg, the alliance negotiated in 1719 and informally agreeing that his grandson, Frederick, should marry Frederick William's daughter Wilhemine, with her brother, later Frederick the Great, to marry a daughter of George II. Frederick William and his wife wanted the choice to be Anne, the eldest daughter, but George I wanted her to marry William IV of Orange instead, and backed the choice of the second daughter Amelia for Frederick. Opposition to Peter the Great, however, caused political problems in London, where Walpole opposed the dispatch of a British fleet to the Baltic and complained about intrigues at Hanover against the ministry in London.

In 1725, in contrast, cooperation between British and Hanoverian goals was more readily obtained. The breakdown of Franco-Spanish relations led that year to an alliance between Spain and Austria that was rumoured to include provisions in favour of 'James III and VIII'. George's visit to Hanover in 1725 became the occasion for active negotiations, including a visit by Frederick William of Prussia. This resulted in the Treaty of Hanover by which the rulers of France, Britain and Prussia guaranteed each other's territories and rights.

The rest of George's reign lay under the shadow of war, until, on 31 May 1727, shortly before his death, a preliminary settlement of international differences, postponing most of them until a peace conference could be held, was reached at Paris. George took an active role in the crisis, which became more serious in 1726 when Prussia, Russia and Brunswick-Wolfenbüttel joined the rival alliance. Anxious about Hanoverian vulnerability to Prussian and Austrian attack, George was able to secure British subsidies to allied Hessian forces from 1726, as well as British pressure on France to move large forces toward the Rhine. An indication of George's activity towards the close of his reign is provided by a letter of January 1727 from Newcastle, then Secretary of State for the Southern Department, to Thomas Robinson, the Secretary at the

Paris embassy, noting that the French envoy had communicated a letter from Morville, the Foreign Minister, suggesting pressure at the Imperial Diet to keep the German rulers neutral. He wrote:

> and though I have not received it back from His Majesty, yet upon my acquaintaining the King with the contents of it, His Majesty commanded me to let you know, that he entirely approved of what was suggested by Mor. de Morville, and that orders should be forthwith sent to Leheup,

the British envoy at the Diet, to cooperate with his French counterpart to this end.[48]

Walpole remained the dominant figure in the ministry in George's last years. George honoured him publicly: with the newly-created Order of the Bath in 1725, and the much older and higher-ranking Order of the Garter the following year. Walpole, the sole commoner with the latter honour, and the first to be promoted to it since 1660, found his Garter a cause of anger and criticism. The award also showed George's careful adaptation to the nature of power, a parallel to his conforming to Anglican liturgy in his Chapel Royal. James II and VII and his son were not willing to make such adaptations.

George's personality encompassed a helpful range of activities. Far from being a militaristic dolt, he had cultural and intellectual interests, including an active engagement with the scientific research of the Royal Society. Indeed, George has been portrayed as a figure of the early Enlightenment, and his well-read mother was certainly in touch with advanced ideas. As an example, George was keen to have his granddaughters inoculated against smallpox. He also planned the university at Göttingen, something brought to fruition during the reign of his son, and founded the Regius Professorships in modern history at the universities of Oxford and Cambridge: they were seen, in part, as a way to help train diplomats. George's patronage of Cambridge was particularly important; for 6000 guineas, he bought the internationally famous library of John Moore, Bishop of Ely, who died in 1714. This collection, of nearly 29,000 books and 1790 manuscripts, more or less doubled the stock of the university library.[49]

Under George I and George II, the Toryism of Oxford ensured that it was treated less favourably. The contrast between the troops sent to Oxford to suppress Jacobite riots and the books given to Cambridge led to rival epigrams. The pro-government one by William Browne, who took his MA from Cambridge in 1714, claimed:

> The King to Oxford sent a troop of horse,
> For Tories own no argument but force;
> With equal care to Cambridge books he sent,
> For Whigs allow no force but argument.

George I's reputation as a supporter of toleration, seen in his attempt to ease the position of Dissenters, can be related to enlightened ideas as well as to prudential political considerations. It encouraged Voltaire to dedicate his *Henriade* to him. When Voltaire took refuge in Britain in 1726, he was helped by George.

George was also a keen supporter of Italian opera in London and a patron of the composer Handel, whom he had appointed *Kapellmeister* at Hanover in 1710, and who in London taught his grand-daughters as well as his daughters by Melusine. During the 1714–15 season at the King's Theatre, Haymarket, George attended twenty-two performances out of a possible forty-four; in 1715–16 he attended seventeen times out of a possible twenty-nine; and in 1716–17 he attended thirteen or fourteen times out of a possible twenty-five. In the 1726–27 season George attended Handel's opera *Admeto* on several occasions. Handel's *Water Music* was first performed, in 1717, as part of an evening of entertainment for the King. George also liked concerts and masquerades, which enjoyed a vogue in London during his reign.[50]

Interested in building, George had the summer palace of Herrenhausen near Hanover extensively refurbished, and the garden greatly enhanced, work on the latter continuing after he left for Britain. The hunting lodge at Göhrde was also rebuilt as a small palace, and used extensively during his visits in 1719, 1720 and 1723. As a sign of his tastes, the palace included a theatre, although the excellent hunting was the major reason why George enjoyed his visits there. In Britain, he was responsible for extensive work on Kensington Palace, including the completion and decoration of new state rooms and the remodelling of the grounds, where George liked to take long evening walks; his daughter-in-law Caroline was to continue this remodelling. At Windsor, the hunting was improved.

George's scientific and cultural interests should not be allowed to divert attention from his clear preferences for drilling his troops and hunting. George fought in 1675–78 in the Dutch war against Louis XIV, and against the Turks in Hungary in 1683–85, was nearly killed fighting the French in the battle of Neerwinden in 1693, led forces into Holstein in 1700, in a successful attempt to put pressure on Frederick IV of Denmark, and launched a totally successful rapid invasion of the Duchy of Wolfenbüttel in 1702. He commanded on the Rhine against the French in the War of the Spanish Succession in 1707–9. Typically, letters from George dating from 1708–10, recently acquired by the British Library, that were sent to Abraham Stanyan, British Envoy Extraordinary to the Swiss cantons, deal with the army's financial needs and introduce officers.[51] Three of George's brothers died in battle: Friedrich August and Karl Philipp, both in 1690 in war with the Turks, and Christian Heinrich in 1703 in the War of the Spanish Succession. In contrast, no later Hanoverian prince was to die in battle, although George III's son, Ernest, Duke of Cumberland, was wounded. Service in the field helped consolidate a prince's reputation as a warrior and, in George's case, presumably compensated for the blow to his manliness caused by Sophia Dorothea's adultery.

George I and the Prince of Wales were reconciled in 1720, but only to the extent of a mutual coldness. Although there was little sign of any difference of opinion between father and son over policy in the 1720s, there was a continued tension over the Prince's position. George refused to have his son as Regent in Britain during his absences in Germany in 1720, 1723, 1725 and 1727, and turned down the younger George's request for a military post in any European conflict that might involve Britain. This challenged the latter's wish to do something useful and to gain renown.

George I's life saw many of the family crises that were to recur among his successors. His failure in marriage was to be matched by George IV, and his terrible relations with his heir by George II and George III. In each case, specific factors played a role, but the common pattern helped to set a tone for the dynasty. It contrasted with the Stuarts, although James II and VII's bad relations with his daughters by his first marriage, Mary and Anne, were important in the political crisis of 1688–89, and crucial to its resolution.

It is easy to see why George I was unpopular, especially as a result of his multifaceted 'Hanoverianism'; but it is also clear that, after having initially pursued very divisive politics, he eventually helped to make the political system work effectively, by the last years of his reign bringing a valuable measure of political stability to the realm. At his death, there was no question that the succession would pass anywhere other than to his son. George I, who had embarked at Greenwich on 14 June, died early on 22 June at Osnabrück en route to Hanover; he had had a stroke on the journey on the 20th. George was buried in Hanover, close to his mother, although it was reported that, in the shape of a large bird, perhaps a raven, a bird renowned for its constancy, he returned to visit Melusine, who from 1728 lived in Twickenham, dying in 1743.

# 5

## *George II*

'But,' replied the King *peevishly*, 'Mr Pitt won't come in'. 'If *that* was done', I said, 'we should have a quiet session.' '*But Mr Pitt won't do my German business*' 'If he comes into your service, Sir, he must be told, he must do your Majesty's business ...' 'But I don't like *Pitt. He won't do my business*'. 'But, unfortunately, Sir, he is the only one who has ability to do the business'.

Thomas, Duke of Newcastle recounting a conversation
with George II, 1756 [1]

The second of the Hanoverian dynasty to rule Britain, George Augustus, the eldest child and only son of George I and Sophia Dorothea, is not easy to evaluate. He left relatively little correspondence, in large part because he appears to have written very little. Born outside Hanover at the palace of Herrenhausen, on 10 November (30 October os) 1683, George was brought up as the heir to his father, with the only major difference to the usual pattern resulting from his parents' divorce in 1694. After that, George saw more of his grandmother, Sophia, although her influence is difficult to gauge. In September 1705, he married the vivacious Princess Caroline of Ansbach (like him born in 1683),[2] who was to exercise considerable influence on him until her death in 1737. Caroline's reputation in England was enhanced by her earlier refusal to abandon the Protestant faith in order to marry 'Charles III', the Habsburg claimant to the throne of Spain, who became the Emperor Charles VI. The contrast between the Queen's bright, sparkling, witty nature, and George's more dour, boorish demeanour led contemporaries, such as Countess Cowper, Lord Hervey, and the Earl of Chesterfield to underrate the influence of the latter. In 1708 George took part in the campaign in the Low Countries against France in the War of the Spanish Succession, serving with bravery at the battle of Oudenaarde, and he never lost his love of military matters.

A naturalised British subject from 1705, and Duke of Cambridge from 1706, George accompanied his father to London in 1714, becoming Prince of Wales that September, although Jacobites disagreed with this designation, leading to the pamphlet *To a Thing They Call Prince of Wales* (1716?). Relations between the two Georges were difficult, and, in 1717, led to a serious rift that was closely linked to a major division within the Whig party. Relations were mended in 1720, although they remained poor. The Prince thereafter played little part in politics. The spectacular disputes with his father of the late 1710s had been replaced by a mutual coldness. The ministry sought to smooth matters, with the Prince being informed of policy through the Lord Privy Seal, the Duke of Devonshire, who had close connections with the Princess, Caroline of Ansbach.[3]

The impact on George II of his parents' divorce is unclear. It was reported that the younger George, who was not allowed to see his mother after the divorce, had sought contact with her, and that in 1727 he displayed her portrait, but the correctness of these reports is unclear, as is the suggestion that his attitude changed when he discovered evidence of her adultery. George II certainly lacked the secure family background his father had enjoyed. In particular, he did not share George I's experience of maternal love and encouragement: Sophia had died shortly before George I became King.

George I's death was seen by 'James III and VIII' to provide an opportunity for him to reach for the throne. Setting off from his court in the papal town of Bologna, James hoped that by the time he reached the English Channel an uprising would have broken out in Britain. Both France and Austria, however, refused him assistance. Despite reports to the contrary, James did not even reach the Austrian Netherlands, from where he could have tried to sail to Britain. Instead, he ended his journey in the duchy of Lorraine, whence, as a result of French pressure on Duke Leopold, he moved first to the papal enclave of Avignon and then back to Italy. James's half-nephew, James, Duke of Liria, son of James, Duke of Berwick, an illegitimate son of James II and VII, reported from Vienna (he was on his way to take up the post of Spanish envoy in Russia) that Austrian support would not be forthcoming unless James could show himself at the head of a good party, and that the Austrians would not let themselves be persuaded that Britain would declare for James.

The Austrians were to be proved correct, for the accession of George passed without disturbance, a marked contrast to the Tory demonstrations that had followed that of George I. Most of the Tory peers, who had not been to court for years, paid their respects to George II, although Charles Caesar informed James that some did so 'hoping to so lull the government asleep that they would disband some of their forces',[4] while those who had hoped for royal favour were swiftly disabused. The proscription of the Tories, and the monopolisation of royal favour by the Whigs, had helped to provoke the '15 rebellion, but there was no comparable response to the continuation of the same situation under George II. The English Jacobites acted as if they accepted proscription, and were unprepared to run the risks of a rising unless assured of considerable foreign assistance; and both Ireland and Scotland were quiet.

George II made a few moves in the direction of the Tories. He was most gracious to those who came to court, sufficiently so that there was speculation that some, such as Sir Thomas Hanmer, who had been reported close to the Prince in 1718, would be raised to the peerage. He also took steps to increase the number of Tory justices of the peace, but he did nothing more than make a few concessions. As Prince of Wales, George had had little to do with the Tories; the aristocratic clique he mixed with being overwhelmingly Whig.

There was still the possibility that the new King would transform the ministry, and the political crisis of 1727 is instructive because it demonstrates the continued power of the monarch and the extent to which others had to adapt to him. Whereas George I, when he came to the throne, knew little about British politics, George II in contrast had already much experience of them, knew many of the politicians, and had his own ideas.

On the day George was proclaimed King, Newcastle wrote to his co-Secretary of State, Townshend, of 'the concern and distraction we are all in here ... we can make no judgement of affairs here, in all probability the Speaker will be the chief man'. Indeed the Honourable Spencer Compton, son of the 3rd Earl of Northampton and MP for Sussex, was held to be a plausible candidate. Throughout George I's reign, he had been Speaker of the House of Commons and Treasurer to the Prince of Wales, and, in 1722, the ministry, seeking to please the Prince, had bestowed on Compton the extremely lucrative office of Paymaster General.

Arthur Onslow, MP for Guildford, who was in London at the time of George II's accession, noted

> that everybody expected, that Mr Compton the Speaker would be the Minister, and Sir Robert Walpole thought so for a few days ... the new King's first inclination and resolution, which was certainly for Mr Compton ... who had long been his treasurer, and very near to him in all his counsels. It went so far as to be almost a formal appointment, the King, for two or three days directing everybody to go to him upon business ... but by the Queen's management, all this was soon overruled.[5]

Many of the statements used to support the interpretation of the events of 1727 that places Caroline's role as central are, however, open to question. Hervey did not begin his memoirs until 1733 or 1734, whilst Onslow's account is based upon papers and correspondence that no longer exist but were transcribed by his son in 1769. These papers were certainly drawn up after Walpole's death in 1745, and their accuracy is open to question.

The notes made by Lord King, the Lord Chancellor, are a more useful source, as they were made at the time of the events recorded, or only shortly afterwards. King's account of the failure of Compton does not mention the Queen, but suggests that George was persuaded by personal experience to continue Walpole in power,

> by his constant application to the King by himself in the mornings, when the Speaker, by reason of the sitting of the House of Commons, was absent, he so worked upon the King, that he not only established himself in favour with him, but prevented the cashiering of many others, who otherwise would have been put out.[6]

There were several obvious reasons why it would have been foolish for George to remove Walpole at once. The accession of a new monarch meant that Parliament had to be summoned, the Civil List settled, and elections held for a new Parliament; this was the case after the accession of every new monarch and helped enhance their ability to ensure a new political dispensation. Walpole was needed for these purposes.

Parliament sat from 27 June (os) to 17 July (os), George finding the royal speech he made at its opening a considerable burden. Harriet Pitt noted, 'I saw him make [it] today, I can't say heard, for His Majesty was in so much confusion he could not put out his voice to be heard'.[7] During the session, Walpole made himself extremely useful to George, securing an enlarged Civil List of £800,000 yearly. As Prince of Wales, George had accumulated substantial debts. Furthermore, he had a reputation for avarice and meanness. Whatever the importance to George of the enlarged Civil List, it is certain that Walpole's command of the House of Commons, and the ease with which he secured parliamentary consent for the new fiscal arrangements, was very impressive, though it is doubtful whether politicians seeking to win royal favour would have found it helpful to oppose the Civil List in Parliament, especially at the very start of the reign.[8]

Possibly as significant was Walpole's success in the elections. The well-informed Saxon envoy Jacques Le Coq suggested that Walpole was given an opportunity to display his skill to the King, and that George had decided to delay any governmental changes until after the elections, in order to be in a state to gratify those who had helped with the elections, and those whose help would be needed in the subsequent Parliament; a sage move by a king who was not rash. If this was indeed so, Walpole certainly passed the test with flying colours. After the petitions to the House about contested election returns were heard, the new House of Commons consisted of 415 ministerial supporters, fifteen opposition Whigs and 128 Tories, a government majority of 272, the largest since George I's accession. The comparable figures after the 1722 election were 389 Whigs and 169 Tories, a majority of 220.[9]

In his lengthy and thoughtful dispatch of 22 July 1727, Le Coq had reported that other reasons were advanced as to why it was against the King's interest to change the government. First, Walpole's influence with Parliament and with the great chartered corporations – the Bank of England, East India Company and South Sea Company – was held to be very important for the creditworthiness and stability of the government. Secondly, to change the government was held to be inadvisable for British foreign policy: the current policy was the product of the ministry, so it was held to be dangerous to replace them by men who were poorly informed about British foreign policy and the European situation. Furthermore, it was felt that such a change would alarm Britain's allies at a tricky diplomatic juncture.

The importance of these last factors in the mind of George is difficult to evaluate. However interested he was in the Civil List, or in the general election, George was probably at least as concerned about the European situation, and, during the first few years of his reign, he was to display far more interest in European than in domestic affairs. Britain's allies certainly expressed some concern about the possibility of a change in the government: Cardinal Fleury pressed George to maintain Walpole in power, and concern was also expressed in The Hague. It is possible that the French view was of great importance to George, as foreign policy depended on a continued alliance with France. Opposition supporters certainly blamed Fleury for Walpole's continuance in office.[10] George also may well have been influenced by seeing Walpole in opposition in 1717–20, which showed that he was too much trouble to be outside government.

Whatever the reasons, Walpole's maintenance of power was clear within a fortnight of George's accession. The achievement, however, was subject to two doubts: first, whether Walpole would be forced to accept many changes in the ministry; and, secondly, whether George would follow the advice of the ministers. It was thought that those associated with George as Prince of Wales, a distinctly aristocratic group, including Compton, and the Earls of Chesterfield, Essex, Grantham and Scarborough would take prominent roles. Aside from Compton, few members of this group possessed any governmental experience, and none, aside from Compton and Scarborough, had distinguished himself in Parliament. They were worthy of prestigious sinecures, but not power. Aside from Compton, the group was relatively young, younger than George, who acceded in his forty-sixth year: Scarborough had been born in 1688 and Chesterfield in 1694. Suggestions were made that George's aristocratic friends would be raised in the peerage and that several would receive dukedoms.

These rumours proved to be widely exaggerated. Though some sound supporters of Walpole lost their places, they soon gained others. George's aristocratic friends won a few positions. Essex gained the Rangership of St James's, one of the more important posts of its type, as it gave access to the monarch. Grantham was raised to the Privy Council and made

Lord Chamberlain to the Queen. Scarborough was appointed Master of
the Horse, Sir Charles Hotham a Groom of the Bedchamber. With all
these men, it is unclear how much personal ambition they possessed
and how far they pressed George for promotion. Most seemed to have
been content with honourable, fashionable and profitable posts in the
household, but to have shown little interest in gaining the more arduous
posts of power. Essex, a flashy womaniser, was to be envoy in Turin
from 1732 to 1736, but, during his embassy, his principal concerns were
seduction and securing leaves of absence so that he could visit the
carnivals of Italy. Hotham's ambition was restricted largely to the army,
where he sought a regiment, a goal not attained until 1732. Highly
intelligent and profoundly melancholic, a courtier who ended his life
in suicide, Scarborough was not noted for his political ambition. John
Scrope, Secretary to the Treasury, suggested that Compton was disin-
clined to accept responsibility for the financial management of the
crown, but his maladroit conduct in June 1727 does not mean that he
was as weak as has been depicted. Compton was outmanoeuvred by
Walpole and lacked his ability, but Walpole took him seriously as a
politician.[11] Chesterfield was more pushy, seeking Paris, the most important of the British embassies, which greatly disturbed the current
envoy, Walpole's brother Horatio.[12] It was believed that George hoped
to appoint Chesterfield Secretary of State after this training. In the event,
Chesterfield received a less influential embassy at The Hague.

On 24 July (os) 1727, Newcastle reassuredly remarked that George 'has
been pleased to make but very few and those immaterial alterations
amongst the late King's servants'. Having mentioned the dismissal of
the Earl of Berkeley, First Lord of the Admiralty since 1717, and no friend
of Walpole, he added 'the other changes are not worth troubling you
with'.[13] Carteret was sent back to Ireland with diminished powers and
the opposition Whigs were not heeded.

Walpole, who had secured not only his own position but also those
of his colleagues and political allies, was still faced with the problem of
defining a relationship with his new master. Five days after George's
proclamation, Hill Mussenden stated, 'all that can be gathered for the
present is that, whatever side be uppermost, they will not have the same
authority, that the last ministry had, since the King seems resolved to
enter into all manner of affairs himself'. George indeed came to the

throne determined to be his own master. He had no intention of being a *roi fainéant*, and made it clear, from the beginning of his reign, that he wished to control all the activities of government. Such a wish of course was not new and, particularly since Louis XIV's bombastic remarks in 1661, many monarchs at their accession to power, spoke of their intention to rule themselves.

Nevertheless, contemporaries noted that the diligent George threw himself into the business of government, wanted to be informed of everything, and worked hard; indeed so hard that fears were expressed about his health. Hill Mussenden claimed that George was determined to sit in person on the Admiralty, Treasury and War Office Boards. When he came to the throne, he spoke of his intention to supervise the Treasury in person, and of his determination to cut pay, particularly for officials who held more than one post. It was believed that he would cut the number of pensions (annual payments; not to do with old age) paid from the Civil List. Le Coq argued that these changes were due not to George's avarice, but to a coherent fiscal and political strategy, an attempt to reduce the need for governmental borrowing and the dependence upon parliamentary grants. There is no independent evidence for this suggestion, but it is symptomatic of the belief that George was making a serious attempt to intervene in the processes of government.

This initial determination persisted and George continued to work hard. Carteret's new instructions as Lord Lieutenant of Ireland, drawn up in October 1727, limited his power over the Irish army and increased that of the King. Two months later, the manuscript newsletter sent regularly from London to George's uncle, Ernst August, Prince Bishop of Osnabrück, reported that George was intervening in the pay of his household and guard officers, and devoting a lot of attention to administration.[14]

George encountered opposition, however, and his wishes were not always translated into action. In July 1727, George told Lord King that he expected to nominate to all benefices and prebendaries which the Lord Chancellor usually nominated to. When King defended his prerogative, George retorted that Lord Cowper, a former Lord Chancellor, had told George that such nominations were a royal right. Two months later, the Sardinian envoy, D'Aix, reported ministerial anger at George's supervision of their activities and at his willingness to listen to others.

Le Coq pinpointed another area of tension when he suggested that George's attempts at financial reform were weakening the position of his ministers by denying them an undisputed control of government patronage. Nevertheless, George did not persevere in his dispute with King over the nominations. He also allowed the Duke of Grafton's views about the appointment of Suffolk JPs to overrule his own wishes to appoint Tories.[15] George's early enthusiasm for intervening in all the departments of government slowly waned, and Walpole's control of financial affairs was reported as unchallenged by the autumn of 1728.[16]

For the British ministers, George's close personal interest in the army was only an occasional nuisance, although they would have preferred to enjoy some of the military patronage he wielded, and there were clashes between King and ministers over the issue until the close of the reign.[17] It was the possible effects of George's martial temperament upon the conduct of foreign policy that most concerned the government, while, from George's accession until the spring of 1730, there was considerable uncertainty as to which ministers enjoyed George's confidence in foreign policy. The French general and politician Marshal Villars, a member of the Conseil d'État, where the dispatches of French diplomats were read out and considered, noted in his diary that George was believed to desire war ardently and to wish to lead his army into battle. Le Coq reported the fear that George would push foreign policy with more vigour, although he argued that the King's warlike penchant would be restrained by his allies' opposition to war, by considerations of state, and by the fact that the views of a Prince of Wales were naturally different from those of a King of Britain.[18] Concern about royal bellicosity, also made British ministers worry about his journeys to Hanover, as, once there, George's apparent propensity for violent solutions might be harder to tame.

From his accession, George, who had his own sources of information and opinions, made it clear that he wished to control foreign policy. At least initially, he read the dispatches of British envoys with great attention,[19] and made his preferences among the diplomatic corps clear. Waldegrave, for example, was informed 'that H.M. expresses a very particular regard for your lordship'.[20] The ministers was worried about George's willingness to take advice from Louis, Seigneur de St-Saphorin, a former envoy in Vienna whom they regarded as unreliable.

It was in German affairs, that George's interests as dynast and ruler of Hanover were displayed most forcefully, a process encouraged from August 1727 until the spring of 1728 by the serious ill-health of Townshend, the British Secretary of State responsible for policy toward the region. Hanoverian grievances against the manner in which Charles VI exercised imperial jurisdictional rights fortified George's determination to force him to be a good Emperor. In an interesting guide to the King's vividness of language and personalisation of issues, he told the Prussian envoy that 'if the Emperor trod upon his toe, H.M. would let him know whom he had to do with'. The Hanoverian Council of Ministers urged their master to make a forthcoming international conference the stage for an airing of Hanoverian grievances against imperial policy, in particular concerns about despotic moves and steps likely to benefit Catholicism.[21]

The issue that caused most immediate problems was relations with Frederick William I of Prussia, who sent Baron Wallenrodt to sound George about the possibility of a new treaty. George's response both to Wallenrodt and to the British envoy in Berlin was curt: the King denied that he had any plans for the marital links with the Prussian royal family that had long been considered. Frederick William was also irritated by George's refusal to publish his father's will, as he believed that this had deprived his wife, Sophia Dorothea, of her father's legacy to her; in fact, George was motivated by his intention of suppressing the provision for the separation of Hanover from Britain. George's response to Frederick William was in part encouraged by his wish to please his ally France, but his distrust of his brother-in-law was also important.[22]

George displayed considerable independence, and showed his personal interest in diplomacy, in his attempts to develop a league of German princes. In August 1727, Horatio Walpole was informed, 'Your Excellency will perhaps think us too full of the scheme for taking care at the Congress of the Liberties of the Germanic Body, as being pretty strong meat for the Cardinal's [Fleury's] digestion: but My Lord Townshend ordered me to tell you that it arises from the King himself, who sees with regret the Emperor gaining such an absolute influence throughout Germany as may make him an overmatch for us and France too'. The Hanoverian envoy at the Imperial Diet in Regensburg received direct orders from London to stir up the German princes against the Emperor, while George drafted Horatio Walpole instructions demanding that France provide a declaration that it would respect the rights of Protestants in the Empire.[23] That winter, royal diplomatic activity included a meeting of over an hour between Le Coq and Queen Caroline, who told him that George wanted an alliance with Saxony.[24]

The nature of the sources, with diplomatic instructions sent by ministers and over their signatures, is such that royal views are generally difficult to evaluate, but the winter of 1727–28 provides indications of George's bellicosity. The deterioration of Anglo-Spanish relations, for example, led to an emphasis on George's personal determination and the role of his dignity:

> the King is most nearly touched with the turn this affair has taken, and will risk the coming to the utmost extremities rather than submit to those scandalous conditions Spain would impose upon him … if the Spanish court persist in their unreasonable proceedings, His Majesty must, and will, sooner enter into a war with that crown than suffer his own honour and royal dignity, and the interests of his people to be treated in so ignominious a manner.[25]

It was reported that George and his favourites, especially the Duke of Argyll, Master-General of the Ordnance (who had reputedly first persuaded him to have extra-marital affairs), had pressed for war, but that Walpole and the Queen were against it.[26] The Lords' address very much put the government's view that peace was preferable, but it also acknowledged George's martial instincts, when it referred to the 'noble self-denial of all the success and glory that might attend your Majesty's arms in the prosecution of a just and necessary war, when put in balance with the ease, quiet, and prosperity of your subjects. It is a disposition of mind truly great in your Majesty … to choose rather to procure peace for your subjects, than to lead them to victories'.

That was also a result that reflected the multiple compromises of British politics, ones that, however uneasily, George was guided to, and which he accepted and utilised. Similarly, George's suggestion, in the autumn of 1728, that the ships of the Ostend Company, the Asian trading company based in the Austrian Netherlands, be seized as a way to intimidate Charles VI was not pursued.[27]

The politics of George II's early years culminated with the resignation

of Townshend in 1730, and his replacement, as Secretary of State for
the Northern Department, by William Stanhope, Lord Harrington. The
difficulty of assessing George's views and role emerges clearly from this
crisis, as both are seen at second hand. George was a monarch prone
to conversation in the royal closet, not an industrious correspondent.
Generally, the crisis is presented in terms of relations between Walpole
and Townshend, George's role being discounted. Had Walpole, however,
been as strong as is believed, he would have removed Townshend before
May 1730. It was widely reported in diplomatic circles in late 1729 that
George preferred Townshend's policies. If this is correct, then the crisis
of 1729–30 is of great importance, as it can be seen as a foretaste of 1742
and 1744, when George was forced to part with Walpole and Carteret
respectively against his better judgement. George's views in the winter
of 1729–30, on both foreign policy and ministerial politics, are in fact
unclear, although he approved the exclusion of other ministers from
knowledge of the secret correspondence between Townshend and the
French diplomat Chavigny, in which the two men tried to settle difficulties over the projected subsidy treaty between Britain and the
Wittelsbach Electors.[28] Walpole's early biographer, William Coxe,
claimed that Townshend fell because the Queen helped Walpole block
his attempt to replace Newcastle by Chesterfield: 'He became more
obsequious to the King's German prejudices, paid his court with un-
ceasing assiduity, and appeared to have gained so much influence that
he thought himself capable of obtaining the appointment of Chesterfield'.[29] Caroline, who had distrusted Townshend for some time,
especially in 1716–17, was also believed to have played a direct role in
the fall of Townshend.

The latter's grandson, Viscount Sydney (after whom the Australian
city was named), wrote a letter many years later that nevertheless
possesses an immediacy missing in other sources. It makes abundantly
clear the court context of ministerial politics, the importance of royal
favour, and the role of personal honour in court and ministerial relationships. After recounting a violent altercation between Townshend
and Walpole, Sydney continued:

> The way in which I have heard this unusual want of temper in Sir Robert
> accounted for was this: the two ministers had some secret, which they had
> agreed to keep to themselves, but they had both imparted it in confidence

to the Queen. Her Majesty was unfortunately jealous of the too great cordiality, which subsisted between those who were to carry on the public business, and thought that a little jealousy of each other might make both more manageable; she therefore thought proper to let each of them know, that the other had trusted her. Sir Robert was just come from making this discovery. The Queen was much concerned and mortified at the effect of her own manoeuvre, never intending or suspecting that matters would have been carried to any violence. She was very sorry to be reduced to choose between them, but had no hesitation in making choice of Sir Robert when she was forced to decide ... Townshend attempted to make a separate personal interest with the King while abroad with him [in 1729], independent of the Queen. It is unnecessary to say that her Majesty on the return of the King overthrew the whole fabric.[30]

Townshend was certainly criticised for his pro-Hanoverian stance. In January 1730, Horatio Walpole complained of Townshend's 'endeavours to make all measures Electoral preferable to all other considerations, which is entirely agreeable to the King's sentiments'.[31] In turn, Townshend criticised his rivals for failing to support Hanoverian interests:

His Lordship has represented us, as giving up Hanover quite, and has worked much upon the King upon that head; and also, that we had neglected pushing the plan of operations ... I must beg you would do all you can about the German points, Mecklenburg etc ... Let us have some brisk resolution about the plan of operations, and some strong assurances about Hanover, and we shall be able to defy him, and all he can do ... Hanover is Lord Townshend's great merit, and we have been all represented as wanting zeal.[32]

Although the Prussian envoy, Benjamin Reichenbach, claimed that Townshend was fed up with George's brutal manners, it was widely accepted that he was George's favoured minister. Reichenbach reported that George did not want him to go, but was obliged to maintain good relations with Walpole in order to obtain money.[33] As in 1733, however, when Walpole was unable to persuade George to dismiss Harrington and Scarborough, so in 1730 Walpole had to wait for Townshend to resign. He appears to have finally decided to do so because of his frustration at the constant opposition of Walpole to his plans. George, however, had his protégé, William Stanhope, succeed Townshend. It was claimed that Walpole and the Queen had attempted to gain the post for Horatio Walpole but had been thwarted by George. True or not, George had gained a pliant Secretary of State from the crisis.

Whatever their differences in 1729–30, George supported Walpole in office until his fall in 1742, a fall that George bitterly regretted. Earlier, in the aftermath of the Excise Crisis in 1733, Walpole was saved by George's staunch determination to back him, which helped to divide the court opposition to the first minister. John Drummond MP then wrote of 'the destruction of Sir Robert, which is not like to happen, for I never saw him easier at court'.[34]

The role of crown-ministry relations in the political instability of 1716–20 and 1743–46 throws light on Walpole's success in avoiding a similar situation. This was a testimony to his political skills, his attention to court intrigue, his personal good relations with Queen Caroline and George II, and the political responsibility of both George I and George II. Caroline's influence was seen as particularly important. In 1720, Lady Cowper observed that the future King 'is governed by the Princess as she is by Walpole'.[35] In 1731, William Pulteney, the leader of the opposition Whigs in the House of Commons, 'alluded to the report that Sir Robert Walpole is only supported by the Queen',[36] while the *Craftsman*, the most prominent opposition newspaper, in its issue of 15 September (os) 1733, described politics in terms of chess, with Walpole as the knight: 'see him jump over the heads of the nobles ... when he is guarded by the Queen, he makes dreadful havoc, and very often checkmates the King'. Indeed, in 1736, Walpole got Caroline to press George against an alliance with Denmark and Sweden.[37]

Confident that the Queen's support had been crucial, the opposition were disappointed in their hope that Walpole would fall after the death of Caroline in 1737. They had exaggerated Caroline's influence and, anyway, as George became older and increasingly irascible, he was less easily led by Caroline. After her death, George, who appreciated Walpole's ability, promised his minister his continued support, as he had earlier done after he came to the throne.[38] This backing was provided until the end of the ministry, as was seen in the disposal of army patronage, which was closely guarded by George and employed to help Walpole,[39] an important indication of the King's views.

George's attitudes were important in politics, but he was not always able to prevail. Foreign diplomats noted that the failure of the government to win divisions on the Westminster election petition after the election of 1741 meant that George was unable to have sympathetic MPs for the constituency where he lived.[40] The fall of Walpole in 1742, in the face of his inability to continue dominating the House of Commons, was a more dramatic display of George's weakness; but he was determined to protect his former minister, and there was to be no repetition of the harrying of Anne's Tory ministers after the accession of George I. Created Earl of Orford on 9 February (os) 1742, a public display of royal approval, Walpole survived the attempts of a secret committee of twenty-one MPs set up to investigate him and discredit his ministry. When, seeking to create an acceptable new ministry, George offered Pulteney office, he made the condition that Walpole should be 'screened from all future resentments'. Pulteney rejected the condition, but assured George, via Newcastle, he was 'by no means a man of blood'.[41] An investigation of the distribution of secret service funds was thwarted when Nicholas Paxton, Solicitor to the Treasury, and John Scrope, Secretary to the Treasury, refused to testify against Walpole, arguing they were accountable only to George as the money had been paid by the King's special warrant.

After his fall, Walpole was believed to retain considerable influence with George, a position similar to that which Bute was reported to hold with George III after his resignation in 1763: it was always simpler to castigate royal views by blaming them on a supposedly evil adviser. In the case of Walpole, he exercised considerable influence on George from his retirement until his death in March 1745. George sought and valued his advice, referring to his 'consummate judgment in the interior and domestic affairs of this kingdom',[42] and Walpole played a major role in ensuring that, in the ministerial rivalry of the period, Henry Pelham, his former protégé (and Newcastle's brother), triumphed over his former rivals, Pulteney and Carteret. In July 1743, Pelham beat Pulteney for the position of First Lord of the Treasury after Compton, ennobled in 1728 as Lord Wilmington, who had replaced Walpole in this position in 1742, died.

George was more concerned about foreign policy than the Treasury, and supported Carteret, who in 1742 became Secretary of State for the Northern Department, the department that dealt with relations with the German states. Newcastle, however, was determined not to yield to

Carteret, and was prepared to thwart George on this point. Walpole told Dudley Ryder that 'the Pelhams [Newcastle and Henry Pelham] and Chancellor [Hardwicke] treat the King in an imprudent manner, not submissive enough, though the King piques himself on not having anybody to dictate to him'.[43] Walpole's final political act was to advise George to yield to the Pelhams and abandon Carteret, a minister who could not lead the Commons.

In 1744 George failed to sustain Carteret in office, despite his having confidence in him as the minister most ready to support George in German politics, and one who also knew German. Carteret was forced to resign on 24 November (os). The crisis continued, however, because George still listened to Carteret. It was renewed in 1746, when George's lack of support for Newcastle and Pelham, the ministers who dominated Parliament, provoked a political crisis in which they forced his hand, by (with their supporters) resigning their posts in the government on 10 and 11 February (os). By withholding his confidence from his ministers, George had undermined their position in Parliament. But this also provoked their desperate resignation at a time of war and rebellion, and left George little room for manoeuvre. The resignations were of short duration: Carteret and Pulteney (now Earl Granville and the Earl of Bath) failed to form a new administration, and, within forty-eight hours, they had abandoned the attempt, forcing George to turn again to his former ministers. The terms of their return included taking William Pitt the Elder, a notable House of Commons opposition Whig speaker, into office, though not in the post he sought. Thereafter, the Pelhams dominated politics until Henry Pelham died in 1754.

The King's self-imposed political rules also ensured limitations upon his effective action. He did not want to turn to the Tories to support the ministry, and wished to employ favourites, especially Carteret; yet he also regarded as essential the Old Corps Whigs, who were implacably opposed to those favourites. With a parliamentary majority, George could possibly have cleared out the Old Corps, as George III was to do in the 1760s; as it was, he remained dependent on the Old Corps in Parliament. This also had a wider political impact. Resentment against a one-party Whig state remained, although, until 1744, George II was not seriously threatened by pro-Jacobite schemes. Unable to dominate the ministry, George, in the mid 1740s, pursued a secret anti-Prussian foreign policy, operating through the Hanoverian government and the British envoy in St Petersburg, the Earl of Hyndford, in a way that contradicted the anti-French emphasis of the British ministry.

The outbreak of war with France in 1743 was followed by an increase in Jacobite activity, culminating in 1745 in the attempt under Charles Edward Stuart, 'Bonnie Prince Charlie', to overthrow Hanoverian rule in Britain. He planned to exploit continued Scottish hostility to the Union and hoped that the French could be encouraged to intervene militarily if a rising had already broken out. This ignored the argument of the Scottish Jacobites that the Prince should come only if accompanied by a substantial force: 6000 men and the funds to pay them. No such force accompanied Charles Edward, but the 'Seven Men of Moidart' who landed at Eriskay had swelled to 1300 when he raised his standard at Glenfinnan in August. The British army in Scotland, part of a military establishment weakened by the need to send most of its troops to resist the French in the Austrian Netherlands, was outmanoeuvred and Charles Edward successfully captured Perth and Edinburgh in September before routing the government army nearby at Prestonpans on 21 September. Having consolidated his position, Charles Edward then avoided the new government army assembled at Newcastle by invading England further west via Carlisle, which fell after a short siege (10–15 November).

The Jacobites then advanced unopposed through Penrith, Lancaster, Preston and Manchester, entering Derby on 4 December, having out-manoeuvred another government army commanded by Cumberland. At this point, the Jacobites held the strategic initiative, with the opposing forces divided, but the Highland chiefs were disappointed by the lack of support promised them by Charles Edward: both assistance from Jacobites and the absence of a French landing in southern England. After bitter debates, the chiefs forced Charles Edward to turn back and he began his retreat north on 6 December. There was to be another Jacobite victory at Falkirk on 17 January 1746, but the initiative was increasingly gained by Cumberland and his larger army won a crushing victory at Culloden on 16 April 1746.[44]

Aside from success in the field, the Hanoverians had held firm during the crisis. George did not panic when the Jacobites advanced as far as Derby, and the suggestion that the crisis proved the need for the division of Hanover and Britain[45] was fruitless. After Culloden not only was the

Protestant establishment affirmed, but, as a result of the destruction of Jacobite hopes, the Hanoverian dynasty was also finally and explicitly accepted by most of the political nation as representing the aspirations and security of the realm.

The problems of ministerial politics proved to be less intense but more drawn out. In 1744, George had refused to grant Pitt the Secretaryship at War he sought, but in 1746 and 1755–57 the King could not prevent his entry into office. In each case, however, George was in very difficult circumstances and, when they were easier, he proved able to insist on his choice of ministers. Thus when Pelham died in 1754 Pitt did not gain the Secretaryship of State freed up by Newcastle's replacement of Pelham at the Treasury. The Secretaryships, particularly the Northern one, which had responsibility for diplomatic relations with the German and Baltic Courts, Russia and the Netherlands, required royal favour, for the monarch played a crucial role in the conduct of foreign policy, and George did not wish to have to deal with Pitt personally in the Closet in any circumstances. The decision for the successive promotions to Secretaryships of Holdernesse in 1751 and Sir Thomas Robinson in 1754 indicated George's determination to have ministers whom he could deal with easily, and a preference for courtiers and men with diplomatic experience over managers of the Commons. Holdernesse had been a Lord of the King's Bedchamber, while Robinson moved from being Master of the Great Wardrobe to the Secretaryship. This exemplified the importance of the Court. Both were also former diplomats, and Robinson's long service at Vienna (1730–48) ensured that he was particularly knowledgeable about the German politics that concerned George.

Robinson was not up to the growing political problems that stemmed from the outbreak of hostilities with France in 1754, but George was unwilling to have Pitt succeed Robinson; instead, the post went to Henry Fox in 1755. This did not lead to stability, as Pitt went into angry opposition, creating difficulties in the Commons, such that, in October 1756, in the aftermath of Admiral Byng's failure to relieve the British garrison in Minorca, Newcastle resigned when he was unable to persuade Pitt to serve under him. The military and political crisis that marked the start of the Seven Years War with France ensured that Newcastle's failure to create a strong ministerial combination eventually forced

George's hand. The King gave Fox authority to form a Fox-Pitt ministry, only for Pitt to reject the idea, Fox's nephew Henry Digby complaining that Pitt 'seemed rather determined to conquer than assist the King'.[46] George, instead, had to accept a Pitt-Devonshire ministry. In this Pitt initially sought to replace Holdernesse at the Northern Department, although an angry George opposed the change, not welcoming the prospect of Pitt taking responsibility for handling relations with the German powers. As royal wishes were important, Pitt therefore took the Southern Secretaryship.

George, however, continued to be no friend to the ministry, which was anyway harmed by Pitt's acute gout and by a failure to retain the political initiative. In February 1757, the King approached Newcastle, making clear his desire to dismiss the ministry. This set in train a course of complicated negotiations, in which George's second son, Cumberland played a major role. It led to Pitt's dismissal on 6 April. Cumberland had not wished to leave Pitt in a senior position when he went abroad to command the forces defending Hanover against a likely French attack. Pitt's dismissal, however, produced a lengthy political crisis, while attempts were made to form a new ministry. After the failure of an attempt to form a Waldegrave-Fox ministry that would have suited George, not least because Earl Waldegrave was a trusted courtier, a Newcastle-Pitt one was finally secured that July. George had told the Duke of Devonshire 'as to Pitt he had not so much objection to him but he thought him too impracticable to act with anybody'.[47] Pitt finally had to accept office in a government committed to supporting the defence of Hanover, a qualified royal victory.

Even while accepting Pitt into office, royal views were still crucial. These related to place as well as policy. As Newcastle noted in June, 'The two great difficulties that seem to arise in forming a plan of administration with Mr Pitt and his friends are first the King's promise of the Pay Office for Mr Fox ... Secondly the difficulty of removing My Lord Winchelsea and reinstating the other Lords of the Admiralty'; the Duchess subsequently adding 'The King insists upon Mr Fox's being Pay Master, and keeping the Admiralty as it is and says he will yield in everything else'.[48] Fox indeed kept the Paymastership.

Pitt had angered George by his criticism of the degree to which British policies favoured Hanover, and that indeed was central to George's concerns: George spent as much time as possible in the Electorate and actively pressed for its territorial expansion. This was not to be. Instead, George's hated nephew, Frederick II, the Great, of Prussia, became the leading ruler in north Germany. George even had to face the humiliation of a French conquest of the Electorate in 1757, although that was swiftly reversed.

More generally, George was not noted as a patron of the arts. He also showed little interest in science and the royal role in the Royal Society declined. Although he was interested in music, George was despised as a boor by his wife's favourite, Lord Hervey, whose comments have so influenced posterity, far too much so.[49] George, as King, was happiest in 1743 when, at Dettingen near Mainz in Germany on 27 June, he became the last British monarch to lead his troops into battle: he displayed great courage under fire, and the battle was a victory over the French that was to be celebrated by Handel in the *Dettingen Te Deum*, first performed later that year. The French had laid a trap for the less numerous British and Allied forces. One part of their army under the Duke of Grammont was deployed in a strong position behind the Dettingen stream, blocking the Allied route, while another threatened the Allied rear. Instead of holding his position, Grammont advanced, only to be driven back in a victory that owed much to superior British musketry.

George, nevertheless, was condemned in Britain for showing favour to his Hanoverian troops during the battle and this, thereafter, was to be a staple of criticism directed at him; Pitt's personal attack on George's conduct in the battle did not endear him to the King. Furthermore, and in the short term more seriously, the victory was not followed up. Political and military indecision, and serious differences of opinion, combined with the effects of poor weather, disease and the absence of an adequate artillery train, ensured that George was unable to make an impact on France's well-fortified eastern frontier. There was nothing to match the determination and unity of command that the Duke of Marlborough had offered in the War of the Spanish Succession. Lack of success led to dissension and disappointment.

As a young man, George had also participated in the battle of Oude-naarde in 1708. He had charged the French at the head of the Hanoverian dragoons, and had his horse shot from under him, an episode that was to be referred to frequently during his reign. Described in the House of Lords address of 7 February (os) 1728 as 'formed by nature for the greatest military achievements', George associated the army with his *gloire*, and believed that the military reviews he conducted were the most obvious and impressive display of his power and importance. He was keen on the army, enjoyed the company of military men, such as Charles Hotham, William Stanhope and Richard Sutton (all three of whom were given diplomatic posts, with Stanhope also becoming a Secretary of State and Earl of Harrington), and was determined to control military patronage. George also kept a close eye on military developments in other countries, followed European campaigns with great interest, keeping hold of a map of the Crimea so that he could follow the Russian campaign in 1736,[50] and showed favour to foreign envoys with a military background, such as Marquis Seyssel d'Aix.

Neither George, nor any member of his family, showed comparable interest in the navy. This reflected their background but helped ensure that the naval triumphs of the period did not reflect direct credit on the royal family. Nor did any member of the family seek to add naval service to that on land as James, Duke of York, later James II and VII, had done. Frederick, Prince of Wales planned, when he came to the throne, to make his son George, later George III, Lord High Admiral and to send another son Henry to sea, but nothing came of this.

George II's personal interest in the army could be a major nuisance to his British ministers. They had less room for making concessions in parliamentary manoeuvring over such issues as the size of the armed forces and the policy of subsidies paid to secure the use of Hessian forces. The impact of George's martial temperament upon his conduct of foreign policy also concerned the government. In Britain, however, George had no particular political agenda, and this was important to the development of political stability. His pragmatism, nevertheless, was accompanied by a certain amount of choleric anger. Presumably passing on information from his brother, the Duke of Newcastle, Henry Pelham told Dudley Ryder in 1753 that, as far as Hanover was concerned, George 'passes his time there much in the same manner as here, and without any more spirit or cheerfulness, but gave rather a freer venture of peevishness when he was among his Hanover ministers than here', which was one way to approach the King's constitutional and political position. In 1750, Newcastle had provided more direct evidence of royal peevishness: over negotiations for a subsidy to the Elector of Cologne, 'The King says he will not be so used, and will not give one single shilling; that his German Ministers are the worst negotiators; that they know no way of succeeding, but *yield*, and *give*'.[51]

The King, however, could prove susceptible to manipulation. In 1727, he had shown a determination to control court appointments when he had dismissed most of his father's court servants, but, five years later, Viscount Perceval recorded a visit from his cousin Mary Dering, Dresser Extraordinary to the King's daughters:

> She gave an instance of how Princes are imposed upon by their ministers. She said that when the King came to the crown his resolution was to continue in his service as chaplains all those who had been so while he was Prince, and to fill up the number belonging to him as King with as many of his father's chaplains as could be admitted, but one of his chaplains he particularly named to be continued on account of some extraordinary services he had done him when Prince. But when the then Lord Chamberlain ... brought him the lists to sign, he did it without further examination than observing the chaplain's name was there, yet afterwards it proved that the man was removed, and neither all his old chaplains, nor many of his father's continued, but a good many new persons placed.[52]

Seven years later, Sarah, Duchess of Marlborough, a caustic critic, wrote, 'It is said, His Majesty is much offended at this proceeding with Spain, but I won't answer for the truth of that report. For I can't imagine by what means His Majesty will be rightly informed of it'.[53] Such a comment could be dismissed as gossip in opposition circles, but, shortly afterwards, Walpole's brother, Horatio, a key diplomat, wrote to an Under-Secretary, promising to continue a confidential correspondence 'on condition that my letters shall not be sent with the packet to Kensington',[54] in other words to the King. Newcastle followed the same policy.[55]

Aside from deliberate efforts to keep him in the dark, there was simply not enough time for George, faced with the size of government business, to supervise all that he wished to control and for him to see that his orders were carried out. Some of the bold claims he made soon after his accession about what he would do as King can be attributed to inexperience and nervous excitement. In the event, in some spheres, such as the church and the law, George's interventions were episodic,

although he could be extremely determined in defence of his prerogatives. The Walpole ministry, for example, was to find it difficult to
persuade George to offer preferment to clerics whom he disliked. As far
as religion was concerned, George was conventionally devout and lacked
Caroline's interest in heterodox theological speculation.

In his last years, the elderly George, while still determined to resist
ministerial appointments that he disliked, was essentially prepared to
leave politics and government to his ministers. Instead, George was more
concerned about foreign policy. Indeed, in 1757, he pressed the Bavarian
envoy on the need for concerted action to preserve German liberty.[56]
In 1751 Mirepoix, the French envoy, had already reported that George
was indifferent to ministerial intrigues and left his ministers with control
over domestic matters and government patronage; being concerned,
instead, essentially with the Electorate and, more specifically, with his
jealousy and fear of Frederick II. That autumn, Newcastle had found
George willing to talk on a confidential basis about foreign affairs, but
'totally silent upon everything at home'.[57] Their relationship, however,
forced George to take an interest. In 1755 Holdernesse, the Secretary of
State who accompanied George to Hanover on his last visit, reported
to Newcastle about an audience at Herrenhausen: 'The King entered
much into conversation upon parliamentary and party matters and said
you had promised to write me word at a proper time, how *some people*
*stood affected to his measures'.*[58]

Politics was affected by disputes within the royal family. With
Caroline, George had had eight children: three boys (one died in in-
fancy) and five girls. His relations with his eldest son, Frederick,
Prince of Wales (1707–51), were particularly difficult, mirroring those of
George with his father. Although he was not faced with parental divorce,
Frederick was deprived of parental company, being left until 1728 in
Hanover, after his parents departed for England in 1714, as a sort of
pledge of the royal family's continued commitment to the Electorate.
His uncle Ernst August, Prince Bishop of Osnabrück, acted as a guardian.
Once in Britain, Frederick developed political links with opposition
Whigs, being increasingly seen as a 'Patriot Prince', and thus as an
antithesis to a Hanoverian King. This was particularly marked in 1736,
when opposition Whigs, or self-styled 'Patriots', congratulated Frederick
on his marriage to Augusta of Saxe-Gotha, while, as the government

discovered, Frederick was encouraged by his uncle by marriage, Frederick William I of Prussia.[59] The Prince's opposition was crucial to the fall of Walpole in 1742, and Frederick, who had reassured opposition leaders in January 1739 that he would never talk to the first minister, refused reconciliation with his father until after Walpole lost office.[60]

Thereafter, Frederick offered support for the government until going into opposition again in 1747. This move played a major role in leading the Pelhams to hold the general election that year, a year earlier than was necessary, because they hoped that this would deny Frederick sufficient time in which to organise support. In this, they were successful. The Prince remained in impotent opposition, although this very opposition challenged the likely longevity of the current political situation. In 1750, when Mirepoix referred to Frederick as inclined to disagree with his father in everything,[61] Frederick would have become King had George lived for only as long as his father had done. Instead, George was to survive his elder son, who unexpectedly died on 20 March (os) 1751. After a post-mortem, Frederick's death was attributed to a blow from a tennis ball three years earlier, although illness rather than accident was probably the cause.

Frederick's death led to concern about the position of George's remaining son, Cumberland, whose influence with his father was increasing, but who had a reputation as an authoritarian militarist. When, on 16 May (os) 1751, the House of Commons debated the Regency Bill after Frederick's death, Pitt, in characteristically offensive mood, suggested that Cumberland was less interested in 'protecting the Crown than' in 'wearing it',[62] and there were even newspaper references to Cumberland acting as a potential Richard III toward Frederick's young sons.

George did not only have problems with his sons. The willingness of another Frederick, his son-in-law Frederick of Hesse-Cassel, to become a Catholic was also a grave concern. George was determined to protect the position of his daughter Mary, Frederick's estranged wife. The 'utmost zeal and assiduity' was called for in ensuring that she obtained an independent financial provision and did not have to live with Frederick.[63]

After Caroline died in 1737, George settled down into a domestic relationship with his already established mistress, Amalia Sophie Marianne von Walmoden. He had met her in Hanover, to which

Caroline did not accompany him: she remained with the children in Britain and acted as regent. Madame Walmoden's second son, John, born in 1736, who was reputed to be the King's child, rose to be a Field Marshal in the Hanoverian army. After Caroline died, George made Madame Walmoden Countess of Yarmouth, and her role became similar to that of Melusine von der Schulenburg under his father. She became an influential political force because of her access to him. As George's confidante, she was alleged to have recommended at least three peerage creations in return for bribes, and was used as a way to convey ideas to George. In October 1756, Pitt went to see her to forward his plan for a ministry nominally headed by Devonshire. Two years later, Pitt told her that if the Habeas Corpus Bill, an unsuccessful attempt to expand the definition of habeas corpus, was not passed, that would compromise his relations with his ministerial colleagues.[64] In the event, Pitt's pressure on his colleagues only angered George. In 1767, however, recycling an old myth, Robert Wood, one of Pitt's Under-Secretaries, claimed that Pitt had had 'the total direction of the old King under Lady Yarmouth and by her means'.[65]

George was regarded as particularly healthy for his age;[66] although there were periods of illness,[67] and foreign commentators, such as the spiteful Frederick II, were interested as to whether he would last for much longer.[68] In 1751, the year in which Prince Frederick died, Lady Anson saw George in the drawing room, noting 'the King looks extremely well'.[69] Age, nevertheless, had an effect on George, and politicians and others anticipated his demise. In 1754, Frederick II noted reports from Hanover that George was nearly blind and indeed, in 1756, growing problems with his sight led the King to want the use of black ink in documents that he had to read.[70] The previous year, the Sardinian envoy, Count Viry, then with George in Hanover, had attributed the King's illness to distress at leaving his beloved Electorate.[71] He had certainly been able to spend a long time on that visit on his favourite activity of reviewing troops.

The political agenda of George's last years was dominated by war. Between 1739 and 1748, the War of Jenkins' Ear, and then the War of Austrian Succession, set Britain against both Spain and, from 1743, France (although war was not declared until 1744). The latter created the framework for a further and wider bout of hostilities with France during the Seven Years War (1756–63), with Spain joining in on the French side in the latter stages after George III had come to the throne. The Seven Years War was played out on a global scale, in Europe, India, North America, West Africa and the West Indies, and demonstrated both the degree to which Britain had become an imperial power and the remarkable impact that disputes between European states could now have on world affairs. In Europe, Britain was allied to Frederick II, who enjoyed an aura of battlefield success that George could not command. Indeed, Frederick was presented to the British public as the Protestant Hero and as a military leader to rank with Caesar.

By the close of George's reign, Britain had smashed the French navy (at the battles of Lagos and Quiberon Bay in 1759) and taken much of the French empire, most dramatically Quebec in 1759, becoming the dominant European power in South Asia and North America. The direct contribution of the by then elderly King to this process was limited. In 1755, indeed, Mirepoix was confident that George did not want war and cared little about the colonies.[72] That was certainly true of his Hanoverian ministers. Even when in Hanover in 1755, however, George remained closely interested in British foreign policy as war with France neared, while, once victories had been won in the Seven Years War, the King was keen to retain any conquests made. After news arrived of successes in the 1758 campaigning season, George was convinced, as he told Pitt, 'that we must keep Cape Breton, and Canada' (the latter as yet unconquered) and regain Minorca by exchanging it with a yet to be captured Martinique. Newcastle thought both men unrealistic.[73] In late 1759, after far more victories had been won, Pitt was willing to negotiate with France, but George wanted to fight on in order to obtain the best peace possible for Hanover, which was involved in the war. The two men also differed over reinforcements for India, where the French were contesting Britain's position. Robert Clive sought assistance from Pitt, finding a ready response, whereas George wanted the troops sent to Germany to keep French forces from Hanover.[74]

The ability of Pitt to direct resources to transoceanic goals was a consequence of the way he, Newcastle, his leading ministerial colleague, and George operated parliamentary monarchy in the late 1750s. Pitt used Newcastle to change George's mind, while George and Newcastle benefited from Pitt's ability to manage Parliament. There were clashes, as in early 1758, when Pitt tried to force George to replace Andrew Mitchell as envoy in Berlin, threatening to resign over the matter.[75] The dispute captured the problems posed by royal power. Berlin was a crucial embassy and Pitt had to take responsibility for carrying government business through the Commons, but envoys were the personal representatives of the King. As an aspect of the ambiguity of the constitution, there was a tension between the parliamentary aspect of government – ministers taking responsibility for the successful management of Parliament – and the departmental one, where different spheres were focused on the crown. This was an inherently unstable situation that Pitt, like other ministers before and after, found frustrating.

The occupation of Hanover by the French in 1757 had led George to consider negotiations with Austria for neutrality for the Electorate, a measure rejected by Pitt as likely to wreck Britain's alliance with Prussia. Pitt pressed George hard for the rapid disavowal of the convention accepting French occupation, refusing in October 1757 to pay the Hanoverian troops while they remained inactive. That winter, Pitt played a major role in securing a political settlement that tied the defence of Hanover to British direction and identified it with the more popular Prussian alliance. He proposed that Britain pay the entire cost of the Army of Observation, the German force designed to protect Hanover, and, in 1758 he won support for the dispatch of British troops to Germany which were designed to assist this army.

At the same time, Britain's military commitment to the Continent created practical problems for the British ministry that required the King's help. Thus, in June 1759, Newcastle was delighted to report that George very much approved a letter he and Holdernesse had drawn up, adding 'As a proof of the King's approbation, His Majesty ordered My Lord Holdernesse to carry the letter to Mr Reiche; and to direct him to prepare a draft of a letter, from the King, to Prince Ferdinand, exactly agreeable to *that*'.[76] Ferdinand of Brunswick (Brunswick-Wolfenbüttel) was the commander of the army in which the British expeditionary force was fighting. It was to win a major victory over the French at Minden on 1 August 1759.

It was at the height of wartime euphoria that George died, on 25 October 1760, the first of the Hanoverian monarchs to die in Britain. Time would tell whether the war abroad, and the new political dispensation that it had created at home, would bring further benefits to the regime of the new King, George III. The private tributes paid to George II when he died are striking, especially as it might not have been thought that the cantankerous monarch would have inspired such respect and affection. Characteristically emotional, Newcastle felt he had 'lost the best King, the best master, and the best friend that ever subject had. God knows what consequences it may have'. Carteret wrote to his daughter that he had 'lost in common with the public an excellent King but also I can say with great truth a most gracious and good friend in particular'. The 'bluestocking' Elizabeth Montagu offered a very personal assessment:

> With him our laws and liberties were safe, he possessed in a great degree the confidence of his people and the respect of foreign governments; and a certain steadiness of character made him of great consequence in these unsettled times. During his long reign we never were subject to the insolence and rapaciousness of favourites, a grievance of all others most intolerable ... His character would not afford subject for epic poetry, but will look well in the sober page of history. Conscious perhaps of this he was too little regardful of sciences and the fine arts; he considered common sense as the best panegyric.

Most, however, turned with relief to the bright promise of a new, young and vigorous King, leaving Sarah Stanley to note, on 7 December 1760: 'I can't help still regretting our late Sovereign, if he had some defects, he had certainly many virtues, and he had experience, which nothing but time can give; yet he seems already to be almost forgotten'.[77]

George II's death also marked the close of an era in British monarchy, the era of seventeenth-century monarchs. Born in 1683 (his father had been born in 1660), he was to be succeeded by a grandson, George III, born fifty-five years later, in 1738. Through good health, George II outlived his eldest son, while his other son, Cumberland, was to die in 1765. Because he was succeeded by his grandson, George III, rather than Frederick, George II was also the last of the dynasty to be born in Germany. Indeed George III never went to Hanover, nor left England. George II's death therefore marked one of the major turning points in the history of the dynasty, one that is underrated by the emphasis on dynasties, rather than other groupings of monarchs, as the building blocs of monarchical history.

George III began a period of English-dominated British monarchy, with Hanover as an appendage, albeit an important one. George II ended a cosmopolitan period that, with the exception of the self-consciously English Anne, had begun with Charles II and James II and VII, both of whom had spent many of their formative years in foreign exile, continued with Dutch William, and culminated with George I and George II. This was a bloc in the history of the British monarchy, not only for that reason, and because it spanned a century (1660–1760), but also because this was the age of Baroque monarchy in Britain. This Baroque character was a matter in part of cultural preferences, which, in the cases of George I and George II, included echoes of Italianate culture and of French style, but also of an identity that, at least in part, Britain and Hanover shared with the rest of Europe.

Issues of chronological demarcation are important, in particular the vitality, alongside the British divide in dynastic terms, of the more general compartmentalisation of the European eighteenth century, and the creation of a chronology that treats its early years as the concluding period of the era of Louis XIV, and then, after a period much of which is in shadow, focuses on Maria Theresa of Austria, George III and the Enlightened Despots. The nature of this chronology, and the extent of this period of shadow, varies by country and subject; but it is certainly true that we know less of the reign of George II (1727–60) than that of George III (1760–1820), the Portugal of John V (1706–50) than that of Joseph I (1750–77) and his minister Pombal, less of the Spain of Philip V (1700–46) and Ferdinand VI (1746–59), than that of Charles III (1759–88), less of the Russia of Catherine I (1725–7), Peter II (1727–30), Anna (1730–40), Ivan VI (1740–41) and Elizabeth (1741–62) than of that of Peter the Great (1689–1725) and Catherine the Great (1762–96), and so on. There have been improvements, but the weight of research and publication continues to fall on the second half of the century. This is true of Austria, Britain, France, Prussia, Russia, Spain and Sweden. Furthermore, work on the first half of the century does not play a major role in accounts of the eighteenth century as a whole.

While this remains the case, it is difficult to establish how best to assess George III and the other rulers of the second half of the century, and to consider the novelty of their policies, and how their aspirations and achievements should be assessed. This is part of a larger problem of deciding how best to relate the two halves of the century. There are essentially two approaches. The first treats the entire century as a unit, so that, in the case of Britain, George III is set alongside his two predecessors. In this perspective, the greater clarity permitted by work on the second half illuminates a longer-term situation. Alternatively, it can be argued that there was significant change during the century, with the later decades being very different from the earlier; this approach is taken in a variety of subjects, including demographics, economic history and imperial regulation, and can also be seen in work on British and French history and on Enlightened Despotism. In each case, however, the detailed chronology of change is different, and the weight placed upon a 'tipping point' or period of transition varies.

If century long units are to be adopted, for the British monarchy, the first half of the eighteenth century in many respects sits more comfortably with the second half of the seventeenth. Although, in specifically Anglican terms, George III was closer to Queen Anne than to George II, there were major changes in the style of power between the two halves of the eighteenth century, not least a decline in the themes and idioms of sacral, or at least providential, monarchy, and, even more, a reduced emphasis on the military role of the crown: George II at Dettingen was a world away from George III visiting farms. This can be linked to a longer-term shift in sensibility from the attitudes, themes and trophes inaccurately, but helpfully, summarised as Baroque, to those summarised as Classical or Neo-classical. The British monarchy was well placed for this transition, as, under the first two Georges, its political position did not depend on Baroque attributes. Indeed, on 29 August (os) 1752, the London newspaper *Old England* had argued that the English monarchy was very different to its French counterpart because the English 'attribute no divinity to their Kings'.

A different aspect of the monarchy's grounding in a position defined in part by its limited authority was offered in May 1756 when Holdernesse wrote to Andrew Mitchell, the British envoy in Berlin and an MP, pointing out that when the Anglo-Prussian treaty had been concluded, a declaration had also been signed to settle the dispute over the Silesian loan, and that the Prussian envoy

> Michel at that period had orders from the King his master, to require an explicit and authentic declaration from the King's servants, touching the treatment his subjects might expect to meet at sea, in case of a war between

England and France; but Mr Michel having been desired to represent to His Prussian Majesty, that no declaration of that kind could be valid, as the King's authority did not reach to cases provided for by law, and that the only method by which the ends which His Prussian Majesty has in view could be obtained would be by a treaty of commerce.

Agreeing, Frederick II had sent a project for a treaty, but Holdernesse advised Mitchell, 'You are sufficiently informed of the nicety with which we are obliged to proceed in cases of this nature, and can explain ... the reasons which have induced me to refer this project to the Board of Trade, and to wait for their report ... though from the forms of government the business is delayed, it is by no means neglected'.[78]

Four years later, referring to another limitation, a French memorandum argued that George II lacked a proper court and that there was scant external pomp or theatre of majesty. The writer claimed that George lived in a town where trade alone was valued,[79] and clearly thought the monarchy weakened by this situation; but, although a lack of pomp by continental standards might have made it difficult to impress foreigners, there are few signs that it weakened George. Instead, the trend in recent decades has been to offer a positive assessment of George, one that emphasises his importance and independence, not least, but not only, by focusing on his role in foreign policy.[80] This remains the appropriate conclusion.

1. George I, portrait by Sir Godfrey Kneller, 1714. (*National Portrait Gallery*)

2. George II, portrait by Charles Jervas, 1727. (*National Portrait Gallery*)

3. George III, portrait by Allan Ramsay, 1761. (*National Portrait Gallery*)

4. Queen Charlotte of Mecklenberg-Strelitz, wife of George III. (*National Portrait Gallery*)

5. George III, portrait by Sir William Beechey, 1800. (*National Portrait Gallery*)

6. George IV, portrait by unknown artist, 1815. (*National Portrait Gallery*)

7. Queen Caroline of Brunswick, portrait by Sir Thomas Lawrence, 1804. (*National Portrait Gallery*)

8. William IV, portrait by Sir Martin Archer Shee, 1800. (*National Portrait Gallery*)

# 6

## George III

I trust with the protection of Divine Providence I shall extricate this country by becoming spirit and activity out of its present difficulties.

George III, 1772 [1]

The outlines of George's career are readily rehearsed, and yet also bear testimony not only to his longevity but also to the fascinating range of issues he had to confront and the major changes that Britain experienced during this reign. George (1738–1820), King of Great Britain and Ireland 1760–1820, Elector of Hanover, 1760–1814, and King of Hanover, 1814–20, was the last monarch to rule the Thirteen Colonies that became the United States of America. Born in London, at Norfolk House, St James's Square, on 24 May (os) 1738 (and 4 June new style), George was the first son of Frederick, Prince of Wales and his wife Augusta.

Frederick died in 1751, leaving his eldest son to succeed him as Prince of Wales. As Prince, George developed a sense of antagonism towards the prevailing political system, which he thought oligarchical and factional. The young Prince, and his adviser and confidant, John Stuart, third Earl of Bute, who was a surrogate father (rather than as was widely alleged his mother, Augusta's lover),[2] favoured the idea of politics without party and a King above faction. To further his goals, George thought it necessary that he personally should take a central political role. This was not only his constitutional role as one of the three elements in Parliament, but also his moral duty.

The two fused in the potent idea of George as a 'Patriot King', a notion that stemmed from Henry, Viscount Bolingbroke's earlier discussion of such a concept in his *Idea of a Patriot King* (1749), which called for a monarch who was virtuous, impartial and powerful enough to override parties. These were ideas supported by Frederick, Prince of

Wales, who, in his youth, had been given a moral course in history by being provided with Clarendon and Burnet to read;[3] and they were inculcated in George as a youth. Influenced by the concept of patriarchal government implicit in Bolingbroke's book, George believed that, in maintaining his right to choose ministers and his ability to block legislation, he was ensuring that he could discharge his functions and, to use a concept that he understood, serve. In this respect, George sought to fulfil the hopes that had focused on his father. The King was to act as a political redeemer, a notion that reflected a powerful optimistic element in the political iconography of kingship.[4]

George and Bute had also been angered by the political realignment of 1757 that brought Pitt and Newcastle into office together. They felt betrayed by Pitt and were ready to oppose the government and to make threats about what the position would be when George became King. Thus, in 1759, George backed Simeon Stuart when he stood against Henry Legge, the Chancellor of the Exchequer and a politician associated with Pitt, in a by-election in Hampshire. The strength of Legge's position led Stuart to back down. Legge was then pressed by Bute to promise support in the next general election:

> he does, out of real friendship to Mr Legge, beseech him to consider very seriously whether after triumphing over the Prince's inclinations at present, Lord Bute hath any method left of removing prejudices that the late unhappy occurrences have strongly impressed the Prince with, than by being enabled to assure him that Mr Legge will as far as shall be in his power cooperate with his Royal Highness's wishes at the next general election.[5]

Legge's refusal angered George, who dismissed him in March 1761.

The notion of the King as redeemer was linked to George's focus on Britain rather than Hanover. George lacked the degree of emotional attachment to, and concern about, the Electorate showed by his two predecessors, and this had already been seen when George was Prince of Wales. An undated letter that he then sent to Bute revealed George's opposition to the dispatch of troops to Germany, as well as his related hostility to his grandfather:

> I shall soon be going to that hated Drawing Room, which I suppose will be fuller than usual, on account of last Monday's news from the foreign

dominions; I fear the troops will now with greater ardour be demanded to keep the French from returning.[6]

George made his views clear in his addition to the draft for his first speech from the throne, although his British theme was to be criticised in the letter of 'Junius' to the king on 19 December 1769 which accused him of having 'renounced the name of Englishman'.

> Born and educated in this country I glory in the name of Britain; and the peculiar happiness of my life, will ever consist, in promoting the welfare of a people, whose loyalty and warm affection to me, I consider as the greatest and most permanent security of my throne.[7]

Although he learned German from an early age,[8] and, like his predecessors, had a German wife (though not a mistress of *any* nationality), George never, despite repeated reports of planned visits,[9] visited the Electorate, before or after his accession. George's early determination to repudiate the policies and methods of his grandfather was shown in his attitude to Hanover, not least in his willingness to break with Frederick II of Prussia without securing the alliance of another power that might guarantee Hanover. Indeed, once he had come to the throne, George consciously presented himself as a British patriot, and was praised on that head. For instance, the *Bath Chronicle* of 25 December 1760 carried an item of London news from the *Monitor*: 'It is said that His Majesty, in consideration of the war with France, has forbid all French wines of any sort to be drank in the palace, not even excepting his own table. It is calculated this will be a saving of at least £40,000 per annum'.

George's popularity was further enhanced by his marriage. The first unmarried monarch to ascend the throne since Charles II in 1660, George married Charlotte of Mecklenburg-Strelitz on 8 September 1761, and the two were crowned in Westminster Abbey on 22 September. Chesterfield wrote from Blackheath on 12 September, 'The town of London and the city of Westminster are gone quite mad with the wedding and the approaching coronation, people think and talk of nothing else'.[10] The coronation in fact was poorly organised, not least because the mislaying of the Sword of State led to a delay of three hours. The banquet was also chaotic, with no places for some of the leading aristocrats, while the Champion's horse backed into George, who lost his temper and berated the acting Earl Marshal after the ceremony.[11]

Given the tendency to focus on George's politics in the 1760s, it is important to note the importance to him and others of his marriage, which was designed to ensure his happiness and to secure the succession. The criteria George exercised in looking for a wife focused on disposition and childbearing ability. He did not seek another Caroline of Ansbach, excluding his cousin Frederica of Saxe Gotha on the grounds that she was interested in philosophy. The initial six women on the list were Protestant princesses, as was necessary for the Elector of Hanover, and all Germans, and the two added were the Princess of Denmark and the eventual choice, Charlotte. Two from the list were judged unacceptable because of socially questionable marriages among their ancestors; a third was seen as too young; and another two were seen as bad-tempered by those who reported to George. Charlotte was eventually left alone in the field.

Despite his popularity on his accession to the throne, George soon became a figure of controversy because of his determination to reign without party. The theme of the King as a dangerous political force exerting a malevolent role in British affairs was strongly revived in the 1760s after two reigns in which criticism of the monarchs had arisen largely from their Hanoverian concerns or from the perspective of a Jacobite loyalism that, in fact, caused most politicians to rally to the Hanoverian dynasty. Politically, George was the most interesting (and longest ruling) of the Hanoverians, although he came young to the throne and had little earlier political experience: one of the most pernicious consequences of the bad relations between the Hanoverians and their heirs was that the latter had no real political apprenticeship (and in George III's case no military one as well). What experience they did have was as a totem of opposition activity, scarcely the most helpful training for the commitments of the throne.

George was not the brightest of monarchs, and most certainly not the most sparkling. He had, however, several qualities worthy of note, not least diligence. Until he became seriously ill, he continued the diligence seen under his predecessors since the accession of James II and VII. As Prince of Wales, George's father Frederick had given few such signs, and, indeed, in his artistic interests, political opportunism and self-indulgence, he had prefigured George IV; but, as Frederick did not become King, he left the task of recreating the monarchical habits associated with Charles II to his grandsons, George III's numerous progeny. If George III was scarcely unique in being industrious, his energies were directed differently from those of his predecessors. In addition, he came to play a role in a political world that had grown accustomed during the last fourteen years of the reign of his elderly grandfather, George II, to a monarch of lesser energy who, although far from being a cipher, accepted the direction of most domestic affairs by his leading ministers.

To many Whigs, the novel practice of seeking Tory support constituted a revolutionary political step, and almost an unconstitutional move on the part of the monarch. George's ostentatious displays of favour towards individual Tories, who had been denied access to the benefits of court approval since the Hanoverian accession reflected, however, his support for the ideas and ideals of non-party governments, not Toryism *per se*. Unlike George I and George II, George III was also not a pragmatist but, instead, had an agenda for Britain. He thought that much about the political system was corrupt and, in part, ascribed this to the size of the national debt. As a consequence, George's moral reformism, which drew on his strong personal piety, was specifically aimed against faction and luxury. In 1763 George complained to the French ambassador about

> the spirit of fermentation and the excessive licence which prevails in England. It was essential to neglect nothing that could check that spirit and to employ firmness as much as moderation. He was very determined not to be the toy of factions ... and his fixed plan was to establish his authority without breaking the law.[12]

Aside from his new agenda for the crown, George, like other rulers, found it difficult to forge acceptable relationships with senior politicians at his accession, something which contributed to the ministerial and political instability of the 1760s. Pitt's attitude towards Bute was unacceptable to George, while both George and Bute felt that Pitt had betrayed them in 1757 by forming a ministry with Newcastle, a sin compounded by his support for the dispatch of troops to Germany in 1758. Pitt himself took few pains to soothe Bute's susceptibilities and clearly felt contempt for the man.

George, however, made his support for his favourite clear. On 27 October 1760 Devonshire recorded in his diary, 'Lord Bute told Mr Pitt that the King would have no meetings held at which he [Bute] was not present, and that for the future everything should be considered and debated in his presence, and then His Majesty would determine as he thought proper'.[13] George broke with the domineering Pitt in 1761 and with Newcastle the following year. Ministerial stability, however, proved elusive. The ambiguity of a number of constitutional points, such as the collective responsibility of the Cabinet and the degree to which the monarch had to choose his ministers from those who had the confidence of Parliament, exacerbated the situation, while what Bute termed 'the violence of party' owed much to the King's conscious abandonment of royal support for government by the Whigs for the Whigs. This helped ensure the end of the cohesion of the Old Corps Whigs, which was an important aspect of the instability of the 1760s. Breaking with the Whigs led to claims that George was connected to Tories, indeed Jacobites, and was also held to indicate that George shared illiberal views on government, in his case an unwanted stress on the royal prerogative, views that were blamed by some on the combined malevolent impact of Princess Augusta and Bute.[14]

These claims were misplaced. George II had been no cipher, a point that emerges more clearly as a result of recent research on the politics of his reign, and George III was motivated not by the desire to return to the Stuarts but by a pious diligence. In so far as he looked back, the model was the fictive 'Patriot King' or, among earlier monarchs, Queen Anne, who had been diligent and a pious Anglican, and who would have liked to rule without party. The pious diligence of George III was, in some respects, a parallel to the pietism seen among north German monarchs in the early eighteenth century, especially Frederick William I of Prussia. George I was affected by similar ideas, although the sense of duty he showed was generally not ostentatiously devout, and neither George I nor his Prussian son-in-law could be accused of being too subservient to the clergy, a charge brought against George III by Horace Walpole.

Whereas George I and George II had devoted much of their energy to foreign policy, George III appeared to herald a new departure. His willingness to break with the Whigs encouraged suspicions about his intentions and offered an apparent echo of Stuart autocracy. Throughout his reign, political opponents believed that George was not only out to increase royal power, but also that he acted in a manipulative way to do so, allegedly undermining politics by the use of secret advisers or of ministers who were not committed to fair government: a group of villains that began with Bute and included Mansfield, Jenkinson, Shelburne, Thurlow and Auckland. This theme helped inspire, and in turn drew heavily on, Edmund Burke's *Thoughts on the Cause of the Present Discontents* (1770), which became a key opposition text.

By the spring of 1763 Bute, whose enthusiasm for high office had never been total, was disillusioned with government. Although the ministry enjoyed solid parliamentary majorities, Bute found the stress of politics, which included exposure to the expression of rabid anti-Scottish sentiment, unbearable. George's continued reliance on him was therefore a weakness, not least because the close association of the two men ensured that the unpopularity of the minister cast a shadow over the public reputation of the monarch. This reliance was not to end when Bute resigned. Indeed, in April 1763, George wrote to him 'thank God I have a friend ... that comforts me and makes me look on my ministers as my tools solely in my public capacity'.[15]

In the event, George found that Bute's resignation that month left him with a ministry under George Grenville, an aggressive individual prone to hector the King. Relations between the two men were poor, not least because George regretted Bute's resignation. George may also have had physical symptoms of porphyria in 1762 and, even more, 1765; the latter led the government to consider urgently a regency in the event of his death.[16] His acute irritability certainly helped to sour his relations with Grenville. Indeed, George was sufficiently dismayed to allow himself to be persuaded by Bute, who initially remained influential, to open negotiations with Pitt in August 1763.[17] They proved abortive because George was not prepared to accept Pitt's demands to control the composition of the government, while Pitt failed to accept George's views. The King approached Pitt again in May 1765, his loathing of Grenville leading him to accept Pitt's demands, although, in the event, the ailing Pitt was unwilling to form a ministry. As a result, the Grenville ministry was replaced in July 1765 by a new one under the Marquess of Rockingham that was not much to the King's wishes. William, Duke of Cumberland, not Bute, was the most influential adviser to George at this juncture.

The volatile political atmosphere in London also contributed to the sense of crisis in the 1760s. Pitt's resignation in 1761 had considerably tempered George's popularity: 'the cry of the people in the taverns and alehouses is *no Pitt, no King*'.[18] On 9 November 1761, when George attended the Lord Mayor's banquet, he received less applause than Pitt. Dissatisfaction in the capital was exploited by a squinting anti-hero, John Wilkes, an entrepreneur of faction. The libertine MP fell foul of his antithesis, George III, as a result of bitter attacks on the government in his newspaper, the *North Briton*. Wilkes's denunciation of the Peace of Paris in number 45, issued on 23 April 1763, with its implication that George had lied in his speech from the throne, as a result of being misled by his ministers, led to a charge of seditious libel. In an outraged defence of royal dignity, as well as its own position, the government, with the full support of George, took a number of retaliatory steps that eventually culminated in Wilkes's expulsion from Parliament, and his repeated re-election for Middlesex. As Wilkes was declared incapable of being returned for Parliament, this thwarting of the popular will served to give opponents the opportunity to stigmatise the royal government.

For George, 'faction' was not a target to be fought only when he replaced his grandfather's ministers in 1761–62. Instead, it was one that he had to confront repeatedly. For example, angered by the policies of the Rockingham ministry of 1765–66, George, hoping 'to extricate this country out of a faction', in July 1766 sent for Pitt, a volte-face that did not, however, create an effective ministry, although it did cause a final breach between George and Bute.

Nevertheless, there was no fundamental political crisis. Instead, after George found an effective political manager, in Frederick, Lord North in January 1770, politics within Britain became far more quiescent. North was able to lead the Commons, manage government business, and maintain a united government, while the reintegration of the Tories into the political mainstream helped heal a long-standing divide dating from the mid seventeenth century.[19] North was helped by the disunited character of the opposition and by a natural rallying of support to the crown, the focus of most politicians' loyalty, a rallying that also took place in response both to the extremism of some of the Wilkesites and to a more general concern about the preservation of order. The absence of a reversionary interest, as George, Prince of Wales was only born in

1762, further helped by removing the alternative of a loyal opposition focused on another member of the royal family. The only other member of the royal family who had sought to play a major role, George's uncle, William, Duke of Cumberland, was far from the succession, due to the numerous progeny of his brother, Frederick Prince of Wales. In any case, Cumberland died in 1765. The collapse of Bute's influence was also important to the King's recovery in popularity, while George was also more adroit than he had been in the early 1760s. Although the absence of a dynastic rival (or alternative dynasty) was valuable, it also forced some opponents to seek more radical methods of attack, helping to make republicanism attractive again in the age of the American Revolution, but this also lessened the appeal of opposition.

In 1773, the painter Sir Joshua Reynolds wrote after his return from the review of the fleet:

> The King is exceeding delighted with his reception at Portsmouth. He said to a person about that he was convinced he was not so unpopular as the newspapers would represent him to be. The acclamations of the people were indeed prodigious. On his return all the country assembled in the towns where he changed horses. At Godalming every man had a branch of a tree in his hand and every woman a nosegay which they presented to the King (the horses moving as slow as possible) till he was up to the knees in flowers, and they all singing in a tumultuous manner, God Save the King. The King was so affected that he could not refrain shedding abundance of tears, and even joined in the chorus.[20]

Hans Stanley, who combined the Governorship of the Isle of Wight with the Cofferership of the Household and being MP for Southampton, reported after spending three days in Portsmouth:

> I am no courtier in saying that one of the parts which I was the most pleased with was the King's address and behaviour. I knew him sufficiently before, to be persuaded that he did not want either politeness, or a certain degree of play and imagination in conversation, but as he has lived so much in retirement, I thought he would have been embarrassed and reserved in so large a company ... but Charles II could not have been more affable, more easy, or more engaging at his table, and would not have had so much discretion and propriety; I did not attend him in his survey of the docks, where none but those of the marine department assisted, but I am told his questions were all manly, sensible, and pertinent, and that he

made every note and observation, from whence this expedition might be a real instruction to him, and not a mere amusement.[21]

Portsmouth was a special case, with huge numbers directly dependent on the crown. Any association with the navy was popular, and this was to be shown anew when George visited Portsmouth in 1778, but the account of the response on the journey back is instructive and suggests that the usual chronology for shifts in George's popularity – a decline from after Pitt's resignation in 1761 and a revival from 1784 – requires revision, a point supported by the degree to which the image of the King as a model of domestic virtue predates 1784 by several years. In particular, the extent of royal unpopularity outside London needs to be qualified. In 1778, George noted his 'thorough satisfaction at the manner in which I have been received by all ranks of people on my late tour'.[22]

By then, in combining his diligence as a royal bureaucrat with his growing willingness to tour, George had successfully blended 'two approaches to the public face of kingship', that of 'his grandfather with his father's English gentleman Prince. These were quite different ideas. George II was a businesslike King, doing his duty as he saw fit. Frederick, in searching for a meaningful role in Britain, effectively took the personal presence ... to the "people"'.[23] George III was both conscientious and publicly approachable, visiting the aristocracy on his travels, but also making himself more generally visible. Thus, staying with the Earl of Ailesbury at Tottenham Park in 1787 on the way back from Weymouth, George III not only played cribbage, drove in an open chaise round Savernake Forest (the King himself driving), and looked at the Earl's collection of prints, but also received an address from the Mayor and Corporation of Marlborough.[24] The following year, George visited the seats of Earl Bathurst and the Earl of Coventry, but opportunities were also provided for him to be seen. *Berrow's Worcester Journal* of 31 July 1788 recorded:

> On Saturday last their Majesties accompanied by the Princesses, passed and repassed through Tewkesbury on their way to and from the seat of the Earl of Coventry. Upon which occasion the inhabitants gave every proof of their loyalty and attachment to their sovereign. A grand triumphant arch was erected across the street at the post office, adorned and decorated with flowers and garlands, and with flags streaming, on the top of the arch

their Majesties' arms were placed and beneath an inscription with those words, 'King George I before his accession to the throne was Baron of Tewkesbury'. 'May the illustrious house of Hanover flourish to the latest posterity'. A band of music was placed on an eminence near the arch, who as their Majesties passed played, 'God Save the King'. The 29th Regiment of Foot was drawn up in form by the Earl of Harrington, and every other method used to testify the pleasure they received from a view of so many branches of the Royal Family.

The capital, however, was the most prominent site for displays of popularity or signs of its absence. It was in London that George was hissed, when he drove to Parliament in 1771 to give his assent to a number of Bills; an apple was also thrown at his carriage.

Signs of a more widespread popularity were seen in the elections: North had little difficulty in winning the general elections of 1774 and 1780, or in keeping the Rockinghamite opposition at bay. The latter was convinced that there was a royal conspiracy against liberty, and provided a paranoid tone to discussion about George, one echoed across the Atlantic, but the number within, or outside, the British political nation who believed that they were suffering under executive tyranny was smaller than the noise they made.

Although North was an active minister, George, who was personally friendly with him (the two men also shared a devout Anglicanism), kept a close eye on politics, and his correspondence was a testimony to his activity. Like William Pitt the Younger later, North wrote regular parliamentary reports for George; in the late 1760s, Grafton had already done so intermittently. North was pressed to take steps to win over or inspire particular parliamentarians,[25] and expected to provide information on topics such as the attendance at pre-sessional meetings.[26] George also took a close interest in division figures, being pleased when the government majority rose in February 1770.[27] In 1774 he expressed concern about the electoral situation in London and Westminster:

Had the City affairs been managed with as much activity prior to Mr Robinson's being in office as he does the Court of Aldermen would not have been composed of a majority favourable to so disgraceful a member as Mr Wilkes; Mr Robinson having fully stated the state of the mayoralty and the meeting at Guildhall for proposing candidates for the county is very agreeable.[28]

... by the conduct of the mob towards Lord Thomas Clinton this day it may be seen that riots will be attempted; Mr Robinson will therefore keep the peace officers in the way during the Westminster Election.[29]

Once fighting had broken out in America in 1775, George kept a close eye on the details of activities linked to the war, as was clearly shown in his correspondence with John Robinson, the Secretary to the Treasury:

> Mr Robinson has the honour to transmit herewith pursuant to His Majesty's orders a précis of the several proceedings at the Treasury relative to America since the first of January last with the correspondence thereon, and also a state of all the provisions furnished by the contractors drawn into one view, together with an account from Mr Adair of the medicines sent for the use of the army.[30]

> Mr Robinson has the honour to send, by Lord North's directions, for H.M.'s inspection, two casks of sour grout [sic], put up with valves in the same manner as the casks shipped for America; and also one of the valves. The cask marked No. 1 has been sometime made and may be nearly fit for use, that marked No. 2 is at present in a state of strong fermentation.[31]

> Mr Robinson has the honour by Lord North's directions to send to H.M. drafts of dispatches to Generals Carleton, Howe, and Burgoyne, and to the Paymaster General and Mr Gordon Commissary at Cork; Mr Robinson finding that the Treasury has occasion to trouble H.M. often on the American business, and East India affairs, has presumed, to have some boxes made in order to save H.M. the trouble of making up packets, and to send inclosed a key in which he humbly hopes he shall not offend.[32]

George's close supervision can be readily illustrated:

> the dispatch to General Carleton is drawn up with the clearness that always is to be found in papers drawn up by Mr Robinson, the proposal to Lord North in the margin that more money should be sent under the head of Extraordinaries seems highly necessary, otherwise the General will during the winter be under the greatest difficulty to issue subsistence to his army, as the pay cannot be issued farther than until the 24th of December. I have signed the warrants. The digesting the several matters of dispute and inquiry under different heads that relate to the affairs of Bengal undoubtedly will be most useful, and I hope with a little management that when Lord North fairly sets his shoulders to that arduous task that he will find it less difficult

than he seems to apprehend; if he would fix his own ideas on the subjects and not give ear to such various counselors, he would be less perplexed, and the right path would certainly be followed.[33]

George's personality emerges clearly in his correspondence, highlighting the problems created by a lack of comparable sources for his two predecessors. His attention to parliamentary and electoral (referring, here, to Parliament, not the Electorate of Hanover) matters was closer than for other Hanoverians, and his comments reflected his belief in order and his instinctive dislike of change:

> It is very extraordinary that Mr [Charles James] Fox should have so large a majority [in Westminster] unless composed of very bad votes, this certainly makes the scrutiny a proper measure ... the fatigue of the winter, which might be greatly diminished if Lord North would let business come forward as soon as possible, and keep Parliament constantly employed whilst assembled, instead of frequently from a wish of putting off the evil of deciding, leaving the House idle which always encourages Opposition to run into speculative maters that ever tend to sap the constitution.[34]

George's determination to maintain royal authority certainly played a major role in the crisis in relations with the American colonies that led to revolution there in 1775. Already, in the Stamp Act crisis of 1765–66, which arose from attempts to increase the taxation from the American colonies, George had been 'more and more grieved at the accounts from America. Where this spirit will end is not to be said; it is undoubtedly the most serious matter that ever came before Parliament. It requires more deliberation, candour and temper than I fear it will meet with'.[35] George had also been unenthusiastic about the Rockingham ministry's compromise that defused the crisis in 1766: an abandonment of the tax, albeit with the insistence, by a Declaratory Act, on the principle of parliamentary sovereignty. George's moves within Britain had already helped to spawn a critical political literature that condemned his alleged despotic attitudes and policies, a literature that influenced the American response to successive ministerial plans to increase its American revenues or to maintain control in the colonies.

During the American War of Independence (1775–83), George sought to stiffen opposition to what he saw as rebellion. He was, in turn, seen by the Americans as the cause of their problems. In a line-cut for Freebetter's *New England Almanack*, Nathan Daboll depicted America spewing back into George's face the tea he is pouring down her throat while she is held down, a powerful image of violated womanhood, as one of George's assistants is lifting her skirt. Britannia, askance, turns away, a vivid rejection of George's earlier association with patriotism.

In November 1774, George had informed North 'blows must decide whether they are to be subject to this country or independent'.[36] On 26 October 1775, opening a new session of Parliament, George declared that it was necessary 'to put a speedy end to these disorders by the most decisive exertions'. George took a part in the planning of strategy, arguing, for example, that the expedition North planned for the Carolinas in early 1776 should aim first for North Carolina, where the Scottish settlers were believed to be favourably inclined.[37] He also pressed for vigour, responding, for example, to Carleton's retreat from Lake Champlain in late 1775 by suggesting that the general was possibly 'too cold and not so active as might be wished',[38] a reasonable response to Carleton's failure to maintain the initiative, but one that was a little surprising given George's lack of military experience.

The war broadened out when first France (1778) and then Spain (1779) joined in against Britain. George had earlier shown an unwillingness to see war with these powers. During the Falkland Islands crisis of 1770, he wrote to North that 'every feeling of humanity as well as the knowledge of the distress war must occasion makes me desirous of preventing it if it can be accomplished provided the honour of this country is preserved', and, on that occasion, he had tried to suggest a way to keep negotiations going.[39] In 1778, however, George's views on the integrity of the empire gave him few options. The impact of his strong convictions and his sense of the need for fortitude was shown clearly. George refused to be dismayed by French entry into the war:

> Lord North must feel as I do the noble conduct of the three fifty gun ships that with so much bravery have driven off separately ships of far superior strength; I doubt not whenever it shall please the Almighty to permit an English fleet fairly to engage any other a most comfortable issue will arise; armed as France and Spain now are no peace could either be durable or much less expensive than a state of war ... I trust in the justness of my cause and the bravery of the nation.

The following month, the King added,

> If Lord North can see with the same degree of enthusiasm I do, the beauty,
> excellence, and perfection of the British constitution as by law established,
> and consider that if any one branch of the empire is allowed to cast off
> its dependency then the others will infallibly follow the example, that
> consequently though an arduous struggle that is worth going through any
> difficulty to preserve to latest posterity what the wisdom of our ancestors
> have carefully transmitted to us; he will not allow despondency to find a
> place in his breast, but resolve not merely out of duty to fill his post, but
> will resolve with vigour to meet every obstacle that may arise he should
> meet with most cordial support from me.[40]

George also displayed a firmness that could seem petulant. It was only
grudgingly that he accepted the concessions offered the American rev-
olutionaries by the Carlisle Commission of 1778. This represented an
acceptance that the war would be ended by compromise, and that the
imperial relationship would have to be substantially altered. In addition,
when in March 1778 North recommended an approach to Pitt the Elder,
since 1766 1st Earl of Chatham, in order to weaken the opposition,
George replied that

> no advantage to this country nor personal danger can ever make me address
> myself for assistance either to Lord Chatham or any other branch of the
> Opposition ... I would rather lose the Crown I now wear than bear the
> ignominy of possessing it under their shackles.

Chatham's demands helped wreck the negotiations, but so also did
George's attitude.[41] George repeatedly rejected North's attempts either
to strengthen the ministry with fresh supporters or to retire.

Chatham's death in May 1778 was followed by a response that made
George's attitude to his commemoration seem pedantic and grudging,
and out of tune with the public mood. On the day of Chatham's death,
the Commons voted unanimously an address for a public funeral and
a monument in Westminster Abbey, a measure that surprised George,
who informed North that he would find it offensive if intended as a
compliment to Chatham's 'general conduct'.[42] That year, George associated himself with the war effort by visiting Portsmouth, as well as
military encampments at Windsor and near Salisbury.

In 1780 George wrote, 'I never have seen any part of Opposition inclined to make the smallest concessions, and no power on Earth shall ever reduce me to deliver myself up into the hands of any of them'.[43] Failure in America, however, particularly the surrender of Cornwallis at Yorktown in October 1781, brought down the North ministry in March 1782, beginning a period of instability that lasted until 1784. George, in 1782, had to turn to the Rockinghamites and accept that peace would entail the abandonment of the Thirteen Colonies, and, in 1783, to accept a coalition ministry headed by the Duke of Portland, the new leader of the Rockinghamites, in which the most prominent members were North and Charles James Fox, formerly bitter enemies of each other.

The formation of the latter ministry demoralised George, and his habitual self-righteousness brought him no solace. The formation of the ministry also helped to contribute to a more general sense of political failure. This suggests that contemporary expectations of the political system were not, as occurred in 1782–84, of frequent changes of government in response to shifts in parliamentary and electoral opinion, but, rather, of a stable ministry responsive to (and thus, if necessary, limited by) responsible parliamentary and popular opinion. The sense of Britain as weak and of George as a failure was not helped by the unsympathetic attitude of foreign rulers, such as Catherine II of Russia and Frederick II of Prussia. Catherine said of George's loss of the Thirteen Colonies, 'Rather than sign the separation of thirteen provinces, like my brother George, I would have shot myself'.[44]

The resolution of the crisis, in the shape of a stable ministry under William Pitt the Younger, second son of Pitt the Elder, was far from inevitable. It was not certain that Pitt would secure a Commons majority simply because George had appointed him to office in December 1783, after the King helped secure the defeat in the Lords of the East India Bill, a crucial item of government business. George's actions, both against the East India Bill and in appointing a first minister who lacked a Commons majority, brought out the lack of agreement about the constitution; they were regarded by some as unconstitutional. Faced by the collective resignation of many office holders, angry at the treatment of North and Fox and unwilling to serve under Pitt, George saw himself as 'on the edge of a precipice'.[45] His grandfather's failure to sustain Carteret in office in 1746 seemed about to be repeated. Commons defeats in January 1784 led Pitt to think of resigning and George to reiterate his willingness to abdicate: he was distressed to find the Commons 'much more willing to enter into any intemperate resolutions of desperate men than I could have imagined', and emphasised his hostility to 'this faction'.[46]

Hanging on, however, helped the new government benefit from a swelling tide in popular opinion, shown in a large number of addresses from counties and boroughs, with over 50,000 signatures in total, in favour of the free exercise of the royal prerogative in choosing ministers. These addresses were also a testimony to the potential popularity of the monarchy. In 1784, however, this was clearly presented in a political dispensation – against the factionalism represented by Fox – while, at George's accession, his popularity had been far more inclusive. The loss of America had been cathartic and the particular circumstances of 1783–84 made it harder to present Fox and North as a 'patriot' opposition. Parliament was dissolved in March 1784 when Pitt felt able to face a general election. The subsequent elections, with many constituencies contested on national political grounds, were very favourable for the ministry. The government had a majority of about 150 seats and won many constituencies with large electorates, including Yorkshire. At a meeting of the Yorkshire freeholders on 25 March, Lord Fauconberg had asked, 'Is George III or Charles James Fox to reign?'.

The election results reflected not only the unpopularity of the Fox-North coalition, and especially distrust of Fox, but also support for George as the symbol, and indeed reality, of stability and continuity, a position very different from two decades earlier. The notion of a 'Patriot King' above faction seemed fulfilled. There was a renewed burst of popularity when George survived an attempt to kill him in 1786: Margaret Nicholson, the culprit, was mentally ill, rather than motivated by political ends.

Despite an irritability that, in part, was possibly a result of poor health, George had also matured in office, becoming a practised politician. His conscientious nature shines through his copious correspondence, while in 1788, his answer to the speech by the Recorder of Worcester was reported to have included 'this patriotic and generous sentiment – "The loyalty and affection which I have experienced amongst my subjects in this part of the Kingdom, and especially on this occasion, are an ample recompense to me for the public service of twenty-eight years"'.[47] This conscientiousness was related not only to George's idea of service but also to his sense of his position as the pivot of an inclusive civil politics. Although very aggrieved if his goodwill was not reciprocated, George felt that the monarch could reach out, beyond the antipathy and factional self-interest of politicians, to a wider, responsible and responsive public opinion. In the mid 1780s, George had therefore played a major role in ensuring the re-creation of a political world that accorded with his aspirations at his accession. Indeed he used royal proclamations to galvanise public opinion on a range of issues. Once crown-elite consensus had been restored – at least in so far as was measured by the crucial criterion, the ability of George to cooperate with a ministry enjoying the support of Parliament – Britain was essentially politically stable. This stability was a reflection of that ability; one that required a willingness to adjust, or even to compromise, by the King.

From 1784, Pitt dominated politics for over two decades, serving as First Lord of the Treasury from December 1783 until 1801, and then again from 1804 until his death in 1806. George was unhappy with some aspects of Pitt's policies, especially his support for parliamentary reform in 1785. Pitt was, nevertheless, very much George's own minister. George was scarcely likely to turn to the Fox-North opposition, whose factiousness he found 'extraordinary',[48] and, during the ministry, there was an essential stability at the centre of established politics. As a result, the King tended to be more in the political background than hitherto. Politically, he found himself opposed by his heir, George, Prince of Wales. The latter was not only opposed to the frugality, virtue and duty of his father, but also to Pitt. Instead, he preferred Fox, who, unlike the Prince, had talent, but, like him, lacked self-control.

George remained politically influential during the long Pitt ministry. The extent to which his serious illness in 1788–89 led to a major political crisis is strong evidence of his continued importance. George's attack of porphyria, which resulted in symptoms of insanity, caused the Regency Crisis of 1788–9. The illness had probably been transmitted to the Hanoverians from the Stuarts via Elizabeth of Bohemia and Sophia,[49] and has sparked the strongest modern interest in the King, most prominently with Alan Bennett's successful play *The Madness of George III* (1991), which was subsequently filmed. Since his attack in 1765, George's health had generally been good, although in 1778 he had 'a little feverish complaint'.[50]

On 17 October 1788 George was taken ill, although he recovered to take a levee on 24 October, and Pitt wrote to him about Baltic developments on 25 October and 5 November. George, however, became delirious while at Windsor on 5 November, and on 7 November it became common knowledge that he was seriously ill. At the time of the attack, George was fifty, and the auguries for a long life were not good. His father had died at the age of forty-four, while, of George's eight siblings, six died before the age of fifty: Edward, Duke of York (1739–1767), Princess Elizabeth (1741–1759), Henry, Duke of Cumberland (1745–1790), Princess Louisa (1749–1768), Frederick (1750–1765), and Caroline Matilda, Queen of Denmark (1751–1775), although Augusta, Duchess of Brunswick (1737–1813), and William, Duke of Gloucester (1743–1805) lived to over sixty.

It soon became apparent in 1788 that it would be necessary to make provisions for a regency, and, also that this arrangement might have to last until George's death, as his recovery seemed problematic. On 15 November Hiley Addington reflected the general view when he wrote to his brother Henry,

> Immediate danger perhaps is not to be apprehended; – but as all accounts agree in declaring His Majesty's disorder to be seated in the brain; which continues notwithstanding the abatement of the fever, surely his case must be hopeless.[51]

Although Queen Charlotte was mentioned, it was clear that, if there was to be a regency, the Prince of Wales, now of age, would be Regent. The ministry would therefore change, as the Prince was close, politically and personally, to Fox. The extent of his likely powers as Regent was unclear, however, and that would have to be determined by Parliament, which met on 20 November, only to be adjourned to await developments in George's health. When, on 3 December, the King's five doctors were examined before the Privy Council, they disagreed as to whether he was likely to recover, though two days later a new doctor, Francis Willis, under whose attention George was to improve, first saw his new patient. Meanwhile politics did not stand still, and there were serious parliamentary clashes on the Regency Bill. On 15 December, George's second son, Frederick, Duke of York spoke against the ministry in the House of Lords, providing a clear view not only of his attitudes but also of those of his elder brother.

Recovery took time and led to much discussion of medical options. The cricket-loving and womanising Duke of Dorset, then ambassador in Paris, suggested that Willis try giving George the 'blood of a jack-ass' to drink. This was unnecessary, as, from early February, George began to improve in time to prevent the creation of a regency, and to thwart the Emperor Joseph II's attempt to dictate arrangements for Hanover. There had also been problems over the position of the ruler in Ireland, as the Dublin Parliament adopted a different position from that of Westminster, in inviting Prince George to assume the royal functions without conditions. In ceding to the Dublin Parliament, in 1782–83, the sort of rights of independent initiative and legislation demanded by the American colonists before their rebellion, the Westminster Parliament appeared to have created an unstable relationship affecting the position of the crown. George's recovery ended the matter. On 8 February, Henry Addington wrote to his father, a doctor who had predicted the King's return to health:

> He has indicated no disposition to violence for several days, and is in general composed and easy. Dr Warren said yesterday that he had not seen him *so near himself* since his illness; and I understand, that the other physicians are of the same opinion: Dr Willis, whose hopes and fears have not been much affected by the fluctuations in the disorder, now declares, that the probability of recovery is greatly strengthened, and that everything is going on to his utmost wishes. Most people, I am sorry that I cannot say all, begin to look cheerful again, and to flatter themselves with the hopes that the interests of the nation may yet be preserved, and that the only consequences of His Majesty's malady may be a knowledge of the faithful attachment of the people at large, and a discovery of those who have proved or forfeited their pretensions to his confidence and favour.

On 19 February, the House of Lords was told that George was in a state of convalescence.[52]

George's recovery, which may have only been partial,[53] also provided an opportunity for a renewed burst of royal popularity, one that was far more focused on George personally than had been the case in 1784. The celebrations provided an opportunity for a focus on the links between crown and God. 'God Save the King' had been the prayer of the nation, helping to underline the importance of religious themes of monarchy. The service of thanksgiving at St Paul's Cathedral on 23 April 1789 provided a dramatic display of the nation's thanks, and one that was more vivid because it was held in London, earlier the centre of Wilkesite opposition. Thanksgiving services were repeated across the country and George's summer travels that year drew crowds, including allegedly 17,000 people in Longleat Park: 'His Majesty, the three Princesses and myself went in an open chaise down the avenue and back again to satisfy the populace who were extremely desirous to see the King'.[54]

There was also renewed confidence in the constitution. In an image that George, with his interest in the astronomical researches of William Herschel would have understood, the 'Address to the Public' in the first volume of *The Senator: or Parliamentary Chronicle* (1791) referred to

> that firmness, beauty, and magnificence of our excellent constitution, founded on the mutual consent of Prince and People; both moving, as it were, in one orb, reciprocally influencing, attracting, and directing each other; whose united power may be compared to a machine for determining the equality of weights.

George had again become a factor to reckon with in the political world, although, as his opposition to the French Revolution and to domestic radicalism matched not only that of the ministers but also the bulk of the British political elite, it is difficult to distinguish the royal role from that of the ministers. The sense that crown, church and elite must join together was captured by Lord Auckland, British envoy in The Hague, who, in November 1792, urged 'every possible form of Proclamations to the People, orders for Fast Days, Speeches from the Throne, Discourses from the Pulpit, Discussions in Parliament etc'.[55]

A year earlier, the King had applauded criticism of the Revolution from the Whigs:

> The letter of Mr Burke and its enclosure [a letter of support to Edmund Burke from Earl Fitzwilliam] both deserve commendation so far as they convey the genuine sentiments of the writers of the bad example set in France to all established governments; yet I am sorry to see Lord Fitzwilliam's resolution of only whispering opinions that ought to do him credit if he publikly avowed them and consequently adopting a conduct that must make the uniformed suppose him indifferent on so material a question.[56]

George's attitude was clearly shown in February 1793 when the French

National Convention declared war on Britain. George found the news: 'highly agreeable ... as the means adopted seems well calculated to rouze such a spirit in this country that I trust will curb the insolence of those despots and be a means of restoring some degree of order to that unprincipled country, whose aim at present is to destroy the foundations of every civilized state'.[57]

George was not an ultra and did not press for the restoration of the Bourbons, but, with his concern for order and legitimacy, he was unhappy about the idea of negotiating with the French republicans, being persuaded to accept such negotiations in 1797 and 1800 only with great reluctance. George's part in encouraging ministerial resolve was shown in a letter to Pitt, characteristically precisely dated by the King to the minute. Writing at 11.10 p. m. on 8 May 1798, George expressed his pleasure that George Tierney's motion in the Commons for a separate peace with France, which would have split the international coalition, had been defeated. He then expressed his support for throwing Fox out of the Privy Council for giving the toast 'Our Sovereign, the People' at a dinner of the Whig Club. Again, characteristically, George was concerned about correct form:

> I am glad to find by Mr Pitt's note that Mr Tierney's motion has been rejected by so handsome a majority. I entirely coincide in the opinion of the propriety of my striking Mr Fox's name out of the list of the Privy Counsellors; but prior notice should be given to the Lord President [of the Council, Pitt's elder brother] that the book may be brought to St James's for that purpose, which intimation I desire Mr Pitt will give to his brother.[58]

The previous year, George had showed his hard side when he insisted that the death sentences decreed for the naval mutineers who had crippled British naval power that year should be enforced. He also publicly associated himself with the war effort. On his holiday in Weymouth in 1794, George saw the Dorset Yeomanry exercise and reviewed the Buckinghamshire Militia. Once returned to Windsor he inspected the Surrey Yeomanry at Epsom and the Prince of Wales's Regiment of Light Dragoons on Ashford Common.[59]

George's obduracy created problems for his ministers when, in the 1790s, he opposed the extension of rights to Catholics in Ireland or

Britain. Arguing that these moves would breach his coronation oath, George stated that he would not give royal assent to such legislation, evidence that the royal veto on legislation was still an active factor. This helped to precipitate Pitt's resignation in 1801 and the fall of the Grenville ministry (the 'Ministry of All the Talents') in 1807. Catholics could not become MPs in the new Parliament created by the Anglo-Irish union of 1801 until 1829, and this may have undermined the Union, although a fair share of informed British political opinion thought it could go forward on that narrow basis. Other influential figures, however, thought George mistaken. William, Lord Grenville, the Foreign Secretary, wrote of the ministry's resignation in 1801:

> [There is] a firm conviction in our mind that the removal of the remaining disqualifications which still affect the Catholics was necessary in order to complete the measure of the Union and was a just return for the support which that body had afforded us in carrying through the Union itself: and further that whatever difficulties any man thinks he sees in the present situation of the country ... the propriety of endeavouring to attach the mass of the population of Ireland to the new united Government was increased by them: and therefore that the measure was no less pressing in point of time than expedient and wise in itself. To all these was opposed an invincible repugnance in the King's mind, grounded in a mistaken but respectable principle of adherence to what he conceives to be the sense of his coronation oath. The question was one which admitted of no compromise, and the time was of the essence of the question itself. Under these circumstances men of honour and public principle could do no otherwise than we have done.[60]

George's attitude also made religious issues even more central in the politics of the early nineteenth century than they might otherwise have been. His firmness, not to say rigidity, which had already been seen in his successful opposition in 1787–90 to the repeal of the Test and Corporation Acts, contrasted with the more flexible attitude of his non-Anglican predecessors, George II, George I, William III and, arguably, Charles II; it also helped to focus the defence of order, hierarchy and continuity much more on religion than would otherwise have been the case in a period of revolutionary threats. George III was motivated not only by his religious convictions, but also by the argument that the position of the Church of England rested on fundamental parliamentary legislation. Any repeal would also challenge constitutional safeguards similarly founded and secured. It is not therefore surprising that Edmund Burke's emphasis, in his *Reflections on the Revolution in France* (1790), both on continuity and on the value of the Glorious Revolution of 1688–89, seen in that light as a response to James II and VII's despotic innovations, found favour with George. Burke became acceptable at court.

More generally, George was an active supporter of the Church of England, with a strong faith. The report, in December 1778, of a plan to kill him en route to the theatre led the King to respond by expressing scepticism, urging investigation, before adding:

> As to my own feelings they always incline me to put trust where it alone can avail in the Almighty Ruler of the Universe who knows what best suits his allwise purposes, this being the week I go to Holy Communion, I had no thoughts of going unto the play.[61]

His response in 1794 to danger was no different, and George also responded calmly to James Hadfield's attempt to shoot him in Drury Lane Theatre during a performance of the *Marriage of Figaro* on 15 May 1800. A devout Anglican, personally pious and noted as such, not least for his responses in divine service, he took his role in the appointment of bishops seriously and was concerned about the pastoral qualities and doctrinal orthodoxy of candidates, an abrupt shift from his two predecessors, who had shared their ministers' determination to use the church in order to maintain Whig strength. George's interest extended to overseas, where the spread of an Anglican presence was encouraged. Thus, an Anglican bishopric for Nova Scotia was created in 1787, while, four years later, an Act provided large endowments to support the church in Upper Canada. George also supported the Naval and Military Bible Society, as well as the Society for the Propagation of the Gospel, while his religious and Hanoverian interests coincided in his support for the German Protestant Mission to the East Indies.

The monarchy became a more potent symbol of national identity and continuity in response to the French Revolution. The distancing of the King from the daily processes of government that increasingly characterised the Pitt years also contributed to his growing popularity. Royal influence and patronage declined with the abolition of sinecures, the diminishing influence of court favourites, and the growing accountability of Parliament. The paranoid Fox, who never freed himself from ideas of royal conspiracies, nevertheless felt able to tell his nephew Holland in 1804, 'There is not a power in Europe, no not even Bonaparte's that is so unlimited' as that in Britain.[62] This authority was very much that of the government, however, rather than simply the monarch – George did not strive to preserve or revive a power for the crown separate from that of Parliament; while, within the government, the political role of the monarch, particularly in the initiation of policy, declined. Fox had a particular reason to be aggrieved as George that year refused to have him made a Secretary of State.

In the 1780s, George had felt already that the monarch could reach out, beyond antipathy and factional self-interest on the part of politicians, to a wider, responsible and responsive royalist public opinion. After the attempt by Margaret Nicolson to assassinate him by stabbing him in the street outside St James's Palace on 2 August 1786, George wrote about 'the interposition of Providence in the late attempt on my life by a poor insane woman ... I have every reason to be satisfied with the impression it has awakened in this country'.[63] The domestic radicalism that accompanied the French Revolution led to an upsurge in republicanism, and indeed to a mob attack on his carriage en route to the opening of Parliament in 1795 and to George being twice fired on in 1800. This was more than countered by a widespread loyalism that focused on the crown. This was seen with the celebration of George's birthday (4 June), which had been impressive and popular from his recovery in 1789, but which was increasingly associated with the struggle with France, with George reviewing volunteers in Hyde Park on his birthday in 1799 and 1800. The public celebration of St George's Day was also a sign of the role of the monarchy in marking the passage of the year.

In 1809, when George celebrated his jubilee (which was timed to coincide with the inception, rather than the completion, of his fiftieth year as King), the public event not only symbolised the stability that he had provided in an age of volatile politics, but also expressed the genuine affection and admiration that his subjects now had for their monarch. The social elite and the bulk of public opinion rallied around the themes of country, crown and church.[64]

George III was a keen family man. Unlike many royal unions of the period, George and his wife, Charlotte of Mecklenburg Strelitz, formed a genuinely close relationship. Sir Joshua Reynolds noted of George's return from Portsmouth in 1773:

> When he came to Kew he was so impatient to see the Queen that he opened the chaise himself and jumped out before any of his attendants could come to his assistance. He seized the Queen, whom he met at the door, round the waist, and carried her in his arms into the room; I trouble with these particulars as everything relating to Kings is worth hearing.

Charlotte shared George's commitment to propriety, piety and philanthropy, and his dislike of ceremonial and expense.[65] The press reported her activities. Thus, *Berrow's Worcester Journal* of 23 October 1788 noted that Charlotte had established a school in Datchet for poor girls to learn spinning: 'a laudable endeavour ... to promote habits of industry ... she is a constant visitor'. Theirs was a particularly long union: Charlotte died in 1818, ensuring that she matched the pattern of royal spouses between the wives of William III and William IV in not surviving the monarch.

As their numerous children grew to adulthood (Charlotte bore a total of nine sons and six daughters), however, there arose a conflict between George and Charlotte's own sense of propriety, and the dissolute life adopted by most of their brood of boys. The members of the younger generation were especially loath to accept the King and Queen's views on marriage and choice of marriage partners, and entered into liaisons which, while often stable and personally fulfilling, hardly redounded to the increasingly respectable, almost prudish image that George wished to promote. The alienation between the generations was represented most strikingly in the endless disputes between the King and the Prince of Wales, and in the very public sense of glee that 'Prinny' demonstrated when his father became too ill to rule.

Gambling, which was a fashionable activity in the aristocratic salons of London, was an activity that captured the difference between parents and sons. George and Charlotte disliked both gambling and what it led to, but to the Princes it both provided and symbolised excitement and style. The fluidity of unconstrained public socialising clearly worried George. Unlike George II, who was very fond of them, George was opposed to masquerades. Religion and religious observance was another major difference between parents and sons, and a focus of the rebelliousness of the elder sons.

George had varied interests. He was a major collector, not least of books, art, maps and scientific instruments,[66] acquiring for £10,000 in 1763 the important art and book collection of Joseph Smith, who had been Consul in Venice. George also liked music, frequently playing the harpsichord, and was interested in science: he revived links with the Royal Society, and was a supporter of the astronomer William Herschel. Born in Hanover, Herschel (1738–1822) had moved from music to astronomy. In 1781 he discovered Uranus, the first planet to be found since antiquity, although Herschel initially thought it was a comet. In honour of the King, Herschel named it the 'Georgium Sidus', a reference to Virgil's *Georgics* that claimed immortality for George. The following year, George met Herschel who subsequently exhibited his telescope before him and was given the new post of court astronomer. George continued to take considerable interest in Herschel's work, funding his construction of a larger telescope, with a grant of £2000 in 1785 and £2000 in 1787, as well as an annual payment of £200 for repairs. This support enabled Herschel to discover the satellites of Uranus. George walked through the thirty-nine foot long telescope tube before the mirror was inserted, reportedly encouraging the Archbishop of Canterbury, John Moore, to follow him, 'Come, my lord bishop, I will show you the way to heaven'.[67] George's scientific interests included a fascination with clocks and barometers, and he paid the Scottish clock-maker Alexander Cumming £1178, a large sum, for a barograph, a mechanical device that recorded changes in atmospheric pressure, completed in 1765. At Kew, George was a patron of botanical science.

Culture was linked to patriotism in the foundation of the Royal Academy in 1768. George's support, not least £5,000 from his Privy Purse for initial funding, and his knighting in 1769 of the academy's president, Joshua Reynolds, was an important part of the sponsoring of British culture. In turn it enhanced monarchy, a pattern that can be traced back to Thornhill's celebration of the new dynasty in paint at Greenwich. Making available the royal apartments in Somerset House from 1771 (the Royal Society and the Society of Antiquaries followed), George continued his interest in the Royal Academy into the 1800s. Painters he favoured included Paul Sandy and Benjamin West. Sandby

(1725–1809), a master of the watercolour, who made numerous drawings of Windsor where he lived, was, like his brother Thomas (1721–1798), one of the twenty-eight original members of the Royal Academy nominated by George. He also taught Queen Charlotte.[68] Thomas Sandy, Deputy Ranger of Windsor Great Park, was made Joint Architect of His Majesty's Works in 1777, following with the Master Carpentership in 1780. Born in Pennsylvania, Benjamin West (1738–1820) came to England in 1763, acquired a reputation as a history painter and was commissioned by George, who admired his *Agrippina*, to paint *The Departure of Regulus from Rome*. George then became an active patron, nominating West to the Royal Academy, appointing him Historical Painter to the King in 1770 and Surveyor of the Royal Pictures in 1790. He also employed him to decorate St George's Hall, Windsor, with eight pictures from the life of a glorious predecessor, Edward III, and to produce thirty-six pictures on the progress of revealed religion for the royal oratory (twenty-eight were executed). The Prince of Wales' pattern of artistic patronage was very different. By 1801, West, who in 1792 succeeded Reynolds as the second President of the Royal Academy, had produced sixty-four pictures and other designs for George, who had paid him £34,187.

George also took a keen interest in music, playing the flute, harpsichord and pianoforte, collecting music, and being a great enthusiast for Handel's oratorios. George played a conspicuous role in the concerts held at Westminster Abbey in 1784 to celebrate the centenary of the composer's birth. Aside from attending the concerts, he also supported the King's Concerts held in London,[69] while he visited Worcester in 1788 for the Three Choirs Festival in the cathedral, and added his own private band to the orchestra. The festival brought together many of George's concerns, as it was intended for the relief of the widows and orphans of the clergy, and included a cathedral service. On 6 August, George heard the *Coronation Anthen*, the overture from *Esther*, and the *Dettingen Te Deum*, the last a reference to his grandfather's brave service to the nation, on 7 August more sacred music by Handel, and on 8 August the *Messiah* and later a 'miscellaneous concert'. The visit also provided an opportunity for George to display royal bounty. He left ten guineas for the workmen at the china factory he visited, £50 for the poor of the city (with another £50 from the Queen), £200 for the clergy widows and orphans, £300 to liberate debtors (twenty-one were set at liberty as a result) and his pardon 'to such criminal prisoners under sentence of transportation, as, from the regularity of their conduct in the gaol, or other favourable circumstances, might (in the judgement of the county magistrates) appear to deserve it'.[70] George was also a frequent visitor to the theatre, including three times in less than a month in Cheltenham in 1788 and frequently on his stays in Weymouth.

Although not a builder on the scale of his son George IV, in large part because he believed in restraining expenditure, George III was very interested in architecture and an important patron. Once he had purchased what was called Queen's House and later Buckingham Palace, George had it altered and furnished as a town residence, not least in order to house his growing library. The fashionable character of the decoration was later matched by the work at Windsor Castle carried out by James Wyatt, from 1796 Surveyor General and Comptroller of the Office of Works, who was George's favourite architect. The castle saw much building and decoration in the then fashionable 'Gothick' style, with George spending over £133,000 from his privy purse: his patronage helped make 'Gothick' the national style.

George's use of the castle combined public and private functions, while his supervision of the tenants on the Windsor estate was also seen as displaying both. The King often walked on the North Terrace, while St George's Chapel was remodelled as part of George's revival of the cult of the Garter, an important aspect of Windsor's role as a setting for exemplary kingship. Windsor, which had been neglected under George II, was the setting for royal ceremonials such as the installation of the Knights of the Order of the Garter held on St George's Day in 1805. The previous year, George and his family had moved permanently into the castle.

Other expenditure included a small castellated palace at Kew, designed by Wyatt in Gothic style, on the site of Richmond Lodge, but never finished and pulled down in 1828. Hampton Court was neglected, becoming grace and favour apartments, rather than a royal residence. In Richmond Park, George replaced the ornamental landscaping carried out under George II and Queen Caroline by the contemporary natural look popularised by Capability Brown.[71]

George was also interested in farming, especially from the 1780s. He visited farms and expected his sons to cultivate a strip on a model farm he had devised, an activity they did not relish. The King's import of merino sheep played a role in improving the British wool stock.[72] It contrasted with George I's focus on improving the stocking of game in the royal forests, although George III was also an active hunter. George III became well known for his agricultural interests, which bridged patriotism and philanthropy, and for his simple life as 'Farmer George'.

This lifestyle, in turn, was a reflection of a number of considerations, not only parsimony and a dislike of show, but also a concern to avoid the consequences of overeating and drunkenness. In the midst of frequently splendid, and certainly ample entertainment, George was cautious in what he ate and drank, trying, for example, not to eat sugar. He was a model of slimness compared with Louis XVIII. Indeed, his poor health in 1788 initially led to the suggestion that the 'abstemious system which His Majesty has invariable pursued' had led to a dropsy as he had drank insufficient wine.[73] George also showed an ease in his contact with people of all ranks that reflected a certainty of position and purpose and a belief that dignity did not lie in social distinction. Indeed, his illness led to a stress on a common humanity, as with the newspaper report that, when already troubled, and shortly before being taken seriously ill, George had remarked 'Lord bless us! The best of us are poor creatures'.[74]

Although his simple life led to satire at his expense, especially on the themes of parsimony and of Farmer George, George's domestication of the monarchy and his lack of ostentatious grandeur was an important contribution to a revival in the popularity of the monarchy. This served it well in the political crisis of the 1790s caused by the French Revolution, acting as a powerful counter to the lifestyle associated with his eldest son. George indeed was the originator of the emphasis on domesticity in the British royal family.[75] The behaviour of the royal family had become increasingly important. It was now played out under a more observant public gaze, one that was far from confined to the contained public sphere of the court. In 1763 Elizabeth, Countess Cornwallis already noted, 'Mr Pitt was alone with the King from twelve o'clock till three yesterday noon at Buckingham House, numbers of people waiting at the gate with anxious countenances the whole time'.[76] As a consequence of this public gaze, the conspicuous contrast between George's behaviour and that of his sons rebounded to the credit of the former.

The contrast between the fate of the British and French monarchies was due to many things, but the differences between the personalities and attitudes of George III and Louis XVI were not unimportant, although these differences should not be pushed too far. Neither man was grand in his manner, Louis shared George's lack of a mistress, and George's attitude to Catholic Emancipation was a pale echo of Louis's refusal to accept the need to work with the revolutionary government. Yet in 1791 Louis fled the capital as part of a scheme to force a change, before being captured at Varennes; whereas, in contrast, George's opposition to ministers and policies he disliked was expressed within the political system. George was also favourably contrasted by British commentators with the tyrannical and bellicose Napoleon.

George was the last ruler of Britain ever to use the title of 'King of France'. The claim, first advanced by Edward III in 1340, was finally dropped from the royal style in 1801, after which George's title was formally expressed as ruler of 'the United Kingdom of Great Britain and Ireland'. Hanover (a title never included in the royal style as exercised in the British Isles) was raised to the status of a separate kingdom in 1814. In spite of the regency exercised by his eldest son from 1811, George held his titles until the very end of his life, by when he had ruled longer than any previous British sovereign, exceeding Henry III's record (1216–72) by reigning for fifty-nine years.

The monarchy, or perhaps the *image* of the monarchy, had been reconstructed during the later years of the reign. The strong patriotism of the long war with France, and the King's virtual disengagement from day-to-day politics, combined fruitfully to facilitate the celebration less of the reality and more of the symbol of monarchy. In this the precondition of the creation of a popular monarchy was (ironically but significantly) the perceived decline in the crown's political authority in a partisan sense. Authority in a non-partisan sense was retained, for example the crown's usefulness as a guardian of the Protestant constitution. Furthermore, unpopular decisions were now blamed on the ministers. George himself contributed to this positive image, not by making a special effort to change but by being himself. In addition, a series of gestures underlined George's commitment to the country. These included the payment of £20,000 from his privy purse to the Voluntary Contribution of 1798, and the extension of taxation to the private income to the crown resulting from the passage of the Crown Private Estates Act of 1800.

With George, family life and political attitudes were closely inter-twined. His concern for a proper conduct of British government and society illuminated his committed Anglicanism, his determination to ensure the proper government of the Church of England, his interest in public morality and, not least, his desire that the royal family should set an example of appropriate behaviour. He did not go to Newmarket (although his horses raced there), forbade dice at court, and shunned masquerades. The report of George's visit to the Theatre Royal, Cheltenham on 15 August 1788, in *Berrow's Worcester Journal* of six days later, noted that when George and Queen Charlotte entered, they ex-pressed 'much satisfaction at Mr Watson's good management, the most perfect order and regularity being observed throughout'.

The flavour of George's attitudes can be gained from his instructions to Colonel Richard Grenville, who had been appointed Governor to Frederick, Duke of York, on his going to Germany to reside as Prince Bishop of Osnabrück. For example:

> Though in this country I highly disapprove of masquerades, I do not put any injunction to his not frequenting them at Hanover, where the Officer of the Guard has power to prevent all irregularities, and in reality it is necessary from the established custom in Germany of not permitting the Bourgeoisie to mix with the Nobility but in mask at Balls and Assemblies ... must attend Divine Worship in the chapel of my palace every Sunday morning.[77]

Frederick himself was urged to read the Bible every morning and evening, not least because it provided the opportunity for self-examination.[78]

George's cultural preferences, particularly his interest in the work of Handel, were related to his moral concerns. Handel said of George, 'While that boy lives, my music will never want a protector',[79] and, in this, as in much else, the boy was father to the man. In contrast, his brother Henry, Duke of Cumberland, who was very fond of music, lacked these moral concerns. The morality expounded by the King extended to the public finances. In 1770 George informed North:

> Your plan for the finances this year is so very honorable that it cannot fail of success, I am the more sanguine on this occasion as it shows in a

most striking manner the fairness of government in their dealings with the stock holders, at the same time that France has in the most base manner deceived those concerned in its funds.[80]

The explicit morality that George displayed helped make him an attractive model for the devout and for those concerned with social order, although it was wearing to those who did not share it, most obviously his sons. George showed many of the virtues applauded by Evangelicals, but he was not restricted in his Anglicanism: although George had his own preferences among clerics and ecclesiastical views, his Anglican orthodoxy was inclusive in practice.

In the royal family, George's legacy was less happy. As so often, parental love and care did not have the desired effect. George's daughters had a particularly difficult life. In 1797, the eldest, Charlotte, married the hereditary Prince of Württemberg, Frederick William Charles, who became Duke in 1797, Elector in 1803 and King in 1806; but the other five complained about living, under their mother's unwelcome dominance, in a 'Nunnery'. Queen Charlotte regularly read sermons to them. Elizabeth was finally, in 1818 at the age of forty-seven, able to marry Frederick, hereditary Prince of Hesse-Homburg, and Mary, in 1816, at the age of forty, married William, Duke of Gloucester, her first cousin, but they had had a long wait for marriage. The other sisters did not marry. Two fell in love, but found their mother unaccommodating. Amelia, the youngest daughter and the King's favourite, fell in love with the much older Colonel Sir Charles Fitzroy. There was rumours that she had secretly married him and had a child, but, in the event, she died in 1810 after long years of tuberculosis and erysipelas. There were also reports of a secret marriage between Princess Augusta and Sir Brent Spencer, one of George III's equerries; the Queen's opposition left them no alternative. Another equerry, General Thomas Garth, probably entered into a secret marriage with Princess Sophia, and in 1800 she secretly bore him a child. George was more indulgent to his daughter-in-law, Caroline, and her daughter his grand-daughter, Charlotte.

As adults, the Princes did not suffer the constraints their sisters encountered, but, in earlier days, the King's love for them was expressed in terms of a carefully-planned emphasis on dutiful conduct and exemplary education. The response was similar to that of many of the American colonists: royal good intentions did not suffice. The King sought to reduce passion to order, but was frequently defeated. Thus, Frederick, Duke of York was a favourite of the King, who tried to ensure not only an exemplary upbringing but also a continuing oversight that included a second marriage ceremony in England;[81] but George had to face his son's ability to lose large sums in gambling and racing.

George, Prince of Wales was also financially irresponsible, and repeatedly incurred debts that he could not meet. George III had to pay £5000 to buy back the love letters that George, Prince of Wales had written his mistress, Mary Robinson, a prominent actress whom he had seen playing Perdita. She was also given a life annuity of £600 and £200 for her daughter (who predeceased George) in return for surrendering the Prince's promise of £20,000 when she came of age. George, Prince of Wales's secret marriage on 15 December 1785 to Maria Fitzherbert was in defiance of the Royal Marriages Act of 1772 under which descendants of George II could only marry before the age of twenty-five with royal permission, while thereafter they had to give a year's notice to the Privy Council and Parliament had not expressly to disapprove of the marriage. Occasionally unfaithful and more constantly difficult, the Prince stayed with Maria until 1794 when he left her for his new mistress Frances, Countess of Jersey. Maria was given a settlement of £3000 a year.

George III's energy also contrasted with the lethargy of his heir. Having arrived at Worcester on the evening of 5 August 1788, on the following morning 'his Majesty, being a very early riser, had surveyed the cathedral and its precincts, and walked to almost every part of the town before seven o'clock'.[82] This was not an hour the Prince of Wales often saw. George III repeated his early morning perambulation the next day. He also made private visits to bishops on his travels – to those of Gloucester and Worcester in 1788; again not an activity that commended itself to his eldest son.

It is customary to emphasise George's differences with his children, but the problems in the royal family were more than just a matter of different generations. Thus, Edward, Duke of York (1739–1767), one of George's younger brothers, did not share the King's religious beliefs (he was a latitudinarian), nor his moral conduct. Freed from the burden, but not the privileges, of royal status, York was able to follow his own wishes. Thus, he visited Italy in 1763–4, the first member of the British royal family to go there as a tourist (although prior to 1714 several members of the house of Brunswick had done so), showing particular interest in Venice. York sailed from Plymouth to Genoa where he spent ten weeks, in part because he was attracted by Angela Serra (Madame Durazzo), an amateur painter with whom he appeared hand in hand at a reception at the Palazzo Ducale.[83] York pressed on via Florence to Rome, where Pope Clement XIII (1758–69) held a reception in his honour and gave him gifts. Cardinal Henry, the Jacobite Duke of York, left Rome in protest at this sign of papal determination to work towards reconciliation with Britain and the Hanoverians, one that owed much to Cardinal Alessandro Albani (1692–1779), who, in his role as Protector of Germans, took an interest in the Hanoverian dynasty.

After Rome, where he also sat for his portrait by Pompeo Batoni, York pressed on to Bologna, Parma, Venice, Padua and Milan, where he was interested in the copy he was given of Beccaria's *Dei delitti e delle pene*, a call for the end of capital punishment. York then returned to Genoa, and sailed back to Dover. On his trip he had been particularly keen on the company of attractive women, but also took part in a round of activities befitting his status, including hunts and receptions. York also heard the castrato Giovanni Manzuoli sing, played the violin and attended scientific experiments. He died in Monaco in 1767 *en route* for a second visit to Italy.

In many respects, York was more similar to their father, Frederick, Prince of Wales, than to his royal brother, George III, while George's son, later George IV, had much in common with his uncle. The contrast between the royal brothers serves as a reminder of the play of contingency; it also acts as a warning against placing too great an emphasis on clashes between generations. The same was true of another brother, William, Duke of Gloucester (1743–1805), who visited Italy in 1770–72, in large part in order to find relief for his asthma, although also in order to meet by arrangement Madame Grovestein. He went to Italy again in 1775–77, but this time with his wife Maria and daughter Sophia. He went again in 1786–87, on this occasion with his family and his mistress, the beautiful Lady Almeira Carpenter, who was officially his wife's lady-in-waiting. Gloucester's royal status made him a Field Marshal, but did not lead him to military fame. The future George IV was himself influenced by his uncle Henry, Duke of Cumberland (1745–90), who had got into trouble in 1770 for an affair with Countess Grosvenor, and whose clandestine marriage to a commoner was a major reason for the King's sponsoring of the Royal Marriages Act. Cumberland introduced the Prince to gambling and encouraged him in drinking and womanising.

George III's sense of royal dignity and a certain lack of charitableness toward those who did not meet his standards was shown by his treatment of his brothers and sons who married secretly against his wishes. His brother William was banished from Court in 1772 and not deemed acceptable until 1780, while his brother Henry's marriage led to his being similarly cut. When he was informed that his son Prince Augustus had married Lady Augusta Murray, George ordered the government to proceed in accordance with the Royal Marriages Act.[84] Authority and morality combined to harm relations within the royal family.

George's recovery after his 1788 attack of porphyria may have been only partial, although he was generally seen as having good health in the 1790s. In February 1801, however, George suddenly became ill, with disturbing signs of a recurrence of the illness of 1788. George on one day seemed near to death, but he recovered and the illness lasted less than a month. There was nothing to match the political crisis of 1788, not least because the Prince of Wales agreed to Pitt's proposal that, if George failed to recover, there would be a restricted regency. George III was given more problems by the determination of Dr Thomas Willis and his brother John to force the King to health by detention and restraint. As he recovered, George was confined until he finally refused to sign any documents unless he was permitted to join the Queen. Far from being mad, George was far more sane than the Willises suggested. The recurrence of the illness led to concern that it would recur anew, however, and this encouraged an attempt to keep him from news that might disturb him, especially after he was ill again for a week in February 1804. In addition, George's sight went in his right eye from 1804–5. The *Times* noted on 7 November 1805: 'His Majesty wears a green shade constantly over his eyes, after candle-light; and, we are sorry to say, he cannot distinguish any person except he be very near, and with the assistance of a glass'.

Christian fortitude, 'that just sense of religion',[85] continued to offer George solace, and he remained politically important, although there were challenges to his views. In April 1804, Pitt went into opposition to the Addington ministry that had been in power since Pitt resigned in

1801 over Catholic Emancipation. Although George still supported Addington, the latter resigned, thus protecting the royal prerogative of choosing ministers, rather than being forced out by parliamentary action, which would have left George with fewer options. Pitt became first minister again in 1804, but died in 1806.

George had little time for the Ministry of all the Talents under Lord Grenville, formed after Pitt's death. To George, Grenville had the obstinacy of his father, George Grenville, and he abhorred his ministerial colleagues, especially Fox. The ministry fell when it was unable to promise George not to raise anew the issue of Catholic Emancipation. The Portland administration (1807–9), which succeeded it, was properly mindful that it was the King's ministry. The government, however, fell over the unsuccessful expedition sent against Antwerp in 1809, the Walcheren expedition, named after the island where many of the troops died of disease. George played a major role in securing the reconstitution of the ministry that October when Spencer Perceval replaced Portland. This was a choice that George wanted: he trusted Perceval, both as an individual and as an Evangelical Protestant who had no truck with Catholic Emancipation. As a result, George did not try to have Canning, Castlereagh or Liverpool, other potential choices, as head of the ministry.

George's health permanently broke down at the close of 1810. The following year, the crown had to be put in commission with the passing of the Regency Act and the appointment of George, Prince of Wales as the King's lieutenant. George became more seriously ill from July 1811 and was exposed to the 1788 system of seclusion and restraint, a policy that, by cutting him off, made him increasingly isolated. Kept in Windsor, where he was out of touch with the world of London, George no longer recognised his family. The situation remained unchanged for the last nine years of George III's life, although Charlotte's death in 1818 led to Frederick, Duke of York, being appointed George's guardian. The King died at Windsor of pneumonia in seclusion, if not obscurity, on 29 January 1820, being succeeded by the Prince of Wales.

# 7

# George IV

never was there an individual less regretted by his fellow creatures than this deceased King.

*Times*, 16 July 1830

Born in St James's Palace, on 12 August 1762, George Augustus Frederick was the first of the fifteen children of George III and Queen Charlotte. Born in the purple, he was given the title of Prince of Wales and Earl of Chester five days after being born, and was brought up in the framework of political and personal morality created by his narrow-minded parents: George III set standards of prudence and austerity that have been characterised (disparagingly) by some modern historians as 'middle-class'. The future George IV waited longer than virtually any previous heir to become King (ensuring that he became King not only long after he was estranged from his wife, but also after the death of his only legitimate child); and his increasing alienation from his father simply added to the sense of exasperation and urgency with which he pursued the trappings of monarchy.

George was not a man able effectively to resist the trend toward a lesser political role for the monarch, however much he might spasmodi-cally insist on his views of his own importance. Furthermore, by the time of his accession, at the age of fifty-seven, George's stamina had already been weakened by laziness, self-indulgence and poor-health. The self-indulgence reflected the degree to which George lacked his father's strong sense of duty, as well as his moral concern; and the absence of both was also reflected in his failure to follow George III's pattern of royal diligence. George IV could scarcely have issued a proclama-tion against vice and immorality as the pious George III did in 1787. Cartoonists may have lampooned George III and Queen Charlotte for austerity and boring parsimony,[1] but they excoriated their sons for extravagance and lust. George IV displayed little concern for this bad press, but he also lacked the political ability to manage scandal in any effective way. Furthermore, the contrast between the two men was not only drawn by caricaturists and opposition figures. Henry Addington, the former Prince Minister, now Home Secretary and Viscount Sidmouth, wrote in February 1820, following the death of George III, 'How much better is it to weep over departed excellence in the nearest and dearest of all connections than to be harassed by living profligacy'.[2]

George was Prince of Wales and then Prince Regent when the great spate of wars with France came to a resounding culmination in the conflict with Napoleon. In an early stage in the conflict with Revolutionary France, in 1793, Sir William Beechey had painted a massive *George III Reviewing the Troops*, a work destroyed in the fire at Windsor Castle in 1992. This depicted an equestrian group of George III, the Prince of Wales, and Frederick, Duke of York reviewing the 10th Hussars and the 3rd Dragoons. York indeed pursued an active military career, but George IV, although he was painted in 1792 by John Raphael Smith wearing the uniform of the Grenadier Guards, with his cavalry in formation in the background,[3] and commanded the Prince of Wales's Regiment of Light Dragoons, which guarded Windsor Castle in late 1794, was no military figure. He was, however, very keen to associate himself with military success, although his pretensions verged on the ridiculous, particularly in 1811, when he made himself Field Marshal, designing a uniform in scarlet that, with its weighty gold embroidery, was reported to weigh 200 pounds. Three years later, George had Sir Thomas Lawrence depict him as a general. Later in life, George used to tell people that he had been at Waterloo (which indeed he visited in 1821, *en route* to Hanover) and would seek confirmation from the Duke of Wellington, winning the tactful reply, 'So you have told me, Sir'.

It might appear ridiculous that, after Waterloo, Napoleon, who had decided to surrender to British forces, as he felt he would meet with better treatment than from his other foes, did so with an appeal to George 'as the most powerful, the most constant, and the most generous of my enemies'. Yet, as Prince Regent, George was the regal focus of Britain's contribution to the victorious last stages of the war with France. George was a firm supporter of Wellington, and was in no doubt that the war had to be pursued to its conclusion in the removal of Napoleon; he was insistent that the war goals included the restoration of Louis XVIII, whereas Britain's allies were much more prepared to leave Napoleon in power in France. George had followed news of the conflict, both Wellington's campaigns in Portugal and Spain, and those of Britain's allies on the Continent with great interest and enthusiasm, and was particularly happy in 1813 when Mecklenburg, his mother's homeland, and Hanover were liberated as Napoleon's forces were pushed from Germany.

Once Napoleon had abdicated in April 1814, George sped Louis XVIII on his way back to Paris and took a major role in the celebrations of victory, which included the visit to Britain of Tsar Alexander I of Russia and King Frederick William III of Prussia. Alexander's lack of sympathy for George made the visit a difficult one for the latter, and he was also disenchanted by the lack of popular applause he received during the celebrations, and by the exhaustion of the round of celebrations, which included a visit to Ascot races, the conferment of honorary degrees in Oxford and a naval review in Portsmouth. Napoleon's return from Elba in 1815 found George firmly behind the government in insisting on fighting for the restoration of Louis XVIII. If he was at a society ball in St James's Square when the official news of victory at Waterloo was brought, that was a reflection of the changing nature of British monarchy – the diligent George III had also never served in battle.

George III's ill-health had led to the establishment of a regency with the passage of a Regency Act: the Prince was sworn in as Regent on 6 February 1811. For the first year, at the insistence of the Prime Minister, Spencer Perceval, and against the wishes of the Whigs, his powers were limited, in case his father recovered, but, in February 1812, the Prince gained the full prerogative powers of the crown. He was not to become King, however, until 29 January 1820. In his youth, Prince George had been closely linked both politically and socially to the Whigs, the politicians who opposed Pitt and those who sought to continue Pitt's legacy, but he shifted his position from 1807. In part, this reflected shifts in British politics, including the character of the Whigs after Fox's death in September 1806, but George's changing attitudes as he got older were also important. He became more conservative, not least with a greater concern about the position of the Anglican Church, and also sought closer relations with his father. Prince George's support for the war led him to oppose what he saw as the Whigs' appeasement of Napoleon: they pressed for negotiations. As Prince Regent, George followed his father in stressing his patriotism, duty and wish for an inclusive ministry. In his first message to the Cabinet after he assumed his full powers in 1812, George stated his wish to pursue goals 'common to the whole nation'.

The continuation of the ministry led the Whigs to accuse George of being a turncoat. Convinced that he was ductile, they emphasised the Tory influence of his associates, not least Isabella, Marchioness of Hertford, with whom he was very close; but this underestimated George's capacity to make his own decisions. In 1812 George tried to bring the Whigs into what he hoped would be a widely inclusive ministry, but he refused to accept their liberal views on Catholic Emancipation and the war. He had also, with familiarity, become satisfied with the ministers he had inherited: he was much older than his father had been when he came to the throne. Furthermore, George did not appreciate the criticisms directed at him by Charles Grey and other Whigs. The assassination of the Prime Minister, Spencer Perceval, in 1812 (the result of a private grudge against the government) led to a renewed attempt to create an all-party ministry, but the existing ministers were opposed to the plan and the Whigs demanded too many places. The scheme failed and the Whigs remained in the political wilderness.

Once he had become King, George immediately set about rectifying what he regarded as an intolerable anomaly in his family life. In 1795 he had married his first-cousin Caroline of Brunswick-Wolfenbüttel, a choice that delighted George III. Motivated by the desire to clear his debts, the Prince had expressed no preference, and he first met Caroline three days before the wedding. Each was disappointed by the other, and, when they first met, the Prince recoiled, drank a brandy, and fled. He was fatter and more ill-natured than she had anticipated, while she lacked a royal demeanour and suffered the consequences of her failure to wash. The Prince's choice of Lady Jersey, as a lady-in-waiting was tactless as Caroline correctly suspected that she was his mistress. A disastrous honeymoon, greatly affected by George's preference for alcohol over his new wife, was followed by steadily deteriorating relations, in which the position of Lady Jersey played a major role. Caroline's demand that Lady Jersey lose her post was rejected by her furious husband.

In 1797 Caroline left Carlton House and set up an independent establishment in Blackheath. Critics of the Prince of Wales presented

Caroline as a wronged woman who had suffered at the hands of a debauched husband. Caroline herself was no saint, but this tended to be overlooked. Meanwhile, Lady Jersey had lost George's favour in 1798, although she was swiftly replaced by Elizabeth Fox, the mistress of Lord Egremont. By George, Elizabeth Fox had a son, George Crole, who received £10,000 and an annuity of £300 after George's death. George, however, hankered anew for Maria Fitzherbert, and they lived together again from 1800. From 1807, George's favour for Isabella, Marchioness of Hertford put this relationship under strain and in December 1809 it came to an end.[4]

George IV and Caroline's only child, Princess Charlotte, born in 1796,[5] died in 1817, a few hours after she gave birth to a stillborn son, and it was clear that the succession would pass, after George's death, to his eldest surviving brother, then Frederick, Duke of York. The new King therefore saw no reason why the (allegedly) disreputable Caroline should have the satisfaction of being crowned Queen. As soon as he became King, George also instructed that the Queen's name be left out from the prayer for the King and royal family, a move that greatly offended Caroline. She returned to England, to be greeted with popular support, especially in London where she arrived on 6 June 1820. Caroline's cause was taken up by radicals keen to demonstrate the hypocrisy of the government and to use Caroline as a symbol of wronged womanhood.[6]

There was indeed a febrile situation, not least because it interacted with a sense of crisis, with ministers fearful of widespread radical action, as well as of an attack on George himself. Addington warned Wellington in March 1821, 'The accounts from Manchester, Leeds, Glasgow etc. are unsatisfactory. A simultaneous explosion appears to be meditated'. There were also threats on George's life, including one stating 'I claim on behalf of thousands of my suffering fellow countrymen to cut off the head of the King'. As a result, that September, George was warned not to return to his cottage in Windsor Forest, as he wished to do. George was sufficiently concerned to instruct Addington to keep him informed about opinion in London and elsewhere.[7]

George saw Caroline as unfaithful and her claims as scandalous, and he was unhappy with ministerial attempts to avoid the scandal of a public breach. The entire episode was very different from that which had faced George's great-great-grandfather, George I, not least because it was played out in public in Britain, whereas George I's difficulties with his wife Sophia Dorothea had been contained to Germany (they occurred twenty years before he came to the throne in Britain) and had been largely private. Thanks in part to George IV's lifestyle, many commentators found themselves in a difficult position in 1820–21. Lord Kenyon noted that the Queen was guilty of treason if guilty of adultery:

> An hereditary monarchy requires every practicable safeguard for the legitimacy of the succession. It is *therefore* justifiable to extend such protection, and to make adultery in the Queen Consort punishable with death. It punishes the offence as a state crime, not as a violation of the marriage vow.

For moral and prudential reasons, Kenyon suggested that divorce was not expedient, and that Caroline should be degraded and banished, a course George did not favour. Aside from Kenyon's concern that the bishops would find themselves in a difficult position if a trial took place in the Lords, he felt that 'the general feelings of the religious and moral portion of the community should be tenderly considered', and added, with a clear reference to royal mores, 'The moral principle of this Nation founded on the first ordinance of God to Social Man would be utterly destroyed by the admission of divorce except to an innocent claimant'. Kenyon subsequently suggested a compromise by which Caroline lived abroad, as he believed it best for the nation if there was no case in the Lords.[8]

To George, however, it was necessary to have a divorce and to prevent Caroline from being crowned, and, like her, he rejected the idea of a compromise. Instead, the government introduced a Bill of Pains and Penalties into the House of Lords to end the marriage and to dethrone Caroline as Queen. The press lapped up the sexual details, which made Caroline's infidelity clear, and engaged in a vicious and personal debate about whether Caroline was a wronged woman, as the *Times* and the radicals argued, or a disgrace to her sex. The testimony included remarks such as Giuseppe Rastelli's claim that 'he saw the Princesses hand in Bergami's breeches'.[9] Lord Sheffield complained of 'transactions I conceive highly degrading to the House'.[10]

Caroline's cause was taken up by the public, and the debate lent focus and interest to political controversy. The small Lords majority for the Bill led the government to withdraw it rather than face a stormy passage in the Commons. Viscount Castlereagh, the Foreign Secretary, explained the government's view: the Queen's guilt was clear, so that her name could not be inserted in the liturgy, and she could not be provided with a royal residence, but she could receive a financial settlement without being obliged to live abroad, although it was hoped that she would do so. He added,

> I trust that this determination to avoid on the one hand everything that could be construed into a wish to commence any new proceedings against the Queen and on the other to abstain from rendering honour to a person whose guilt has been so loudly pronounced will meet with the general approbation of those who are well disposed to the present government.[11]

George was furious about the withdrawal of the Bill, but he benefited from growing popular disquiet about Caroline's personal life, especially the evidence that she had had affairs with foreign servants. As a result, in February 1821, the Commons rejected by a large majority an opposition motion that Caroline's name be restored to the liturgy. Nevertheless, there had been much that was ridiculous and degrading about the controversy.[12]

Although the government felt obliged to abandon its campaign against Caroline, she was successfully denied coronation. The lavish coronation of the King alone was held on 19 July 1821. George was determined that it was to be a spectacle, and planned the ceremony accordingly. Aside from a crown enhanced by an unprecedented high number of borrowed jewels – so that a total of 12,532 diamonds were used in the setting, and the wearing of exotic robes, the staging was carefully prepared. Parliament had granted the sum of £240,000 to meet the costs – a marked contrast with the £70,000 spent on George III's coronation; a contrast that cannot be accounted for by inflation since 1761. The King wore ornate and heavy clothes, including, on his entry into Westminster Abbey, a black velvet hat carrying a large plume of ostrich feathers from which a heron's plume emerged, while his gold-bordered crimson velvet train was so long and heavy that nine pages were needed to support it.

George and Caroline took a very contrasting part in 1821. Caroline's demand that she be crowned, with or separately from George, who refused to receive her at court, had been rejected by both George and the Privy Council. Caroline's letter of protest and remonstrance brought together a variety of reasons, including her exalted background, but focused on her position as a touchstone of wider rights:

> the authority of ancient usage cannot be rejected without shaking that foundation upon which the most important rights and institutions of the country depend ... Her Majesty believed that she exchanged the protection of her family for that of a Royal Husband and of a free and noble minded nation. From Your Majesty the Queen has experienced only the bitter disappointment of every hope she had indulged – in the attachment of the people she has found that powerful and decided protection which has ever been her steady support and her unfailing consolation. Submission from a subject to injuries of a private nature may be matter of expedience, from a wife it may be the matter of necessity, but it never can be the duty of a Queen to acquiesce in the infringement of those rights which belong to her constitutional character.

The petition was rejected, with the Council deciding that the Queen Consort was not entitled as of right to be crowned,[13] and there was also criticism of the radicals who took up the Queen's cause. George Cruickshank produced a caricature *The Radical Ladder* depicting Caroline reaching for the crown with the help of radical agitators looking to the French Revolution as a model. When, on the day of the coronation, she arrived at the Abbey, entry was refused and the door shut in her face.

The public response to George's coronation, a ceremony of great pomp and expense, was repeated acclamation, and the event fulfilled its purpose of fostering popular loyalty. Although radical sentiment remained strong, there had also been a rallying of support to George by the time of his coronation. Indeed, the Bishop of Hereford felt able to write,

> I verily believe there existed throughout the nation a spirit of loyalty unparalleled for many years. In most places, measures were taken to make the lower orders substantially feel the importance of the day; they were feasted with what they seldom taste, and that most plentifully. Such

language speaks home to them intelligibly, and the remembrance of the
festival and of the occasion will be indelible.[14]

George's coronation was followed in 1821–22 by popular visits to Ireland,
Hanover and Scotland; the first to Ireland and Scotland by the monarch
for over a century. George's wearing of Highland dress was particularly
successful in courting popularity in Scotland, while his visit to Ireland
saw him at his best, able to respond to people and circumstances and
to present himself in a benign and accessible fashion. The Irish responded well to him, and George to the Irish. George sailed to Ireland
via the English Channel, anchoring off Weymouth, and then via Plas
Newydd in Wales. He stayed at Plas Newydd with the Marquess of
Anglesey,[15] who had lost a leg at Waterloo and been Lord High Steward
at George's coronation, and was a General at the time of George's visit.
This was George's only visit to Wales: he had had no inauguration
ceremony as Prince of Wales.

Plans for the visit to Ireland were affected by the Queen's final illness,
which led George to postpone his public entry into Dublin. Caroline
died three weeks after the coronation. The Prime Minister, the Earl of
Liverpool, was very anxious that George should swallow his bitterness
and show appropriate sorrow: 'He will surely yield to the public feeling
at such a moment'. Citing his concern that there should be a marked
difference between the funeral and that of his mother, George did not
share the government's view that there should be a general mourning
for the Queen.[16] Indeed, he remarked on 'the blessing, which the protecting Hand of God, in his mercy, has bestowed upon me, in this recent
event ... it has literally turned one almost quite topsy-turvey'. The
government also wanted George to stay at Plas Newydd until after the
Queen's body was embarked for its journey to Brunswick, but George
was eager to get to Ireland to see his mistress, Elizabeth, Lady Conyngham. This was no secret. Addington, who accompanied George,
commented, 'There are attractions here by which I grieve to think he
was powerfully influenced'. Subsequently, he was dismayed by George's
wish to visit her twice at Slane.[17]

Large crowds met George when he landed in Ireland on 12 August,
his birthday, and thereafter he was surrounded with people. George,
who much enjoyed the fuss, conspicuously associated himself with Irish

themes: on his royal entry into Dublin, he carried a hat decorated with a big bunch of shamrock, while he requested the wearing of Irish goods at the drawing room held in the Viceregal Lodge, echoing an affectation Caroline of Ansbach had adopted in the 1730s by wearing Irish linen. A triumph of showmanship, George's visit brought little of substance, as there was no willingness on the King's part to respond to the address from the Catholic bishops or the presentation of a laurel crown by Daniel O'Connell, and no move toward the cause of Catholic Emancipation. Indeed, a careful distinction had been drawn between the addresses from the Established Church, Dublin Corporation and the University of Dublin, which were to be presented to George while he was on the throne, and those from the Presbyterians, the Catholic bishops and the Quakers, which were to be presented in the Closet.[17] Furthermore, the last stage of George's trip was spoiled by poor health – 'an attack in his bowels', which led him to leave a dinner at Trinity College early – and by his anger about the riot in London on 14 September when the movement of Caroline's body through the capital had been blocked:

> The King is in a very uncomfortable state of mind. The circumstances attending the Queen's funeral he is frequently recurring to, in a manner which shows a degree of chagrin, and irritation beyond what I have ever observed in him. These feelings have not affected his general behaviour, and deportment, so as to attract the observation, except of a very few: but the actual expression of them has not been so confined, and limited as could be wished.[19]

Indeed, George was very critical of Liverpool.

Nevertheless, the significance of gestures was not, and should not be, underrated: George had been to Ireland. Although the visit was essentially to Dublin (with the addition of a private trip to the Conynghams' seat, Slane), that was an appropriate response to the time available, the problems of internal travel (it rained heavily en route to Slane and this badly affected the surface of most Irish roads), and the extent to which polite society and the Irish political world focused on the capital.

George sailed from Ireland on 3 September 1821 and, having briefly returned to England, set off from Ramsgate for Hanover on 25 September: he snubbed Dover because it had given Caroline a favourable reception in 1820. Although George left on a fine day, the crossing was rough and the fishing boat he transferred into in order to enter Calais harbour nearly sank. From there, George pressed on to Brussels, where his ability as a mimic enlivened dinner with William I of the Netherlands. Wellington showed George the battlefield of Waterloo, the King being interested to see where Anglesey had lost his leg; but George was already showing signs of ill-health. The Earl of Clancarty, the envoy to the Netherlands, wrote from Brussels:

> The King had, originally upon his arrival here, intended to have gone forward on his journey from hence yesterday morning after divine service, but finding himself somewhat indisposed, he thought it more prudent to postpone his further journey till today. The event has fully justified His Majesty's change of intention; by a few hours quiet, and repose, towards the middle of the day and yesterday the King felt himself entirely restored.[20]

Travelling on, via Namur, Aachen, Düsseldorf and Osnabrück, where George was greeted rapturously by his subjects, George reached Hanover on 7 October. Castlereagh, now Second Marquess of Londonderry, noted, three days later, that everything had gone as well as could be wished and that George had 'borne his journey (notwithstanding some complaint in his bowels) remarkably well'. Indeed, George's skill in making himself agreeable to a new audience was seen with his facility in speaking German. Londonderry added:

> the King has been highly gratified by the attentions everywhere shown him ... he feels himself quite happy, and at home amongst the Hanoverians – at the same time, I believe his thoughts are already turning homewards ... We shall have more military display than the Irish festivities afforded and a boar *chasse* is preparing; the rest of the time will be full up with balls and an excursion to Göttingen.[21]

As so often during the reign, George's precarious health had an effect. Far less fit than George I and George II, both of whom continued to visit Hanover at a greater age (George II until he was seventy-two), George IV was also a much less experienced traveller. Londonderry reported,

> You will not be surprised, after so much traveling by sea and land, coupled as we know has been the case, with considerable anxiety of mind, that the

gout should have shown itself upon the slightest provocation – being on horseback on Saturday for several hours reviewing his troops, and having a charger, not as tranquil under his weight, as his horse in Dublin was, His Majesty's knee got a twist.[22]

George had to convalesce, but he soon recovered sufficiently to take part in the social round expected of him:

> The King is well enough to receive company at dinner. Tomorrow he will have audiences. Friday he is to visit his stud, and manège, which is upon a very large scale, and on Saturday His Majesty will take leave by showing himself at the theatre. As the King proposes to stop at Göttingen on his way the disappointment occasioned by his illness will have been in some measure repaired.

In an echo of the past, George's visit also provided an opportunity for diplomatic discussion with other leading figures, as the Austrian Chancellor, Metternich, visited Hanover; however, as a sign of the times, Metternich was there to see Londonderry, not George.[23] Whereas on the last visit by a ruling member of the dynasty, that by George II in 1755, the ruler had played a central role in the negotiations handled at Hanover, that was no longer the case; although, in his early years as King George IV used the Hanoverian diplomatic service extensively, claiming that this provided him with information not otherwise available to his British ministers. Pressure from Canning, the Foreign Secretary, in 1825 brought to an end this embryonic *secret du Electeur-roi*.[24]

In 1822 George continued his visits to his dominions by visiting Scotland. The focus there on the capital was also appropriate. George reached Scotland on the *Royal George*, sailing in his yacht from Greenwich to Leith, and sailing back from Queensferry. He did not have therefore to face the long journey by land through England, but the railways that were to speed Queen Victorian's journeys to Scotland had not yet been built. As a sign of changing technology, steam tugs were used to help the *Royal George* cope with contrary winds, but in Scotland, George visited Newbattle Abbey, the seat of the Marquess of Lothian, rather than the commercial centre of Glasgow. Aside from wearing Highland dress of a lavish type, and renewing public interest in clans and tartans, George on his visit also favoured Scottish music and dances, as well as Glenlivet and Atholl brose: the previous year, he had enjoyed

Irish whiskey punch. What George made of the sermon he heard preached by the Moderator of the Church of Scotland, against lust and in favour of marital harmony, is unknown, but George was accustomed to the consequences of his position as a public defender of the moral order.[25] The expectation that George's reception in Edinburgh, as in Dublin and Hanover, would be more favourable than it was in London, the centre of disaffection, was proved correct.

After his tour of his kingdoms, however, George retreated from the public aspect of monarchy. Indeed, after 1823, he made no public appearances in London except for the ceremonial opening and proroguing of Parliament. Instead, he spent most of his time at his favourite haunts of Brighton and Windsor, much of it in the company of his mistress, Elizabeth, Lady Conyngham, who, like Ladies Jersey and Hertford, was no youngster: George's preference for women in their forties and fifties attracted comment. Older than George, Lady Jersey had been a grand-mother when their relationship started. The daughter of a self-made Yorkshire businessman, Lady Conyngham was considered a parvenue and a gold-digger. She had replaced Lady Hertford as favourite in late 1819 and gave George, who was initially intoxicated by her, a new optimism. Her husband's appointment as Lord Steward of the Household in 1821, when she was fifty-five, the year in which her relationship with George was closest, aided their contact, although propriety was main-tained to the extent of George and Lady Conyngham not living under the same roof. Nevertheless, the lavish presents, especially of jewellery, and clear public regard that George showed for Lady Conyngham was such that the relationship was no secret. Indeed, the King insisted that she sit close to him throughout the coronation. Her presence there was rewarded with repeated looks that struck some as indecent. She, however, was a peremptory individual and could irritate the King, who was also to complain that she bored him. George's affections were not restricted to her, although, with increasing age, he seems to have been seeking affectionate company rather than sex. In July 1822, George wrote as 'a most affectionate friend' from Carlton House, possibly to a 'Mrs M.'; the recipient is unclear:

You may easily imagine, warm and sincere as my affections are towards you, I have had but little rest, since we separated last night. The fear, that

I may, possibly and unfortunately in a hurried moment, when my mind
and Heart being torn in fifty different ways from fifty different causes have
let an unjust or a hasty expression escape me to any one (but most especially
to You, who I so *truly love* and who are so *invaluable* to *Me* as my *friend*)
is to *me*, a sensation much *too painful* to be *endured*; therefore, let me
*implore* of You, to come to me, *be it but for a moment*, the *very first thing*
you do this morning, for I shall hate myself until I have the opportunity
of expressing *personally* to You, those pure and Genuine feelings of affection
for You, which will never cease to live in *my Heart*, so long as that Heart,
itself continues to beat. I am much too unhappy to say more . . .[26]

One of the reasons why George showed himself so rarely in London
in his later years as King was that he was very unpopular there, but he
also felt ridiculous as a result of his girth and, albeit with the surplus
due to acute hypochondria, was affected by poor health. Indeed he had
been badly ill with a chest infection when he became King in 1820.
Addington then noted: 'The situation of his present Majesty was extremely alarming during the greater part of Tuesday night: but the
formidable symptoms have gradually given way, and all apprehensions
of a fatal result appear to be over'. The fear, however, of 'a fresh attack,
to resist which his constitution may have become unequal' led to action:
'The quantity of blood taken from him in the course of twelve or thirteen
hours by the advice of Dr Tierney was enormous, and to that advice
the preservation of H.M.'s life is, through the blessing of Providence,
to be ascribed'. Ten days later, he added: 'The King's health gradually
improves but there are very painful obstacles to a rapid recovery'.[27]
Renewed ill-health led Liverpool to note in July 1820, 'The King's
progress to recovery is but slow'.[28] His post-mortem in 1830 revealed
deep-seated causes of ill-health: both arteriosclerosis and a bladder
tumour.

George's reign was a rather sad, as well as at times ludicrous, postlude
to the great days of his career as Prince Regent, when, as the leader of
fashionable society, he had created a new, alternative image of royalty
and a new standard of English and international elegance: the Brighton
Pavilion stands today as testimony to his idiosyncratically high sense of
taste. Initially, as Prince of Wales, George's building had essentially been
for private purposes, and was decorative, rather than a work of state.
Carlton House on Pall Mall, which George had been granted in 1783 as

his first independent residence, required restoration, but George had it extensively rebuilt by the architect Henry Holland, and the building was also lavishly decorated, providing a setting for impressive, and always expensive, entertainments. This contributed directly to the Prince's debts and helped poison relations between George and his father.

Carlton House was not alone. From 1783, the Prince spent summers at Brighton, newly fashionable as a result of the belief that sea bathing was healthy. Needing a residence, George had a house transformed into a villa by 1787. Subsequently, the Brighton Pavilion was enhanced, with fresh construction and exuberant decoration. The dome, built from 1804, was designed in what was seen as an Indian fashion, and the metamorphosis of what had been a classical villa into an oriental pleasure palace was also accomplished by the furnishings, which again were in an Indian style. The style did not commend itself to all, and the bitter obituary in The *Times* on 28 June 1830, a masterpiece of malice, referred to 'the mountebank Pavilion, or cluster of pagodas at Brighton'.

As King, George was responsible for the rebuilding, from 1825, of Buckingham House, in order to make it a palace, a major work of state. He also supported John Nash, the architect there, in his work on what became Regent's Park and on the building of Regent Street. The work on the palace was particularly controversial, in large part due to serious cost overruns that led to marked public and parliamentary criticism, as well as to Nash's dismissal soon after George's death. The work remained unfinished under George, which contributed to a sense of feckless expenditure. The entire episode harmed George's reputation: he was blamed for the cost; and, indeed, he was partly responsible because he frequently changed his mind about what he wanted.[29]

George was also a major patron of the arts, not least of the leading British painters of the age. Reynolds and Gainsborough received early patronage, while Romney and Hoppner, especially the latter, were both supported thereafter. Hoppner's position as George's favourite painter was taken from the early 1810s by Lawrence, who was knighted by George the following year, and who painted the portraits of those who had secured the defeat of Napoleon that line the Waterloo Gallery at Windsor. Lawrence succeeded Benjamin West as President of the Royal Academy in 1820, and George was a keen patron of the institution, regularly attending its exhibitions and dinners. Other British painters

he supported included George Stubbs, from whom he purchased eight-
een works, and David Wilkie. George's approval of the idea of a national
gallery was important in securing government backing, and in 1823 it
spent £57,000 buying the collection of the financier John Julius Anger-
stein which was to be the basis of this gallery. George was also an active
purchaser of old masters, being especially fond of Flemish and Dutch
paintings, buying works by Cuyp, Pieter de Hooch, Rembrandt, Ruys-
dael, Jan Steen, Teniers, and Van Dyck, including the latter's triple
portrait of Charles I. Other *objets d'art* that attracted his knowledgeable
interest included bronzes, furniture and porcelain. George was fond of
the ornate decoration of French furniture and this affected British
furniture makers.

Initially as King, George showed himself in considerable style. The
list of courtiers and servants requiring lodging at Phoenix Park in 1821
was impressive:

His Majesty – requiring for his private apartments a Bedroom, a Sitting
room adjoining, and a Page's waiting room.

    4 Pages of the Backstairs in constant attendance
    4 Pages of the presence (2nd class of servants)
    4 Footmen
    Sir Benjamin Bloomfield
    Valet
    2 Footmen
    Equerry in Waiting
    1 servant
    Gentlemen of the Wine Cellar, Confectioner, Pastry Cook, 2 Master
    Cooks, Table Decker, and from 10 to 12 Cooks and servants belonging
    to the Kitchen.
    The above must be lodged where the King resides.
    The Lord Steward of His Majesty's Household
    The Lord Chamberlain
    The Master of the Horse
    The Groom of the Stole
    4 Valets and 8 Footmen
    4 Lords of the Bedchamber
    4 Valets and 4 Footmen
    4 Grooms of the Bedchamber

8 Equerries and Aidedecamps
4 Gentlemen Ushers
16 Servants
Secretary to the Lord Steward
1 Clerk
1 Servant
Secretary to the Lord Chamberlain
1 Clerk
1 Servant
Clerk Comptroller of the Kitchen
1 Servant
3 Clerks
2nd Gentleman of the Wine Cellar
2nd Confectioner and his Assistant
2nd Table Decker
3 Silver Scullery Men
4 Principal Cooks
3 Apprentices
Physician, Surgeon, and Apothecary to the Person
20 Gentlemen Pensioners and 4 Officers
Stable Department – numbers not known.[30]

Once he became reclusive, George cut a far less impressive figure. The contrast with the restored Bourbons in France is striking. Under the reigns of Louis XVIII (1814–24) and Charles X (1824–30), the French court was used to strengthen the relationship between crown and elite and crown and church. Far from anxiously teetering on the brink of revolution, the restored Bourbons maintained an enormous and spectacular court and an elaborate social life during an age of energy and optimism,[31] although Charles X was to be deposed in 1830 while George IV died without losing his throne. Nevertheless, it was the restoration French court, not that of George, that set the tone and fashion for court life throughout Europe, whether in female dress in England, mourning in Naples or receptions in Turin.

George's range of interests, however, was impressive. He backed the Literary Fund's support for indigent writers, had literary interests, secured the return of the Stuart papers to Britain, sponsored the copying of a collection of papyri found at Herculaneum, and was interested in animals. His menagerie reflected the spreading sway of British power and included kangaroos, an ostrich, a zebra, and a leopard, and the giraffe presented in 1827 by Mehmet Ali, the Pasha of Egypt.

Politically, George benefited from the stability of the ministry of the Earl of Liverpool (1812–27), in much the same way that George III had benefited from that of Pitt the Younger. After Liverpool had a stroke and retired, however, George found politics troubling. The crisis of Liverpool's succession was eventually resolved by making George Canning head of the government, against the initial wishes of the King, but Canning's death in August 1827 reopened the political situation. Keen not to turn to Wellington, whom he distrusted politically, George helped to put in a government under Frederick, Lord Goderich, a former Chancellor of the Exchequer, but the agreeable Goderich was weak and could not control his colleagues. Disillusioned with Goderich, whose willingness to blubber did not impress the King, George accepted his resignation in January 1828 and finally turned to Wellington. George insisted that the government should not push through Catholic Emancipation; indeed he had obliged Canning to appoint a Chief Secretary for Ireland who did not support Emancipation.

Wellington, however, saw Emancipation as necessary, and pressed George hard on the issue, urging him to ignore the contrary advice of his brother, Ernest, Duke of Cumberland. As George, who, in his anger, threatened Wellington with abdication, had no alternative ministers to turn to, he finally agreed, under pressure from the Duke, to sign the Catholic Relief Act on 13 April 1829. The willingness of George to bow to necessity defined this last stage of his reign, but it left him bitter and deflated.

George might have been earlier termed the 'First Gentleman in Europe', but, as monarch, he lacked charisma, and was widely believed to have no sense of integrity; although he has recently benefited from sympathetic reassessment.[32] His reign was a lost opportunity for assertive monarchy. In some respects, the history of the British monarchy has often been such. James I and VI failed to unify England and Scotland, and his Stuart successors found it impossible to create a domestic consensus or to win glory abroad, while the 'Glorious Revolution' did not produce an uncontested succession, nor lead to the accession of vigorous monarchs with children. Whereas Georges I, II and III were not without success, under George IV, especially after the royal visit to

Scotland, the British monarchy blatantly lacked flair, and George himself acquired a general and sustained unpopularity that was greater than
that of the earlier Hanoverians. No later British monarch has been so
unpopular on the eve of his or her death as George was when he died
on 26 June 1830.

The deaths of his brother Edward, in 1820, and even more Frederick
in 1827, had an affect on George, helping turn his hypochondria toward
thoughts of mortality. They also brought problems to sort out. Thus,
Wellington wrote to George's confidant, Sir William Knighton, after
Frederick's death,

> Before I would take charge of the enclosed paper I was made certain that
> there was no male by which the unfortunate person to whom it related
> could bring under His Majesty's notice unless I could interest you in her
> favour; and I shall not think it proper that I should know of the circum-
> stances therein stated without at least giving you the option of laying before
> the King, knowing as I do His Majesty's affection for his late brother, and
> how keenly he feels everything that can affect his reputation and honour.[33]

Close to his end George was very sickly and heavily drugged with
laudanum, but he still ate heavily and showed a variety of interests.
Alongside concern about racing, including eagerness for news of the
results of races and for details about horses he wished to buy, came
signs of religious devotion. George read the Bible frequently, took solace
in receiving the sacrament, and declared his repentance of his youth,
saying that he hoped the mercy he had shown others would be offered
him. The King's decline took several months, during which he displayed
considerable courage and calm. In his last moments, he looked at Sir
Watkin Waller, who was holding his hand, and said 'My boy, this is
death!'[34] He then fell back dead in his chair; the rupture of a blood
vessel in his stomach had killed him.

The funeral, in Windsor on 15 July, saw few signs of grief. The
Unitarian *Monthly Repository*'s obituary declared: 'He was too regardless
of the decorum which his father so steadily maintained for it to be
decent in religionists to become his apologists'.

# 8

# *William IV*

if ever there was a Sovereign entitled to the character, his Majesty
may truly be styled 'a Patriot King!'

Earl Grey, House of Lords, debate on accession
of Queen Victoria, 1837

After the dismal story of the last years of George III, and the unpopular,
and largely purposeless, reign of George IV, William IV's reign (1830–37)
can be seen as beginning the process of revival that was to culminate
in the development of imperial splendour under Victoria and Edward
VII.[1] Born on 21 August 1765 in Buckingham Palace, William was the
third son of George III and Queen Charlotte. His father, who had become
more interested in the navy after his visit to Portsmouth in 1773,[2] decided
that William should enter the navy, making plans to that end in 1778.
William did so in 1779, beginning as an able seaman and (in 1780)
becoming a midshipman. William's early naval experiences made him
popular, and certainly more accessible than his royal brothers. Various
stories did the rounds about his willingness to mess in and accept the
name William Guelph as a form of address from his shipmates.

George III was keen that naval life should not mean that William
acquired inappropriate habits, and distance did not prevent him from
keeping an eye on his son, or indeed on his other children. In 1779
George arranged that Henry Majendie, whose father, John, had instructed Queen Charlotte in English and been tutor to the Prince of
Wales and his second son, Frederick, Duke of York, should teach
William on board the *Prince George*; Majendie was listed as a midshipman. In 1781 Majendie was to be appointed William's preceptor. He
clearly commended himself to George, becoming a Canon of Windsor
in 1785, Vicar of Windsor and a Canon of St Paul's in 1798, and Bishop
of Chester in 1800.

In 1780, however, William caused concern by disorderly behaviour in London, leading George III to have him returned to his ship. In 1781, George wrote of 'the anxiety I have for the success of my endeavours to fit my children for the various stations they may fill, and that they may be useful and a credit to their family'.[3] Worry about William led George to write in 1783 to Colonel Richard Grenville, Governor of Frederick, Duke of York, then residing in Germany as Prince Bishop of Osnabrück:

> I hope speedily to send William to Germany not thinking this a safe place on many accounts for one of his age and not less so who by having been two years abroad must expect more liberty than I can approve on this side of the water … Frederick has succeeded so well that his example cannot be too closely followed … William is rather giddy and has rather too much the manners of his profession [the navy], polishing and composure are the ingredients wanting to make him a charming character.

The following year, George wrote to William:

> I am glad you propose being more regular in your correspondence, it is impossible you cannot want for topics if you take pains to improve your mind; the natural attendance whilst at sea certainly was no advantage to your manners nor could your education be so closely followed as could be wished either in your station as a prince or as an officer for seamanship is but a very small part of the requisites necessary in superior commands and for want of which the service has on many opportunities most fatally suffered. The knowledge of the springs that actuate men is necessary to know how to turn them to the pursuits that are honorable to themselves or of utility to the state; that you may by diligence become what it must be your own desire as well as that of those who wish you well will ever be my objective.[4]

William's political leanings were in support of his brothers George and Frederick in the 1780s, although he tried to balance this with continuing regard and affection for his parents. This, however, was a difficult goal and broke down on occasion. There was the Regency Crisis itself (when the Queen's attitude towards William upset him) and the business of him threatening to stand for Parliament for Totnes in protest at the delay in granting him his dukedom (and the financial provision attached to it). This helped stimulate his promotion to his titles (celebrated with a party at Willis's Subscription Rooms in June 1789) but he seems to have tired of his brother George's Carlton House set and preferred the attractions provided by his new and more private establishments at Roehampton and, subsequently, Bushy.

From 1789, the young William received social and professional promotion. Created Earl of Munster and Duke of Clarence and St Andrews in 1789, William, who had only been promoted to be Lieutenant in 1785, became a Rear-Admiral in 1790, a Vice-Admiral in 1794, an Admiral in 1799, and, in 1811, Admiral of the Fleet, and thus Commander-in-Chief, a step that blocked the promotion of other officers. It was not until 1821, when George IV promoted Earl St Vincent, a distinguished veteran of the French Revolutionary War, that there was a second such commander. In 1827, William's naval glory culminated when he was made Lord High Admiral, a post recreated for him (Prince George of Denmark had held it), and one that superseded the Board of Admiralty.

The late eighteenth and early nineteenth centuries was the period of British naval triumph and hegemony, but the Duke of Clarence was not responsible for any successes. He had seen active service during the War of American Independence, off Gibraltar, in the West Indies, the Channel and in North American waters, and commanded ships in peacetime in 1786–90, acquiring a reputation as a martinet, as indeed did his brother Edward, Duke of Kent, in Gibraltar in 1790–91 and 1802–3. Appointed Captain of the *Pegasus* in 1786, William quarrelled over discipline with his experienced First-Lieutenant, Isaac Schomberg, leading Schomberg to apply, unsuccessfully, for a court martial, before being superseded. In 1788 William transferred to the *Andromeda* and, in 1790, to the *Valiant*. The latter was part of the large fleet assembled as war seemed likely with Spain in the Nootka Sound crisis over competing claims on what became the coast of British Columbia. Deprived by the revolutionary crisis of the prospect of French assistance, Spain backed down, however, ensuring that William did not gain further wartime experience. William also acquired a preference for alcohol and smoking from his naval life, as well as a bluff manner and rough speech.

Edward, Duke of Kent's career in some respects matched that of his elder brother. Sent as a colonel to Gibraltar in 1790, his first command, he was appointed to Canada the following year. Aside from service in command of a brigade in the West Indies, Edward remained there, from 1796 as a Lieutenant-General, until, in 1798 as a result of ill-health, he returned to England. Promotion was not delayed. In 1799 Edward became Duke of Kent and Strathern, Earl of Dublin, a General, and Commander-in-Chief of the forces in North America. However, ill-health led him to return in 1800. Sent to Gibraltar as Governor in 1802, Kent provoked a mutiny by banning the troops from entering the wine-shops. The mutiny was rapidly crushed, but Kent was recalled and refused permission to return. In 1805 he became a Field-Marshal, but without command.

Similarly, after 1790, despite his naval rank and experience, Clarence did not serve afloat, other than for brief ceremonial purposes. In 1814 he commanded the naval escort for Louis XVIII when he returned to France from exile in Britain, as well as the British fleet when it was reviewed by the Prince Regent and the allied sovereigns at Spithead. In 1828, however, Clarence, who had become heir to the throne on the death of Frederick, Duke of York in January 1827 (William acted as chief mourner), put to sea in command of the Channel Fleet, despite the view of George IV, the Prime Minister (Wellington) and the head of the Admiralty Board, Sir George Cockburn, that his position as Lord High Admiral did not give him the authority to exercise military command. Their complaints led to Clarence's resignation. More was at stake than this cruise. It had been assumed that the Board of Admiralty would continue to operate as the Lord High Admiral's Council, and would direct the navy. Clarence, in contrast, thought that rank and experience entitled him to direct affairs, and he also committed more money to naval expenditure and the condition of officers and sailors than the government had envisaged. His interest in reforming not only the system of punishments and promotions but also naval gunnery were all contributory factors to the difficulties culminating in his resignation and the abolition of the office.[5] This was scarcely a career to match that of Horatio Nelson, who, indeed, served with William in the West Indies and was a friend. When Nelson married in 1787, William gave away the bride, and Nelson praised his abilities as an officer; but there are no signs that he had the capability to be an effective admiral; in any case he was never given a chance to do so. This did not prevent a pride in British military strength that was to be seen not only in William's praise for Wellington but also in his pressure for a strong naval presence in the Mediterranean in the face of international threats[6] and his firmness in the international crisis of 1836 when he declared his enthusiasm for the excitement of war, an enthusiasm also glimpsed on earlier occasions.

George IV's reign was so unedifying that the ascent of William to the throne in 1830 was seen as a relief. Despite his own failings, and there were many, his reputation was enhanced by being compared to his unlamented brother.

William's reign was dominated by the issue of political reform, and, specifically, by pressure to change the electoral franchise and make it more representative. This was opposed by the Tories, who dominated the House of Lords. The general election that resulted from William's accession was followed, in November 1830, by the defeat of the Tory government under Wellington, who had declared his opposition to parliamentary reform. A Whig government under Lord Grey followed. Grey supported reform not least because he feared that, without it, there would be a revolution; this appeared to be the lesson of the successful French revolution of 1830 that overthrew Charles X. The Reform Bill, however, introduced into the Commons by Lord John Russell on 1 March 1831, was defeated at the committee stage in April 1831 after passing the second reading by only one vote. Grey then sought a dissolution of Parliament, preparatory to a new election designed to lead to a more reform-minded Commons. William's agreement to this dissolution, and thus to the second general election in quick succession, was very popular among supporters of reform. He could, instead, have sought to appoint another Prime Minister.

The second Reform Bill passed the Commons in September 1831, after the general election had returned Grey with a very large majority, but it was thrown out by the Tory-dominated Lords on 8 October 1831. While the prospects of a compromise Bill were probed in discussions, there was much popular agitation, including bitter riots in Bristol, Derby and Nottingham. A third Reform Bill, which reflected modifications arising from the recent discussions, was introduced in the Commons on 12 December 1831, passing its second reading with a large majority on 18 December. The attitude of the Lords, however, remained crucial and it was unclear that the modifications would ensure sufficient support.

The King was asked to appoint enough peers to secure the success of the Bill. William, who respected the position of the House of Lords, and was worried both about the content and tendency of the Reform Bill and by Grey's inability to distance his policy from that of the radical Whigs, nevertheless felt that he had to support the government. Reluctantly he agreed, on 15 January 1832, to create enough peers to support passage of the Bill in the Lords, if such a course was necessary, and also to press the peers to pass the measure. In the event, however, the government's request that May for the creation of fifty peers seemed unreasonable to William: he had only been thinking of about twenty-one.

Having passed its third reading in the Commons by 355 votes to 239 on 22 March 1832, the Bill went to the Lords four days later. Its second reading there was secured on 14 April, but by a majority of only nine, on a division of 184 to 175. This majority was judged insufficient by Grey. After being amended in committee, the Bill went back to the Lords for its third reading, only to meet with defeat on an amendment on 7 May by a majority of 161 to 116. Grey then asked William for fifty new peers, and, when the King refused on 9 May, he resigned. William accepted the resignation of the ministry and turned to the Tories, asking first Robert Peel (who refused) and then Wellington to form a government.

Handicapped by Tory divisions, Wellington failed, obliging William, who did not wish to see another general election and the disruption and uncertainty that would cause, to turn to Grey and to accept the need to create peers as the Whigs wished. He recalled Grey, as Wellington advised, on 15 May and agreed to create new peers if necessary three days later. Rather than doing so, however, William was responsible for a circular letter to Tory peers that led many to decide to abstain, as Wellington promised to do. Under this pressure, the Lords yielded, passing the third reading on 4 June. With the royal assent, the Reform Act became law on 7 June 1832. When it came to the crunch, the King had been led to back Grey by the widespread support for reform, by the view that the choice was between reform and widespread disorder, but also, in the crisis created by Tory divisions, by Grey's opposition to further changes, and by the sense that the Reform Bill would not be followed by a total transformation of British politics.

In fact, what became the First Reform Act was the first major change to the franchise and political geography of England and Wales since the short-lived Interregnum constitutions of the 1650s. A notionally uniform borough franchise was established, based on households rated at £10 annually. As a result, the English electorate increased by 50 per cent, to include sections of the middle class, so that about one-fifth of all adult males could vote after 1832. Separate Acts were also passed for Ireland and Scotland. The distribution of seats was radically altered in order to reward growing towns, such as Birmingham, Blackburn, Bolton, Bradford, Leeds, Manchester, Oldham, Sheffield and Sunderland, that had not, hitherto, had their own MPs and also under-represented counties. By transferring seats to the north of England, the Act reflected the major shift in fortunes arising from industrialisation and increased the political weight of a part of the country with which the royal family had few links; the long-term implications of which for the monarchy were unclear. Nevertheless, the Act helped underline the extent of popular representation through, and participation in, the electoral system, and this sustained the broad popular acceptance of the political system.

Despite his hostility to the radicals, William himself was publicly reputed to be a zealous supporter of reform; a marked contrast with Charles X of France, who lost his throne in 1830. In the cartoon, *The Reformers' Attack on the Old Rotten Tree*, which advocated electoral reform, William was portrayed on 'Constitution Hill', applauding the process of reform and surrounded by respectful figures representing England, Scotland and Ireland. Similarly, in *The Balance of Power in 1831*, the Whigs were depicted sitting on the lower end of the seesaw, which was weighted down by the crown and the press, most prominently the *Times*, while the Tories were up in the air.

William was seen as wanting to be a 'constitutional' monarch – which, indeed, he sought to be. Unlike George IV, William had no prejudice against the Whigs, and had been willing to cooperate with Grey's attempt to form a ministry. William's concessions to the Whigs during the crisis had been offered grudgingly, but, when faced with the prospect of incurring the wrath of the populace by thwarting reform, William's tendency was to give way. His alleged support for the Bill was used extensively, and to considerable effect, by supporters of reform in the 1831 election, while, more generally, William's service to the state was popular: mainly his naval service, but also to a lesser extent his ultimate flexibility over reform. William's opposition to reform in 1832 was blamed on his wife, Queen Adelaide, his brother Cumberland, or his sisters – but not on the King himself. The contrast between the large number of pubs named after William and the small number named after George IV is instructive. William also certainly benefited from the popularity of the navy.

Any lasting assessment of William's political role is complicated by his dismissal of Melbourne's Whig ministry in 1834, 'the last time a British monarch dismissed his ministers and called on others to take their place';[7] although there were later instances in Canada, South Africa and Australia. Melbourne (the fathering of whose brother, George, was improbably attributed to George IV as Prince of Wales[8]) had become Prime Minister in July 1834 when Grey, angered by his colleagues' disunity over the proposed appropriation of Irish Church revenues for lay uses, resigned. William, whose effort to get Melbourne to form a coalition with the Tories was unsuccessful, nevertheless both liked and backed him, not least because he felt he could trust him to oppose radicalism. Indeed, William had clashed with Grey in 1832 over what he felt was the latter's willingness to discourage opposition to radicalism on the Continent. This had led William to demand that his consent be obtained for all instructions to British diplomats, and Grey to offer his resignation; although that crisis had been settled.[9]

Once Melbourne was in office, however, the two men differed over the church. Melbourne wished to make Lord John Russell, later Prime Minister in 1846–52 and 1865–66, Leader of the House of Commons, but William would not accept this: Russell's support for the use of church revenues for secular purposes was seen by William as a threat to the rights of the church that was a breach of his coronation oath, an echo of George III's and George IV's concerns over Catholic Emancipation.

Using the excuse that the government was divided on the issue, William dismissed it on 14 November 1834, the dismissal reflecting his conviction that he had the right to choose the government and that, while that government needed to command parliamentary support, it also needed to be his government and to back him. George IV, however, had not pushed through such a step, and it struck many contemporaries as a disturbing development. They saw parallels with the controversial actions of William's father, George III, in 1783–84. Crucially the sequel was different: Pitt had won the 1784 election, but the Tories, under Sir Robert Peel, lost the 1835 election, although they did gain an additional ninety-eight seats. The election results did not stop Peel trying to continue in office, but defeats in the Commons led him to resign on

8 April 1835, having been in office for one hundred days. Melbourne returned to office on 11 April after the Whigs had rejected William's pressure for a coalition.

Queen Adelaide took Peel's failure both to create a Commons majority and in the subsequent election as a sign of incipient revolution, but this greatly exaggerated the extent of instability in 1834–35. Even in 1831–32, the disturbances, although violent, were relatively modest, considering the issue at stake and the apparent difficulty of ensuring a satisfactory constitutional outcome. William adapted well to Melbourne's return to office. He had to see Russell become Home Secretary, but Melbourne was careful not to alienate the elderly King, while William, in turn, accepted the new state of constitutional monarchy, although there were quarrels and disagreements reflecting the difficulties of 'bedding down' a new practice of politics.[10] Fortunately for William, Melbourne's ministry rested on Tory support and was adaptable to Tory views. Melbourne was largely concerned to consolidate Grey's legacy rather than to press on with radical reforms,[11] while Peel, who was no ultra-Tory, was more comfortable with Melbourne than with many Tories. William could share this view. Nevertheless, he had to accept that crown and Lords could not prevail together against the Commons.

A sense of stabilisation was helped by the extent to which the Reform Act of 1832, while bringing important changes, did not amount to a constitutional revolution, and did not lead to a social one. The political system remained under the control of the socially prominent, both directly and indirectly, a situation that matched William's wishes. Thus, John, Viscount Althorp, who became the 3rd Earl Spencer in 1834, was Chairman of the Northamptonshire quarter sessions from 1806 until his death in 1845, while, from 1803 until 1906, every heir to the Marquessate of Bristol sat at one time or another as MP for West Suffolk or for the borough of Bury St Edmunds, adjacent to the family seat of Ickworth.

Thanks to his impulsive and well-meaning personality, William was frequently ebullient and somewhat eccentric: his conversations went off at a tangent, leading him to be dubbed 'Silly Billy'. Having become King, William did not throw off his unbuttoned style. He regarded himself as a friend of his brother George, but displayed little grief during his funeral, instead talking loudly and leaving before the coffin had been laid in the vault. At one level, William's lack of dignity was the result of a welcome (to some) openness and bumptious eccentricity, but at another there were echoes of his father's behaviour when affected by porphyria, a hereditary disease. William was particularly unpredictable in the spring, but there was nothing to compare to George III's condition in 1788 and 1801. William also did not face the difficulties his father had confronted, especially terrible relations with his son and heir. When Lord High Admiral in 1827–28, William's conduct was regarded as particularly strange and difficult. William's mannerisms had been prefigured by his uncle, Henry, Duke of Cumberland (1745–90), who had also risen in the navy – to be an admiral in 1782. Cumberland, who was regarded as eccentric, was noted for his lack of interest in maintaining his dignity, which included, on one occasion, attempting to play among the musicians in a public concert.[12]

Once on the throne, William behaved in a fashion very different from his royal predecessors. Indeed, his obituary in *The Gentleman's Magazine* referred to 'the substitution of a most obvious desire of popularity ... for the secluded habits' of George IV's last years. He enjoyed walking round the capital without show or ceremony, but had to be dissuaded from doing so as he received unwelcome attention from the populace. He was also discouraged from his habit of inviting new acquaintances to dinner at the palace. The King's unbuttoned style of speechifying also did not impress all with its fulsomeness.

William's 'unroyal' demeanour and habits were also seen with the 'half-coronation', in which economy took precedence over display. The theatre of majesty was not on display. Aside from holding a less expensive coronation, there was no state banquet in the evening; indeed, that for George IV on 18 July 1821 was the last to be held. As a result, there was a slackening in the ritual of monarchy: the banquet had included the appearance of the armour-clad King's Champion to challenge any who contested the royal claim to the throne, as well as the High Constable backing his horse down Westminster Hall from the King's Table and had seen the consumption of 7,742 pounds of beef, 7,133 pounds of veal, 2,474 pounds of mutton, 100 dozen bottles of champagne, 100 gallons of iced punch, and 350 bottles of port and sherry.

The abandonment of much of the *gloire* associated with George IV was also seen with the fate of his plan to make Buckingham House a major palace. The architect, John Nash, took the blame for the cost and was sacked. William chose not to live in the palace and preferred instead to continue to reside in Clarence House, which was more modest. Indeed William proposed to Wellington that the palace be converted into a barracks.

William's lack of pretentiousness and easy style were widely, but not universally, popular and seen as conveying integrity. A democratic myth grew up about William because the populace confused his easy going nature with an inclination toward political reform. A tendency toward eccentric behaviour, if not silliness, had mattered little when cloaked in obscurity, but, in the spotlight of the monarchy, it exposed William to public scrutiny. For many, this revealed him to be an honest and generous man of good will; but others saw William's tendency to move freely among the people or make unpredictable remarks as a vulgarisation of the crown. There was also a tendency to characterise William as rather dim-witted and to doubt his mental health.[13]

William's personal life certainly caused less offence than that of George IV. There was a story, subsequently proved unfounded, that William had contracted a secret marriage (during a sojourn in Hanover in the mid 1780s) to a Caroline von Linsingen and sired a son by her. William's love life was rich and varied, but he was genuinely attached both to Dorothy Jordan and subsequently Queen Adelaide. Between 1790 and 1811 William lived publicly, but quietly, with the actress Dorothy Jordan. Residing at Bushy (William was Ranger of Bushy Park), they had ten children and lived in an affectionate manner.[14] When the succession obliged William to part with Dorothy, she was 'pensioned off' in a settlement which included an annual allowance, house and coach money and support for her daughters by two previous liaisons. After his elevation to the throne, William created George, the eldest of the FitzClarences, Earl of Munster, a title he had held: George shot himself in 1842. William had left Mrs Jordan for both financial and status reasons: he wanted to marry, in large part in order to clear his debts; but, prior to 1818, he had no success, and exposed himself to ridicule by his efforts.

After the death of the Prince Regent's young daughter, Charlotte, in 1817, William, whose position as George III's third son (with the second, Frederick, Duke of York, being childless) in the succession was now dramatically different, married a wife appropriate to his station: Adelaide, elder daughter of Duke George of Saxe-Meiningen. Similarly, the fourth and seventh sons of George III, the Dukes of Kent and Cambridge, married: Edward, Duke of Kent put aside Madame de St-Laurent, who he had met in Canada, and who had been his mistress for twenty-seven years, in order to marry Maria Louisa Victoria of Saxe-Coburg (1786–1861), the widowed Dowager Princess of Leiningen-Dachsburg-Hardenburg, a union that led in 1819 to the birth of the future Queen Victoria. The speedy betrothals of the elderly Royal Dukes – William was fifty-two – was ridiculed as unseemly and expensive.[15] The betrothals owed most to the need to provide the throne with an heir and thus secure the dynasty, but William, like his brother Edward, was further encouraged by the hope that an appropriate marriage might lead Parliament to pay off their debts. They were indeed given an increase in their annual income from £18,000 to £24,000 each, although the increase was not as large as originally proposed.

The German marriages of the Princes underlined one consequence of the Hanoverian dynasty. Whereas William III, his wife, Mary II, and Anne had all had Protestant marriages, these had not been with Germans: Mary had married William of Orange and Anne Prince George of Denmark. In contrast, all four Georges had German wives, as did Frederick, Prince of Wales, while George IV's daughter Charlotte had a German husband, the handsome Leopold of Saxe-Coburg, who, in 1831, became King of Belgium. There were very few other links: George III's sister Caroline Matilda disastrously married the heir to the Danish throne; his brother, William, Duke of Gloucester, married Maria, the widow of the 2nd Earl Waldegrave; and another brother, Henry, Duke of Cumberland, married Anne, the daughter of the 1st Earl of Carhampton who was also the widow of Christopher Horton. The emphasis on German wives was, however, clear in the case of George III's children, both men and women. Thus in 1815 Ernest, Duke of Cumberland married his cousin, Frederica of Mecklenburg-Strelitz, a widow, while in 1818 Adolphus, Duke of Cambridge married Augusta Wilhelmina Louisa, the third daughter of the Landgrave of Hesse-Cassel.

These German marriages helped differentiate the monarchy from the aristocracy, members of which did not respond to the Hanoverian accession by seeking German spouses. They also created a tension within the royal family, one that led to and was accentuated by the Royal

Marriages Act of 1772 with its emphasis on the approval of the monarch. The contrasting marriages of George IV – secretly and illegally to Mrs Fitzherbert and legally to Princess Caroline – were a consequence, contributing greatly to the strife in the royal family. To save bother and presumably expense, William and his brother Edward were married at the same time in a double wedding at Kew Palace on 11 July 1818.

Adelaide had two miscarriages and bore William two daughters, but both died in infancy, one, in 1820, after only a few hours; the other, Princess Elizabeth, in March 1821 aged only three months. Due to William's financial problems, the couple went to Hanover, but they returned to live at Bushy, where Adelaide had to put up with the memory of Dorothy Jordan, before moving to Clarence House in 1824. A good sort denied, by the death of her children, any outlet for her maternal instincts, Adelaide was a kind stepmother to the FitzClarence children, which added much to her attractions to William, and was also to be loving to their children.

The capital of the new colony of South Australia was named after the Queen, an important instance of a wider process of naming by which the royal family left its mark on the world. This process is readily apparent, especially in areas where the end of imperial control was not accompanied by a determination to reject the legacy of the past. The royal nomenclature of place is most pronounced for the Hanoverian period, when empire was largely a case of North America and the West Indies. In contrast, there has been a rejection of imperial names across much of the Victorian and Edwardian empire, especially in parts of Africa; Salisbury, for example, becoming Harare.

Across the world, Georgetowns and Charlottes testified to the reach of British power under the Hanoverians. Thus Georgetown (1735) in South Carolina was followed by Charlottesville (1744) in Virginia, and Charlotte (1750) in North Carolina, the towns providing an Hanoverian imprint in colonies, such as the Carolinas and New York, named after the Stuarts; while the westward expansion and consequent political expansion of existing colonies led to references to the new dynasty as with Brunswick and Lunenburg counties in Virginia. The royal colony of Georgia was also a testimony to the territorial expansion of British North America under the new dynasty.

In modern Canada, Île Saint-Jean, once captured from the French in

1758, was renamed Prince Edward Island. It soon had three counties, Kings, Queens and Prince, a capital at Charlottetown and another major settlement at Princetown. On the Canadian mainland, the colony of New Brunswick, created in 1784, had among its counties Kings, Queens and Charlotte, and its capital at Fredericton. Nova Scotia's counties included Kings, Queens, Cumberland and Lunenburg, and towns including Lunenburg and Windsor. In the St Lawrence Valley in Quebec after the War of American Independence, Loyalists settled in newly-surveyed townships that included Charlottesburg, Osnabruck, Williamsburg, Edwardsburg, Augusta, Kingston, Fredericksburg and Adolphustown. Guelph was a land grant to the west of Lake Ontario, and York was the settlement on that lake subsequently renamed Toronto. There was a Fort George opposite the American Fort Niagara. Posts in the fur-trading Canada interior that stretched north and west of the Great Lakes included Frederick House, Fort Charlotte, Fort William, Cumberland Houses, Fort George, and Fort Augustus I, II, III in the distant North Saskatchewan Valley. Fort George in the Rockies was joined in 1814 by New Fort George on the estuary of the Columbia river.

In addition, warships were exploring what for Britain was the 'dark side' of the Earth: the Pacific. Sailing across the Pacific in 1767, Philip Carteret 'discovered' Osnaburg, Duke of Gloucester and Queen Charlotte Islands, each named after a member of the royal family, as well as New Hanover. George III Maundy coins were supplied to Captain James Cook for burial in newly-'discovered' lands in the name of the King. Earlier, the British presence in Malaysia had begun with the establishment of a British base on the island of Penang by Francis Light in 1786: George Town was the name given to the settlement.

At the same time, it is noticeable that the use in naming of names and titles derived from the royal family declined in the early nineteenth century. There was, of course, no shortage of Georgetowns and Fort Georges, but it is still instructive to consider the dominant use instead of ministerial names in Australia and, subsequently, New Zealand. In the former, Adelaide was the most conspicuous royal name (although there was also, for example, King George Sound), contrasting rather obviously with Sydney, named after the Home Secretary, as well as Melbourne and Stanley. In New Zealand, the settlements made – Wellington (1840), Auckland (1841), and Nelson (1842) – reflected military heroes and governmental figures, rather than royalty. This was an aspect of a more profound change toward a society increasingly defined in terms of public norms of behaviour, in which the role of the royal family depended on their obvious conformity to the norms: George III played an important role in this exemplary morality, but there was then a gap until Victoria returned to the task.

When William himself died in 1837, he was succeeded by Victoria, the daughter of George III's fourth son, Edward, Duke of Kent, who had died in 1820. She had been in effect adopted by William and Adelaide as the daughter they could not have. William greatly disliked Victoria's mother, Maria Louisa Victoria, whom he publicly insulted at a banquet in 1836. A crucial part of this rift was that the Duchess had snubbed Adelaide by failing to attend her birthday celebrations (which preceded those of William by eight days), arriving only in time for those of the King. William was determined to survive until Victoria, whom he liked, came of age, on 24 May 1837, so that the Duchess of Kent should not be Regent, a position she had been appointed to in 1830 in the event of William dying while Victoria was still a minor. Despite falling seriously ill on 20 May, William succeeded in his objective, dying finally a month later, early on 20 June. He had already quarrelled with the Duchess over Victoria's establishment, as he wanted one for her that was completely separate from her mother's. William also disagreed with the Duchess over a partner for Victoria. He wanted the Prince of Orange, while the Duchess wanted Albert of Saxe-Coburg, and Melbourne wanted Victoria's cousin, later 2nd Duke of Cambridge.

William's ultimate flexibility over reform showed that his was not the cause of the reactionary ultras. Indeed, from William's reign on, the British monarchy was not conspicuously associated with the forces of political conservatism, as it would have been if for example his brother Ernest, Duke of Cumberland, had been King. Once he had succeeded to the throne of Hanover in 1837, Ernest moved against liberalism, revoking the *Staatsgrundgesetz*, the 1833 constitution granted by William, and sacking seven Göttingen professors who complained. William had also in 1831 in response to pro-reform disturbances in the kingdom, dismissed the Hanoverian leading minister, Count Ernst Friedrich Herbert von Münster, who was increasingly reactionary, and in 1833 he had agreed to the *Ablösungsordnung* that freed the peasants from the medieval feudal labour services they owed their chiefly aristocratic landowners.

A new constitution for Hanover was granted in 1840, and Ernest was convinced that his policies brought both popularity and stability,[16] but his attitudes led him to be a *bête noire* for British liberals. Earlier, while only Duke of Cumberland, Ernest had had considerable influence over George IV and had bolstered him in his opposition to reform. Cumberland had actively opposed the repeal of the Test and Corporation Acts and condemned Catholic Emancipation in the House of Lords, presenting himself as continuing the policies of George III. Cumberland's position was also demonstrated by his position as Grand Master of the Orange lodges of Ireland. Cumberland, however, was not King. Similarly, if (as seems possible) Edward VIII's political sympathies would have led in the direction of an assertive conservatism, his abdication in 1936 represented another failure for the possibility for assertive monarchy.

When William IV became King, Cumberland lost the influence he had enjoyed under George IV. This shift was demonstrated when the colonelcy of the Royal Horse Guards he had received from George in 1827 was limited when the regiment was placed under the authority of the Commander-in-Chief of the army. Seeing this as an insult, Cumberland resigned the colonelcy. In Parliament, he opposed reform and government policies including the Reform Act, the Poor Law Amendment Act of 1834 and the Municipal Corporations Act of 1835.

The latter were aspects of the legislation of William's reign that helped to sweep away the *ancien régime*. They ensured that the reign was very much a period of transition and, in many respects, more deserving of grouping with the reign of Victoria than with those of the first four Georges. Thus, in 1833, there was both a Factory Act and a Bank Charter Act. The second established the notes of the Bank of England for sums of £5 or more as legal tender throughout England and Wales – a measure of national standardisation. It also added the accountability that was a steadily greater theme of public affairs: the Bank was required to publish its accounts on a quarterly base. The abolition of slavery that year was a more prominent part of this wider reform drive, and one that clashed with earlier opposition by George III, and indeed William, to moves against the slave trade. The reforming Liberal middle-class culture of the period regarded slavery as abhorrent, anachronistic and associated with everything it deplored.

The Poor Law Amendment Act, which followed in 1834, created a centrally controlled bureaucracy, rather than the earlier, varied system of local provision. Local parishes now had to join together into 'unions' to support workhouses, which were to replace home relief. The Act ensured that workhouses and the deliberate harshness of the workhouse regime – which was intended to provide no better a standard of living than that of the lowest class of labourer outside – were an important part of the legacy of William's reign. Indeed, the notion of reformed legislation as linked with a particular reign was particularly the case for that of William.

The Municipal Corporations Act of 1835 was another important legacy of the reign. It standardised the position in England and Wales, replacing self-selecting oligarchic corporations, mostly run by Tories, and giving elected borough councils, based on a franchise of rated occupiers, control over the local police, markets and street lighting. This Act was to be the basis of an upsurge in urban politics, and it was in the towns that the middle classes first came to achieve freedom of political expression. The Tithe Commutation Act of 1836 was another important measure of standardisation, in this case part of a reform of the Church of England that stemmed from the work of the Ecclesiastical Commission. The limited character of opposition from both William and others to this remoulding of state and country was important. The widespread sense of public accountability was captured in the *Sherborne Mercury* of 6 February 1837, under the heading 'Reform Meeting at Lyme Regis':

> A public meeting was held on Thursday the 26th instant [January], at the Guildhall in this borough, the Mayor in the chair, for the purpose of enabling their respected representative, William Pinney, Esq., to state his opinions upon the leading political questions of the day, and to take the sense of his constituents on his parliamentary conduct during the past session.

There was, nevertheless, nothing predictable about political developments, especially in 1827–32, and a different attitude on the part of the last two Hanoverian monarchs might well have proved crucial. So also would have been a different position for the monarchy. That does not imply that the 'wrong' course was followed, but simply that British political culture in the early nineteenth century was changed by the decline of the monarchy in the person of one of its most flamboyant and, in many respects, pathetic figures, the self-centred George IV, a man of more sensibility than sense. William helped bequeath a secure monarchy to his neophyte niece in 1837 in part because, although he had a clear and diligent commitment to what he saw as effective government,[17] he was willing to be a bystander in the era of reform.

The process of reform, which, in due course, opened the way for considerable further constitutional, political and social change in the nineteenth and early twentieth centuries, was carried through with the active support or passive consent of successive monarchs, creating a sense that the monarchy was on the side of progress. This enduring belief contributed in a very real sense to the survival and further prospering of monarchy in Britain.

# 9

# *Hanover*

If the Court of Vienna is sincerely desirous to renew the perfect friendship and harmony which so long subsisted between them and us, they will of themselves see the necessity of doing His Majesty as Elector justice upon several points, upon which the King, and his father, have so long, and with so much reason, complained.

Instructions to Lord Waldegrave,
envoy in Vienna, 1729 [1]

The joy that greeted George IV on his trip to Hanover was genuine. The Marquess of Londonderry, the Foreign Secretary, wrote:

> The King's illness has been a great mortification to the good people here. With this important exception, every thing has gone off as well as possible; and it is impossible to witness ... more decisive proofs of attachment than the Hanoverians have shown towards the King and his family.[2]

George indeed enjoyed the visit, especially his popularity. That, however, was not only to be the sole visit that he made, either as King or earlier, but also the only visit made by a King of both Kingdoms: Hanover (which had become a kingdom in 1814) and Britain. Although William IV had visited Hanover after his marriage, he did not do so as King. The contrast between this situation and that under the first two Hanoverians underlines the difficulty of moving from the history of individual monarchs to that of the dynasty as a while. For George I and George II the dynasty's identity and agenda were heavily bound up with their native Hanover, but this appeared far less the case thereafter. It has recently, however, been suggested that George III, who, alone of the monarchs, at no stage during his life visited Hanover, became far more interested in the Electorate during his reign, in part as he became frustrated with the political situation in Britain but also because Hanover came under greater threat, first from the imperial pretensions of Joseph II and then from Prussian and Napoleonic expansionism.

These threats disappeared, however, with the coming of peace in 1814–15, when Hanover gained royal status and considerable territories. Neither George IV nor William IV therefore needed to take much interest in the Electorate. The territorial aggrandisement pursued so avidly by George I and George II was no longer a prospect, and Hanover appeared a satisfied power. If British power was a partial guarantor of this situation, it was also an aspect of a more general stabilisation that the major powers pursued after the Napoleonic Wars, and Hanover owed as much, if not more, to the Austro-Prussian order that prevailed in the German Confederation. When that order was replaced by disunity, the kingdom found itself in ultimately fatal difficulties: Austrian defeat in 1866 ensured that the map of north Germany would be redrawn by Prussia as it had been by Napoleon from 1806.

If, as members of the dynasty, George III and George IV and William IV pursued Electoral (from 1814 royal Hanoverian) goals, these were largely therefore reactive or passive; although a more active stance derived from the search for German Protestant spouses. The role of dynastic chance is also suggested by the death of Frederick, Duke of York in 1827. Had he lived to succeed George IV, the throne would have been occupied by a monarch who had much more experience of Hanover than William IV, in large part from his long tenure as Prince Bishop of Osnabrück, and one far more committed to the Continent. This, however, was not to be and the brothers who most closely resembled Frederick, Ernest and Adolphus, came after William in the succession. As a result, there were no echoes of the first two Georges, and it is unsurprising that contention about the pursuit of dynastic and Hanoverian interests focused, and still focuses, on them.

The Act of Settlement of 1701, under which the Hanoverians succeeded, stated that no war should be fought for the defence of interests that were not British without parliamentary consent, and that this consent should also be required before the monarch could leave Britain. The latter clause was repealed before George I's accession. He visited Hanover on five occasions during his reigns – in 1716, 1719, 1720, 1723 and 1725 – without having to seek approval from Parliament or from his British ministers. In 1727, George I died on his way to Hanover.

George II, who had left Hanover in 1714 and stayed in Britain while Prince of Wales, revisited the Electorate in 1729, 1732, 1735, 1736, 1740, 1741, 1743, 1745, 1748, 1750, 1752 and 1755. Many ministers were unhappy about the long absences of George I and George II and sought to limit them,[3] while there was also criticism in the press.[4] Opposition from his British ministers and from the Duchess of Kendal led George I to abandon plans to visit Hanover in 1722: as they warned, the Jacobites were hopeful that his absence would provide an opportunity for action.[5] In 1755, Earl Poulett found no support when he tried to persuade the House of Lords to address against George II's forthcoming trip to Hanover, but the King was aware that his ministers privately shared Poulett's views:

> The King was asking at court today, what was to become of Lord Poulett's motion? And being answered, dropped for want of a second, he asked the Duke of Newcastle, why *he* had not agreed to second it, as he had frequently expressed his wishes for his (the King's) staying at home. The King lately asking the Lord Chancellor, whether he did love now and then to visit his seat in Cambridgeshire; the Chancellor answered *Yes, but not in term time.*[6]

Poulett was forbidden the entrées at court, but, by avoiding public criticism, the ministers were able to maintain their stance.

The provision that no war could be fought for non-British interests without parliamentary approval was not reversed, and was, in theory, a major restriction of royal powers, greatly limiting any attempt to use British foreign policy for the support of Hanover. In contrast, there was no Parliament to be answerable to in Hanover, only regional Estates until an assembly for the entire kingdom was established in 1814, and the Elector was responsible for conducting foreign policy. Not once, however, was this parliamentary control driven home, for, far from preventing the King from acting, the Act of Settlement essentially emphasised the need for parliamentary management, and, therefore, the more general point of the practical power, rather than the formal authority, of the monarch in the political system.

This was certainly the view of critics. In January 1744 Richard Tucker suggested to his brother John, an opposition MP, that if the motion for subsidising Hanoverian troops was carried, as in fact it was to be, 'I think the nation were as good desire the administration to determine among themselves what is necessary and not give gentlemen the trouble of leaving their houses to cloak their measures with the ceremony of a consultation or giving advice'.[7] *A Letter to the Archbishop of York*, a Jacobite work of 1745, attacked 'the immoderate increase of national debts and taxes, lavished away to support' and aggrandise Hanover. Thomas Potter failed to persuade the Commons in December 1755 that recent treaties entered into to protect Hanover were violations of the Act of Settlement. The *Monitor*, an influential Pittite newspaper, complained on 18 November 1758 that 'bad ministers, without applying to Parliament, have agreed to take part in the defence of foreign dominions, under false pretences of British interest, and then found means to secure a majority in both houses'.

Aside from this political point, the terms of the Act of Settlement proved very ambiguous and unhelpful in practice. The relationship between royal rights as King and obligations as Elector constituted a new area for debate over the prerogative, one that was defined only after much disagreement. The views of George I and George II were most contentious in the late 1710s, with regard to Sweden and Russia, and in 1740–55, especially 1740–48, with regard to the Prussia of Frederick II. In both cases, this led to political disputes in Britain, as some ministers contested the royal interpretation of British interests. These criticisms have received insufficient attention, as the non-interventionist tradition of ministerial thought has generally been considered in terms of the financial concerns expressed by Walpole and Henry Pelham. There were, in fact, other intelligent reasons for doubting the wisdom of diplomatic initiatives and commitments arising essentially from the Hanoverian connection. Thus, with regard to opposition to Peter the Great in 1719–21, the Russian conquest from Sweden of Estonia, Ingria and Livonia can be seen as a challenge to British commercial interests in the Baltic. Against this, Russian economic growth was to be a fruitful basis for expanding British trade, and, whatever the supposed threat from Russia, it was not in Britain's interest to play the leading role in creating or sustaining an anti-Russian alliance of weak and divided powers. As a result of hostility to Russia, Britain was drawn into support of Denmark and meddling in Swedish politics, but neither power could contribute materially to Britain's international strength.[8]

George I was most concerned about Russia, not least because of the marriage of relatives of Peter the Great to the Dukes of Holstein-Gottorp and Mecklenburg, both of whom had disputes with him. In contrast, George II was more worried about Prussia, although in the event, conflict with another Protestant Crown broke out first with Denmark: a dispute over the territory of Steinhorst in the winter of 1738–39. This was swiftly resolved, in large part because Christian VI of Denmark lacked international support. British diplomats were used to secure backing for George's Electoral interests.[9]

Under Frederick William I (1713–40), the Prussian army appreciably increased in size. Whereas Frederick William's relations with his uncle and father-in-law, George I, although not always close, were generally respectful, those with his cousin and brother-in-law, George II, began poor, rapidly worsened, and never really improved. This gave a new direction to the legacy of confrontation left by George I. At his death in 1727, Britain, in alliance with France and the Dutch, was opposed to Spain, with which Britain had serious points in dispute, as well as to Austria, Prussia and Russia. None of the latter had serious points of dispute with Britain, but all of them were hostile until 1731, in large part as a consequence of the Hanoverian connection. Hessian troops were hired by Britain for the protection of Hanover and, in the face of domestic criticism and references to the Act of Settlement, ministers were obliged to argue that Hanoverian needs arose from its dynastic link with Britain, although the points at issue with Prussia and Russia were in fact largely Electoral in character.

From the outset of his reign, in response to concern about the possibility of an Austro-Prussian attack on Hanover, George II sought to develop a system of German alliances and to persuade France to threaten Prussia and Austria. Newcastle noted, 'His Majesty thinks that great attention should be had to the affairs of the North'. George also wished to defend the position of the Protestants in the Empire, while, in the peace congress that opened at Soissons in 1728, he wanted Hanoverian interests in Bremen, Verden and Hadeln discussed.[10] George was particularly concerned about the decree on the Mecklenburg dispute issued by the Aulic Council in Vienna on 11 May 1728; this angered him because it threatened the Hanoverian position in the duchy, by including Prussia among the administering powers, and because it emanated from a body subject to the control of the Emperor rather than the Imperial Diet where the German princes were represented.[11] George's concern was readily seen in an anxious letter from Townshend to Horatio Walpole:

> His Majesty's thoughts upon the points of Mecklenburg and Sleswig, on which he is very earnest and would not suffer the least delay to be made ... I never saw the King more displeased in my life than he was upon reading what was said in this project and your dispatches upon those two articles ... For God's sake, Dear Horace, do your best, both your reputation and mine are at stake.[12]

Austrian support for the claims of the Duke of Holstein-Gottorp led to George's concern that his restoration would endanger Hanover's hold on Bremen and Verden, and the British plenipotentiaries at the Congress were instructed to press the French to stand firm over this issue, as well as over Mecklenburg and East Friesland.[13] The representative of the Duke of Mecklenburg at The Hague had suggested to Chesterfield 'that he thought the King's Hanover dominions were so much concerned in the fate of Mecklenburg that they might almost give the law to His Majesty upon this occasion'. Although Townshend endorsed Chesterfield's rejection of this suggestion,[14] the key to much British policy lay in George's support of his interpretation of Hanoverian interests. At this stage, George himself, rather than any of his Hanoverian ministers, was the crucial figure. Those in the German Chancery in London – Jobst and Andreas von der Reiche and Johann Philipp von Hattorf – enjoyed little power, and the few contemporaries who considered their role gave it scant prominence. Although Bothmer survived until 1732, he lacked influence with George II, who, according to foreign envoys in Hanover with the King in 1729, either denied information about negotiations to the Hanoverian ministers or backed Townshend against them. Count Watsdorf, appointed Saxon envoy in London in 1730, was ordered to attach himself to the British ministers, and informed that they had the direction in all matters, including even those involving Hanoverian interests, whilst the Electoral ministers were excluded from any role.[15]

Having come close to war with Prussia in 1729, George II sought to breathe fresh life into the Hanoverian-Prussian dynastic relationship by arranging the marriage of a daughter to the Prussian heir, the future Frederick II, and of Frederick, Prince of Wales to a Prussian Princess, a scheme initially envisaged by George I. This fell victim, however, in

1730 to changing diplomatic interests and to Frederick William's violent suspicion of George II. The negotiations included a proposal for the separation of Hanover from Britain. In response to the Prussian suggestion that, if there was to be a marriage between Crown Prince Frederick of Prussia and Princess Amelia, one of them should be created Stadtholder of Hanover, and the Electorate placed under their authority, George was willing for Amelia to be Stadtholder on condition she and Frederick first live in England,[16] a condition that Frederick William I could not have been expected to accept. George's independent links to Crown Prince Frederick further aroused Frederick William's fury when the Prince sought to escape from Prussia in 1730. For the rest of the decade, relations remained poor. This was an added reason why it was important that the Second Treaty of Vienna – the reconciliation with Austria in March 1731 – brought Hanover security. Although Hanoverian territorial demands were shelved, albeit temporarily, the treaty was far from representing a defeat for George because he was only partly motivated by expansion. Security against Prussian pressure was more important.

Poor relations did not prevent rumours of renewed links between the two powers, rumours that included a new dynastic union. Thus British newspapers in January 1739 carried a report from Hanover:

> The report which has been spread that the King of Great Britain will take a tour hither next summer is confirmed by our last letters from London, which add, that his Britannick Majesty's principal view in taking that journey, is to have an interview with the King of Prussia, in order to conclude a double marriage between the two royal families, and agree upon some measures proper to be put in execution for the support of the Protestant interest. It is likewise reported that their Britannick and Prussian Majesties will conclude a treaty of alliance together, which some other princes and states will be invited to come into; and that the design of this treaty is to prevent anything that may disturb the repose and tranquility of the Empire.[17]

There was to be no such visit or alliance, but, instead, a Franco-Prussian agreement; and the failure to improve relations angered a number of diplomats who believed that a Prussian alliance was necessary for Britain. Despite their hopes that one could be negotiated, a number of disputes arising from Hanoverian interests kept the rulers, and therefore the powers, apart. Prussian recruiting for the army in neighbouring dominions particularly irritated George II. Horatio Walpole complained about the 'humours ... little views founded on jealousy etc ... pitiful notions' of George II and Frederick William I.[18] It was scarcely surprising that British ministers were not especially concerned about the, to them, unimportant Hanoverian interests, such as the succession to East Friesland, which was contested with Prussia. The British envoy in Vienna complained in 1739 that Hanoverian demands over East Friesland 'gives a real concern to those here who wish well to us, and a pretext to others to countercarry us in everything else'.[19] In 1738, ministers had to worry that another succession dispute, the Jülich-Berg question, would lead to a Prussian invasion of Hanover that would affect Britain. There was also a serious personal animus between the two monarchs. Robert Trevor had observed in 1729, 'You certainly know, that our King's contempt for his brother-in-law is as great as one man can have for another, and I dread the probable consequences of a rancour so violent and so reciprocal'.[20]

The prospect of a major conflict condemning the Electorate to be the advance guard, or forlorn hope, of an Anglo-French coalition attacked by Austria, Prussia or Russia disappeared in 1731, when the Second Treaty of Vienna was negotiated with Austria. In subsequent diplomatic realignments, Prussia became isolated, while Anglo-Russian relations eased with the commercial treaty of 1734. George II and his ministers hoped that the accession in 1740 to the Prussian throne of Frederick II, who had been given money secretly by George in the 1730s, would improve the situation. Had it done so, and good Anglo-Hanoverian-Prussian relations begun, then it is probable that Hanover would have been both secure and not an issue in British public debate. Frederick chose, however, to follow an independent course, repaying his uncle's money and attacking Austria, beginning the War of the Austrian Succession (1740–48).

The failure to create an Anglo-Hanoverian-Prussian alignment was attributed by some contemporaries to personal rivalry, dynastic competition and Hanoverian interests, but more was at stake. It was naïve to imagine that Frederick would tie himself to Britain, which since 1739 had been involved in the War of Jenkins' Ear with Spain, with the prospect of France coming to Spain's assistance. Furthermore, opportunity beckoned for Frederick in the shape of the Habsburg succession when Charles VI died. This led to his attack on Austria.

Bereft of Prussian assistance, George II had no military prospect of resisting a threatened French invasion of Hanover in 1741. He was obliged, on 25 September (ns), to accept a neutrality convention that led him to vote for Charles Albert, Elector of Bavaria, the French candidate for the imperial throne. This measure, entered into strictly in an Electoral capacity, was nevertheless disliked by his British ministers, who correctly feared that Electoral measures would be interpreted as affecting British conduct both at home and abroad. The convention hindered British attempts to create a pro-Austrian alliance, while, in Britain, it embittered discussion about foreign policy in Walpole's last session as first minister. The convention was also viewed as evidence of a ministerial failure to defend national interests, especially when (allegedly as a result of a secret clause, that did not, in fact, exist) the British fleet failed to prevent Spanish forces designed to attack Austrian Italy from landing in Italy.

Neutrality was probably the best option for Hanover. There was a long tradition of German Princes being neutral in disputes between the great powers, and, militarily, the Electorate was no more able to defend itself in 1741 than it had been in 1716 or 1729, when threatened by Russia and Prussia respectively. Indeed, an obvious feature of most German principalities, including Hanover, was that they did not take part in the increase in military strength that characterised the leading powers, a group that Prussia was able to join only with considerable difficulty. Hanover, moreover, was not protected, as was Britain, by insularity and a navy. Having failed in 1741 to create an effective alliance that could prevent Frederick II from gaining Silesia, there was no doubt of George II's second-rank status in northern Germany. This was clearly demonstrated when Frederick gained East Friesland on the death of the last Prince in 1744, a measure that George futilely complained about for years.

Neutrality, however, suited neither George nor his British ministers. Both devoted the years from 1741 until 1755 to an attempt to recreate the Grand Alliance that had fought France in the War of the Spanish Succession (1701–14; with Britain as a participant 1702–13). This attempt, however, was confused in purpose between opposition to France, the principal British goal, and hostility to Prussia, the view of George and, increasingly, of Austria. Hanover served as a means for conducting anti-Prussian negotiations that George knew would not please his British ministers, while, in 1748, the Hanoverian ministers successfully encouraged Newcastle to intervene actively in German politics, a policy that led him to cooperate increasingly with them.[21]

Fears centred on Hanoverian vulnerability helped to put British diplomacy on the defensive, as in 1753 when a Prussian attack on Hanover was anticipated, and in 1755–56 when, as conflict between Britain and France in North America became more serious, worry about Hanover resulted in a change in the direction of British policy. Concern about a French or French-sponsored Prussian attack on Hanover led George II, then on his last visit to the Electorate, to respond favourably to discussions with Frederick through his Brunswick-Wolfenbüttel relatives. The latter played an important role in the history of the royal dynasty, from George I's invasion of Brunswick-Wolfenbüttel in 1702 and his will to George IV's marital difficulties.[22]

Diplomatic measures in support of Hanover were accompanied by subsidy treaties to hire troops to aid its defence. The cost of the latter made not only the Hanoverian link but also the position of the crown controversial. Thus in January 1744 the Earl of Sandwich, then an opposition Whig, urged the House of Lords to heed what he saw as the general national opposition to Hanover:

> It may be hoped that these sentiments will be adopted, and these resolutions formed by every man who hears, what is echoed through the nation, that the British have been considered as subordinate to their own mercenaries; mercenaries whose service was never rated at so high a price before, and who never deserved even the petty price at which their lives used to be valued; that foreign slaves were exalted above the freemen of Great Britain, even by the King of Great Britain, and that on all occasions, on which one nation could be preferred to the other, the preference was given to the darling Hanoverians.

The previous month, the Lords' protest over the payment of Hanoverian troops had referred to the wider importance of good relations between crown and nation:

> the willingness of the States General [Dutch] ... or any other power in Europe, to enter into a closer conjunction with us, at this critical time, must chiefly depend upon the idea they shall conceive of the state of this

nation at home, especially with regard to the greater or lesser degree of union and harmony, which shall appear to subsist between His Majesty and his People.[23]

In turn, George I and George II used Hanover as an issue with which to judge courtiers and ministers. Viscount Cobham, explaining the resignation of his commission in 1743, claimed 'I have already felt severe marks of His Majesty's displeasure for differing in opinion with his ministers in Parliament'.[24]

If Hanover led to the Anglo-Prussian Convention of Westminster of January 1756, which guaranteed the respective possessions of George II and Frederick II, as well as German neutrality, that was intended to supplement, not replace, British agreements with Austria and Russia; instead, the convention helped lead to the collapse of these alliances. The Hanoverian government's hope in the subsequent struggle that it would be possible to secure neutrality for the Electorate and its allies – Hesse-Cassel, Wolfenbüttel and Prussian Westphalia – was rendered fruitless by the determination of France to attack Prussia from the west. It was the Electorate that reaped the failure of this diplomatic strategy when, in 1757, French forces overran it. William, Duke of Cumberland, with the 'Army of Observation' of Hanoverians and allied German forces, was defeated by the French at Hastenbeck on 26 July. On 8 September, the outnumbered and outmanoeuvred Cumberland signed the Convention of Klosterzeven, disbanding his army and leaving the French in control of Hanover. Frederick II, attacked by Austria, France, Russia and Sweden, could not defend Hanover as well.

Like the neutrality convention of 1741, Klosterzeven revealed the limited value to Hanover of its ruler's great power diplomacy. The emptiness of such a policy without significant military force had been displayed. Although George II had benefited from, and fostered, the willingness of Carteret and Newcastle to support an active continental diplomacy that entailed the creation of an international system that would guarantee Hanover, the weakness of both policy and arrangements had been revealed in 1756–57. Hanover's place in great power diplomacy, instead, stemmed from its vulnerability and its consequent use by other states to try to affect British policy.

The impact of Hanoverian interests on the attitudes and policies of George III, and on British foreign policy during his reign, was for long relatively neglected. In part, this reflected their lesser prominence compared to the situation under George I and George II, and in part the newly-acceded George III's deliberate association with British concerns. In 1751, this had been predicted by the diplomat Sir Charles Hanbury-Williams:

> The grief at Hanover for the death of the late Prince of Wales [Frederick] is very great. They look upon themselves (and I hope with reason) as likely to become in reality a province subservient to the interests of Great Britain, and it is high time they should be so for during my stay at Hanover last summer I saw so much of the insolence of those ministers that it made me sick. But now I think the scene must change for tis impossible that a Prince [George III] not born there can possibly like such a poor scrubby town and such barren and melancholic country.[25]

Indeed, in 1761 George III 'gloried in the name of Britain',[26] and also abandoned his grandfather's attempt to acquire Hildesheim as a reward to Hanover for its participation in the Seven Years War. In response to the direction of policy, Newcastle became far less concerned about the King's Hanoverian advisors and, instead, was worried about Bute.

In recent decades, however, there has been a marked revival of interest in the role of Hanover during the reign.[27] The fruitful nature and high quality of this work, and its understandable focus on signs of Hanover's importance, have led to a tendency to exaggerate the latter. Indeed, although George III did not take revenues out of Hanover, the absence of the ruler was in part responsible for the relative lack of political, economic and social change in the Electorate, certainly compared to that in those German states, such as Prussia, where the 'Enlightened Despots' took a more interventionist role. Nevertheless, there were episodes in which concerns about the Electorate did have a major impact on British policymaking.

Hanover had not played a major role in the 1760s. George III was more concerned about domestic and imperial topics, and foreign policy was dominated by relations with France and Spain, more specifically disputes over colonial interests. Indeed, angered by George's lack of interest in backing the Elector Palatine against the decision of the Imperial Aulic Council in the Elector's dispute with the city of Aachen, the Palatine foreign minister complained that George was overly pro-Austrian and insufficiently forceful.[28]

Hanover played a more prominent role in the 1770s. The possibility that Britain would take a firm line in response to the seizure by Austria, Prussia and Russia of much of Poland in 1772 in the First Partition of Poland was regarded as lessened by the threat of an attack on Hanover. A London report in the *Bristol Gazette and Public Advertiser* of 30 April 1772 noted:

> It is generally imagined by those who seem best acquainted with the secret springs of government, that the dread of a Prussian army in the Electorate of Hanover has altered the intentions of our court relative to the propriety of sending a squadron up the Baltic.

Relations between Hanover and Austria deteriorated in the 1770s, as the Electoral government opposed what it saw as the Emperor Joseph II's dictatorial attitude in the Empire, while Joseph was angered by Hanoverian independence in the Imperial Diet. In 1774 the Austrian envoy in London threatened to suspend all relations with Hanover, while in Vienna they were regarded as broken. The Hanoverian minister attached to George in London from 1771 until 1795, Johann Friedrich Carl von Alvensleben, declared that Joseph was the chief, but not the master, of the Empire. Tension was reflected in the British press, with a report that the Austrian envoy had declared that 'If the King of Great Britain avowed the language lately held by his Electoral minister, he must expect the Emperor to oppose him in every step he took in the Empire'.[29]

Antagonism between Joseph II and George as Elector led the latter towards Frederick II of Prussia, and it is not surprising that, during the War of the Bavarian Succession (1778–79), the Elector adopted a pro-Prussian position, to the anger of British diplomats such as Robert Murray Keith, envoy in Vienna, who feared that this policy was needlessly irritating to Joseph.[30] George's growing interest in German politics reflected, to a considerable extent, his opposition to change in the Empire, a sentiment that most German rulers shared. This helped to perpetuate the decentralised imperial political system at a time when, in most of Europe, attempts were being made to strengthen central government. Just as George I had opposed the efforts of the Emperor Charles VI to stress the authority of imperial courts over disputes between German rulers, and George II had sought to stop Frederick II's invasion of Silesia and the development of two-power Austro-Prussian preponderance in the Empire, so George III was concerned about

Joseph II's attempt to increase Austrian power within the Empire. Generally happy to see Austria strong in Italy and eastern Europe, the Electors of Hanover were deeply concerned about Austrian power and the use of imperial authority inside the Empire. There was a genuine problem in combining Hanoverian policy and, in particular, the need to respond to specific issues and initiatives by other German states, with the British aspiration for better relations with Austria. It was too easy to British diplomats and ministers who sought the latter, and who believed that it was in Austria's interests, to blame their failure on Hanover, underestimating the impact of other factors that lessened the chances of better relations.

Although suspicious about Prussian intentions, George and his Hanoverian ministers moved closer to Prussia in 1784,[31] and news of the Austrian plan to exchange the Austrian Netherlands for Bavaria lent urgency to this alignment. Frederick, Duke of York, George's favourite son, who was resident as Prince Bishop of Osnabrück, was tangible proof of George's growing personal commitment to Hanover, and played a major role in the negotiations. He also warned George that Joseph II's brother, Max Franz, who in 1784 became Prince Bishop of Münster on Hanover's borders, was also seeking the coadjutorship (succession) of the prince-bishoprics of Paderborn and Hildesheim.[32] The latter extended to within a few miles of the city of Hanover and helped separate it from the southern portion of the Electorate. Habsburg power so close was unwelcome.

George responded rapidly to Prussian approaches in early 1785,[33] more so than his Hanoverian ministers, who had to be pushed on by George and York, a contrast that was hardly new; indeed, the tendency in British public debate to treat Hanover as a unit motivated by clear Hanoverian concerns was generally inaccurate. At Berlin, on 23 July 1785, representatives of Prussia, Hanover and Saxony signed a treaty agreeing to the preservation of the imperial system as currently constituted, to cooperation at the Imperial Diet, and to opposition to the Bavarian exchange and any similar further projects.[34] The resulting *Fürstenbund*, or League of Princes, which grew rapidly in the following months, met with serious Austrian and Russian complaints which were held to harm British diplomatic interests, particularly the hope of improved relations with the two powers.

Hanoverian participation in the *Fürstenbund* led to an upsurge of criticism in the British press of specific aspects of the Hanoverian connection, such as the patronage of German plays, music and army officers by the royal family, and the 'Germanic' habit of excluding the public from royal gardens. This was extended to the education of royal princes at Göttingen: in 1786, Princes Ernest, Augustus and Adolphus were sent there to university. Moves against British trade in both Austria and Russia were blamed on the *Fürstenbund*.[35] The *Fürstenbund* also led to a widely-held view that George was controlling British policy for the benefit of Hanover and Prussia. George indeed took an active role in seeking the support of German Princes for the league. Fox and Viscount Stormont, both leading opposition politicians, told the Austrian envoy that George was not only very attached to Hanover but also kept his British ministers in the dark about German affairs. The leading Austrian minister, Prince Kaunitz, also asked how the British ministry could believe an Austrian alliance possible, given George's views.[36] Indeed, the Russian envoy in London, Count Vorontsov, reported George as greatly influenced by Alvensleben and York, both of whom had Prussian links, and as overriding Pitt. In practice, this *secret du roi* was largely restricted to German politics, rather than dominating the whole of foreign policy. Thus, at a crucial moment in the Dutch crisis in 1787, York saw Frederick William II of Prussia on behalf of George, but it was to discuss the coadjutorship of Mainz, on which Hanover and Prussia were cooperating, not Dutch affairs.[37] In 1791, Frederick married Frederica, Princess Royal of Prussia, although they swiftly separated.

Frederick's marriage, which involved trying issues of etiquette as well as practicalities, such as York's concern that Frederica's trousseau should not incur import duties,[38] is a reminder, like the dispatch of the Princes to Göttingen, that the links between the royal family and Germany were many and varied. As Elector, George III encouraged the development of Hanover, particularly its economy and its educational facilities, although this was largely a matter of responding to initiatives by the ministerial council in Hanover. George's personal commitment emerges more clearly in cultural matters, as he wished to ensure a princely effect in his Hanover palaces. Aside from having the palace of Herrenhausen restored, and having two carriages made in London and sent over to Hanover in 1781, George played an active role in creating the largest and best-documented silver service of any made for a German court in the eighteenth century: he was determined on having a new service in Hanover, and one in the new Neoclassical style, rather than a Rococo one. Most of the inherited silver service, a Rococo design, was melted to pay for the new service. Sample designs for a new service were commissioned from the French goldsmith Robert-Joseph Auguste in 1772, and the first pieces were sent to London for George to approve them. The last delivery was made in 1786, by when a service for seventy-two people was available. All was prepared for George's long-promised visit. More mundanely, George had turnips and ham imported from Hanover for the royal table in England.[39]

The wars with France led to a crisis for Hanover, greater and more sustained than any it had hitherto faced. A subsidy treaty between Britain and Hanover was concluded in 1793, but France was not the sole power that had to be confronted. Prussia's decision to leave the war in 1795 led to a neutrality for North Germany to which George adhered as Elector, but a neutrality in which the Electorate was still menaced.[40] In 1801, Prussia, which had long wished to seize Hanover, did so with the encouragement of Paul I of Russia and Napoleon, using the excuse of British actions against the Armed Neutrality of Baltic powers. Prussia, however, restored control that October when Alexander I of Russia reversed his assassinated father's policies, encouraged by the entry of a British fleet into the Baltic after the Danish fleet had been crushed by Nelson off Copenhagen on 2 April. The entire episode showed Hanover's vulnerability, and also its dependence on British assistance. Left to its own devices, it would simply have been another principality vulnerable to Prussian schemes, as a result of the disruption created, or encouraged, by the French wars.

The Peace of Amiens of 1802 between Britain and France brought temporary respite, but, after war resumed the following year, the French rapidly occupied the entire Electorate of Hanover, although supposedly neutral, despite Prussian and Russian requests for the observance of this neutrality. On 3 June the Hanoverian army capitulated by the Convention of Suhlingen. The royal linen, the silver furniture and plate, and the white horses of the Hanover stud, were hastily evacuated; the silver, amounting to seventy crates, arriving in London in December 1803.

Frederick William III of Prussia was himself still keen to acquire

Hanover. In 1803 he decided to occupy it once French troops withdrew, and, by a secret article in the Potsdam Convention with Russia of 3 November, bound Alexander I to press Britain to cede Hanover to him. The outbreak of the War of the Third Coalition in 1805 freed Hanover from French occupation, but Napoleon's victory over the Austrians and Russians at Austerlitz on 2 December 1805 changed the situation, making Frederick William's possession of Hanover dependent on Napoleon. Accordingly, in a treaty signed at Schönbrunn on 15 December 1805, Prussia got Hanover, fulfilling Napoleon's goal of harming the chances of an Anglo-Prussian reconciliation, but it had to accept support for French objectives in Europe and to cede territory to France and its ally Bavaria. Frederick William occupied Hanover, although he did not annex it because that might have entailed war with Britain.

In 1805, the British had sent troops to north Germany to act against France and to restore Electoral authority in Hanover, but Prussia's decision to back Napoleon made the expedition redundant and the force was evacuated. The Ministry of All the Talents, which succeeded the Pitt government after the death of William Pitt in 1806, was reduced to seeking the return of Hanover as part of a peace treaty with France that Napoleon was unwilling, despite negotiations in 1806, to concede.[41] Instead, the fate of the former Electorate was settled by Napoleon's victory over Prussia at Jena in 1806 – he moved rapidly and decisively after good relations collapsed – and it was transferred to become part of a shifting world of French client states and territorial arrangements. The Hanoverians were among the less keen of the subjects of the new kingdom of Westphalia created in 1807 for Napoleon's brother Jerome Bonaparte: in 1810 the Electorate was totally incorporated into the new kingdom. Many fought on in exile for George III, serving from 1803 in the King's German Legion, mostly in Portugal, Spain and Sicily; their action helped greatly to reduce anti-Hanoverian sentiment in Britain. Meanwhile, George III had shown his continued concern in February 1805 by organising a patriotic celebration with a German theme in Windsor Castle. German music was performed and the Hanover silver was used for the meal. The following year, George declared that the occupation of Hanover affected the honour of his crown, and that he would never cede the Electorate.

The Congress of Vienna of 1814–15, which brought the Napoleonic

Wars to a close, saw not only Britain's status as the strongest imperial power confirmed but also a strengthening of Hanover. During the wars, territorial borders had shifted, but the common theme had been the extinction of Hanoverian independence. The Congress saw the recreation of an independent Hanover, as well as its gain of royal status, proclaimed by the Prince Regent on 26 October 1814 and swiftly recognised at the Congress. Hanover also gained territory, so that in 1815 it was the fourth largest state in Germany, after Austria, Prussia and Bavaria, and the fifth largest in population. Although this was impressive, it has to be set in context. As a German monarchy, Hanover was far from unique: Bavaria, Prussia, Saxony and Württemberg were also kingdoms. Secondly, the territorial gains were modest. Hanover gained East Friesland, Hildesheim and Osnabrück at last, and also part of the former prince bishopric of Münster, but these gains were far less than those of Prussia, and were also less impressive than the gains made by Bavaria and Württemberg over the French Revolutionary and Napoleonic period. Unlike Prussia, which gained much of the Rhineland as a result of the Vienna settlement, Hanover remained only a regional presence. Even that had weaknesses: Lauenburg was lost to Denmark, while, far from Hanover absorbing neighbouring principalities, Hamburg and Bremen remained Imperial Free Cities, and Oldenburg, Brunswick, Lippe-Detmold and Schaumburg-Lippe continued to be independent. Territorially, the continued independence of Oldenburg was the biggest anomaly, but it was necessary for dynastic reasons, as the house was linked to the Russian royal family. Furthermore, dynastic links between Hanover and the house of Brunswick (formerly Brunswick-Wolfenbüttel), which had continued with the marriages of George III's sister Augusta and of the Prince Regent, and also with the houses of Lippe, were such that their acquisition would not have seemed appropriate.

British diplomatic influence might have helped Hanover, but it did more for the house of Orange, which gained the crown of the United Netherlands and added rule over what became Belgium to its position in what became the Netherlands, an arrangement that was to be overturned by rebellion in 1830. The two houses were related as a consequence of the marriage of Anne, the Princess Royal, to William IV of Orange in 1734. Furthermore, another British ally, the kingdom of Sardinia, also did well from the Congress, gaining not only the restoration of its territories but also the hitherto independent republic of Genoa. The continued exposure of Hanover to possible invasion had been shown in January 1815 when a difference between the powers over the future of Saxony, with Britain, France and Austria signing a secret treaty for mutual defence in the event of war with Prussia and Russia over Prussia's control of Saxony, was followed by Hanover's accession to the treaty, which underlined its vulnerability in the event of war: in this case, to a Prussian and Russian attack which fortunately did not come as the issue was settled.

Once the new territorial settlement was in place, Hanover had to absorb its new acquisitions, repair the damage of occupation, and adjust to the new German constitution also created by the Congress. Prussia had sought to dominate the new German Confederation in cooperation with Austria, but was thwarted by the opposition of the second-rank German states, especially Bavaria and Württemberg. The result was a loose confederation of states that were inherently independent, but this left Hanover in a very different situation to Bavaria and Württemberg, as Prussia clearly dominated northern Germany. Adaptation to shifts in German power, specifically Prussian policy, dominated Hanoverian politics thereafter. William IV was a keen opponent of Prussian domination, but this adaptation was far less central to the British ministry than had been the case a century earlier.[42] This was reflected in governmental arrangements. Although, on his visit to Hanover in 1821 (in which he used the silver service evacuated in 1803 and returned in 1814), George IV was crowned and met with an enthusiastic response, not least by speaking German, he and William IV, who never visited it as King, did not display the close attention shown under George I. Also, although Count Ernst Friedrich Herbert von Münster, the head of the German Chancery in London, was influential with George IV, who trusted him, he was, as far as the British ministers were concerned, no Bernstorff or Bothmer. Münster had supported the idea of a larger Hanover to restrict Prussia's expansion and help ensure that Germany was not dominated by an Austro-Prussian dualism, but while he remained important after the war he was no challenge to Castlereagh's position.

George III's youngest son, Adolphus, Duke of Cambridge, who had been Colonel in Chief of the King's German Legion, was appointed in 1813 Military Governor of Hanover, in which capacity he attended the

1814 Guildhall banquet for the allied sovereigns held to celebrate Napoleon's defeat. From 1816, Adolphus was General Governor, a position he held until the death of William IV; while in February 1831 he was made Viceroy which shifted the weight of government more to Hanover, and was linked to the dismissal of the reactionary Münster. The role of the German Chancery was diminished, as the Viceroy was given authority to run domestic policy. William IV was to be informed of decisions, but his prior consent was not required. William also retained control of foreign policy. Earlier, Cambridge had been unable to create strong links between British and Hanoverian policymaking. In part, this reflected personality and institutional arrangements – Cambridge was not a key figure, while, as governor, although popular, he lacked significant power over the Hanoverian ministry, a situation that reflected the coherence and institutional tradition of the latter;[43] but there were also important long-term shifts.

The non-political interests linking Britain and Hanover had always been slight. They became more so as Britain developed an increasingly oceanic identity, while a stronger sense of Hanoverian interest and identity was seen in 1824 when an order from London that six thousand troops be sent to Portugal was rejected by the Hanoverian ministers, drawing attention both to the opposition of the Hanoverian Estates, a body set up in 1814, and to recent regulations that decreed that Hanoverian troops should not be used abroad for foreign ends. In the 1830s, Palmerston, the British Foreign Secretary, had scant influence over Hanoverian policy.[44] Although Hanover benefited from the link with Britain, for example from the access to British consular services, there was no comparison with the economic partnership between England and Scotland, with the latter contributing much to, and profiting greatly from, British imperial expansion. Hanover's enforced membership of Napoleon's Continental System had cut economic links with Britain and underlined its very different economic alignment. In theory, there was a complementarity between Hanover and Britain that could have served as the basis of strong links: Hanover was agricultural and Britain needed to import food to feed its rapidly growing population. In turn, Hanover lacked a strong industrial base, and could have served not only as a market but also as the base for British exports to elsewhere in Germany; indeed it served as a market for British industrial goods until 1837.

The prospect of greater economic cooperation, however, lacked strong political backing and fell foul of growing German protectionist pressure. In some respects, this was symptomatic of a new political order, one that was increasingly focused on the politics of trade and that employed trade in order to define political identity. Hanover had not joined the Prussian-organised Customs Union created in 1818; instead, concerned about Prussian moves, Hanover helped to found the Central German Customs Union in 1828. It also did not join the Prussian-dominated *Zollverein* or German Customs Union founded in 1834, becoming instead part of a tax union with Brunswick and Oldenburg. In 1851, however, Hanover joined the *Zollverein*. Already, in the late 1830s, there had been anger in Britain over Hanoverian tolls which affected British trade via the Elbe, the major route for British goods entering Germany.[45]

The religious rationale, in the shape of British anti-Catholicism, that had led to the Hanoverian succession now seemed irrelevant and, at least legally, had been largely dismantled in Britain, although it continued to affect the marital options of the royal family. In the face of growing Prussian power, an independent Hanover also seemed irrelevant: once the personal union ended in 1837, this issue was not something that greatly concerned British ministers or the British public; the Hanoverian connection had not put down deep roots, and King Ernest's revocation of the 1833 constitution affected British attitudes, angering the Whigs and embarrassing the Tories. The role of the Hanoverian line became less important once, from 1840, Victoria had a child. A keen admirer of Prussia, who had lived for much of the 1820s in Berlin, King Ernest died in 1851, having overcome radical tendencies in Hanover during the Year of Revolutions in 1848. He was succeeded by George V of Hanover, his only son, who was blind. Like his grandfather, George III, George V was very keen on music.

Hanover itself was overrun by the Prussians in 1866 when it supported Austria in the Austro-Prussian Seven Weeks War. The Hanoverians under General Alexander von Arentschildt defeated the troops of the Prussian General Edward Moritz von Flies at Langensalza on 27 June, but, due to their being cut off from all supplies and now outnumbered, had to surrender to von Falckenstein two days later.[46] As a result the Prussians overran Hanover and Hesse-Cassel, which were annexed by Prussia, thus uniting Prussia with its Rhenish territories. Queen Victoria's muted response included the view that it would not be expedient to protest about the annexation, and that 'a reunion of Hanover with this Country is by no means an event to be desired'.[47] Refusing to accept the annexation and never giving up his royal title, although he did not adopt that of Duke of Cumberland after 1866, George V went into exile in Vienna, taking the silver service with him, and lived until 1878.

George's claim was inherited by his son Ernst August (1845–1923), who did adopt the title Duke of Cumberland. He did not renounce the claim to Hanover in exchange for the duchy of Brunswick in 1913, but the German Emperor Wilhelm II did not insist on this point: William IV, in 1836, had agreed with the Duke of Brunswick that if the male line of Hanover or Brunswick became extinct the other would inherit. In 1913, Wilhelm II's daughter Victoria Louise married Ernst August's son, another Ernst August (1887–1953). The duchy of Brunswick was lost when the Weimar Republic was founded after the First World War, while the Cumberland title was removed by the British crown in response to the elder Ernst August's role in the war. The line continued with another Ernst August (1914–87), whose sister Frederica married the future King Paul of Greece in 1947, becoming the mother of King Constantine of Greece, who was driven from the throne in 1967, and of Sophia, who married King Juan-Carlos of Spain. Ernst August successfully won his legal case to be declared a British subject. His son, another Ernst August (1954-), who in 1999 married Princess Caroline of Monaco, uses the title Prince of Hanover.

# Achievement

Parties are now abolished, and the King is King of his united and
unanimous people, and enjoys their confidence and love to such a
degree, that were I not as fully convinced as I am of his Majesty's
heart, and the moderation of his will, I should tremble for the
liberties of my country.

Philip, 4th Earl of Chesterfield on the early months
of George III's reign, 1761 [1]

The seventeenth century in British history attracts popular attention as
the age in which the constitution was contested: Charles I was executed,
James II and VII driven from the throne, and parliamentary government
established.[2] In contrast, the Hanoverian age appears less heroic and
less important: the imagination moves from re-enacting the Civil War
battles of the 1640s to recreating the apparently more peaceful and
stable world of Jane Austen of the 1790s.

This approach underrates the drama of the Hanoverian age, whether
Bonnie Prince Charlie's troops marching to Derby in 1745 or the British
troops bombarded into surrender at Yorktown in 1781, or the crises that
in fact challenged Austen's Britain, with Nelson dying as the French and
Spanish fleets were smashed at Trafalgar in 1805. Politically, the period
also saw both the working through of earlier events, and a process of
adaptation and change in constitutional and governmental arrangements. To kill a King, as in 1649, attracts attention, but it is much harder
to get a political system to work, and that was the crucial role played
by the monarchs and ministers of the Hanoverian age.

Parliamentary monarchy is the usual formula used to describe the
system, but its neatness is deceptive. If rulers were constrained, or at
least affected, by the need to find ministers who could manage Parliament, the nuances of that relationship still contained plentiful material

for dispute. The crucial issue, as the Hanoverians all saw, was the appointment of ministers, and that is why it bulks so large in this account, but generally it was only necessary for the monarch to find ministries acceptable to himself. Acceptance by Parliament would follow in normal circumstances, as, by a mixture of patronage and moral support from the monarch, and loyalty from most MPs, the King's choice commanded a majority. The alternative advocated by Charles James Fox – parliamentary majorities, rather than royal choice, as the basis of ministries – was a minority view in the 1780s. Fox was a maverick who wanted to change the constitution and whose ideas were widely rejected; hence the erosion of Fox and North's majority in the Commons against Pitt the Younger in early 1784 and the verdict of the subsequent general election in favour of Pitt and George. There was a whiff of republicanism about Fox and his friends that put them well outside the general run of politicians angling for power, for republicanism had scant support among the political elite.

In the absence of unified parties with clear leadership on the modern pattern, let alone with a continuous nationwide organisation, it was possible for the ruler to seek to create a ministry around the most acceptable politician who might be able to manage Parliament, and, conversely, to keep at a distance those whom he disliked. As a result, ministers sought to persuade the King to view their rivals critically, as Newcastle was able to persuade George II to do of the Duke of Bedford and the Earl of Sandwich in 1751.[3] Secondly, even if the monarch had to accept ministers who were not his first choice, as in 1720, 1742, 1744, 1746, 1757, 1763, 1765, 1782, 1783, 1806, 1828, 1832 and 1835, it was possible for him to try to use a ministry that could manage Parliament in order to win support for royal interests. George I and George II were reasonably successful in this. Major politicians sought to win the cooperation of the crown, not to limit its power. If royal wishes were thwarted, as over the jettisoning of the government's international and domestic policies in 1720, or later over Catholic Emancipation in 1828 and, far less overtly, parliamentary reform in 1832, this was presented as a bowing to necessity in which the ministers assisted the monarch to that end. Under George I and George II there was general satisfaction, indeed a considerable measure of complacency in Whig circles, about the Revolution Settlement, in so far as the constitution was concerned, and critics of disturbing features in the political system tended to blame ministerial corruption rather than royal activity. There was a separate, although linked, Jacobite critique of monarch and ministers, but that had little influence in political circles, especially after the institution of one-party Whig government following the accession of George I in 1714.

The tendency to blame ministers, rather than the crown, was hardly novel, the evil minister having been a persistent theme of political diatribe for centuries, but it was accentuated by the annual meeting of Parliament that stemmed from the financial provisions of the Revolution Settlement. This also led to an increased stress on parliamentary man-agement, the resulting focusing of patronage on parliamentary votes, and the need for George I and George II, foreign rulers who spent considerable time abroad and were unsure of domestic politics, to rely on British managers, rather as local expertise directed control towards parliamentary 'undertakers' in Dublin. This practice had advantages for the crown, although it was not the case that George I and George II were able simply to follow their own policies, while political tension was focused on their first ministers, especially Sunderland, Walpole and Carteret. The Kings had to be willing at least on occasion to adapt their policies to ministerial needs. Nevertheless, especially if their policies did not involve cost, the Kings enjoyed considerable leeway, because these policies, however unpopular, did not cause anxieties to the extent that those of Charles II and, still more James II and VII, had done.

From the reign of George III, the situation changed. George III, George IV and William IV found that ministries they did not want, such as those of Rockingham, Fox-North, and Melbourne, sought to push through unacceptable policies. There were several reasons for this shift. First, whereas Whig ministries had been bound to George I and George II by a fear of Jacobitism, this, due to the weakness of Jacobitism after Culloden, was no longer so from the late 1740s. Indeed, the room for manoeuvre enjoyed by the elderly George II in the political crisis of 1754–57 was lessened by the impossibility of uniting Whigs on an anti-Jacobite and anti-Tory platform, although this worked in his favour as well, as he did not want to be constrained by a united Whig ministry as he had been in 1746.

Secondly, the accession of George III was followed by a more troubling agenda in domestic and imperial politics. George I and George II had concentrated their attention on foreign policy, in particular, on the details of German affairs. Although subsidies for Hanover and the conduct of Hanoverian troops caused outrage in 1742–44, it was difficult to arouse public or sustained political interest in the details of German politics. Indeed, this helped explain the contrast between the fate of these monarchs and those of the Stuarts. Allowing for the extraordinary agitation in 1742–44 over the subsidising of Hanoverian troops, there was a contrast between the consequences of Charles II's secret negotiations with Louis XIV of France preparatory to their joint attack upon the Dutch in 1672, negotiations in which, in broad terms, Charles promised to declare his conversion to Catholicism and to restore the religion to England, and the attempt by George I, in 1719–20, to create a European coalition to drive the Russians from their recent Baltic conquests; or that by George II in 1750–53, to procure the election of the Habsburg heir, the future Joseph II, as King of the Romans and, therefore, next Emperor. Both of the latter steps could be, and were, presented as measures that were not in Britain's interests, although ministerial apologists disagreed. Each, instead, especially the former, could be seen as designed to further Hanoverian views. Yet neither was particularly controversial because they were not central to British political debate, and the costs (and, in the first case, economic disruption) entailed did not impact greatly on the domestic situation. War had weakened Stuart monarchs because doubts about their domestic intentions led politicians to seek to use the opportunities that parliamentary control over war finance presented to curtail their power. Among the groups with parliamentary influence, these anxieties were less strong in the case of the Hanoverians. They, in turn, were freer to pursue their policies than the Stuarts had been, and war had less detrimental consequences on their power than it had for the Stuarts, even though it could affect their freedom to choose the first minister or political manager, as in 1742, 1744, 1746, 1756, and 1757.

The Hanoverians were very different from the Stuarts in that despite High Church concerns, especially in 1714–22, their attitudes and policies did not rouse fears about religion, nor their religion fears about their attitudes and policies, with all the capacity for engendering tension that these fears aroused. The importance of this is now more evident as work on the period increasingly stresses the centrality of religion to senses of identity and its importance in politics. This perspective necessarily leads to a stress on the attraction of the Hanoverians over the Stuarts. It also downplays the role of pressure for constitutional change as the driver of politics. Whereas politics could oppose monarch to at least part of the nation, as with the Wilkesite agitation of the 1760s, religion did not provide such difficulties, at least in England, Wales and Hanover, although the situation was less happy in Scotland and Ireland. In Scotland, the numerous Episcopalians were alienated by the consequences of the Revolution Settlement, which replaced them as the Established Church by the Presbyterians. In Ireland, the Presbyterians and, even more, the Catholics were alienated by the Anglican ascendancy. Thus, an emphasis on the role of religious factors in political identities and disputes directs attention to the British question, or rather questions. This was a situation shared with the Tudors and the Stuarts, but one in which the Hanoverians were happy to follow advice. Not least this was because they lacked any personal commitment to Scotland or Ireland; certainly, to the details of their politics. Thus, in Scotland, the working through of the consequences of the Union continued, and the monarchs did nothing to discourage stabilisation, while, in Ireland, there was an acceptance of Union, although, crucially, George III thwarted his ministers' support for Catholic Emancipation.

From the accession of George III in 1760 the Hanoverian issue receded as a source of contention. George was not particularly associated in the public mind with the Electorate, most clearly because he never went there, while the end of the Jacobite challenge helped reduce the Whig emphasis on the value of the Protestant Succession and, even more, the polemical focus on Hanover by opposition politicians. In contrast, George was more associated with domestic issues that were contentious in their own right and in which the role of the monarch was particularly sensitive. This was true of the choice of ministers in the 1760s and early 1780s, of policy towards the North American colonies from 1765 until 1783, and of Catholic Emancipation.

Linked to the contentiousness of these domestic issues was the willingness and ability of some politicians to create a coherent connection or party that focused much of its ideology and energy on hostility to what was seen as royal attitudes and views. The theme of the King as a pernicious political force taking a malevolent role in British affairs was strongly revived in the 1760s, after two reigns in which criticism of the monarch arose largely from their Hanoverian concerns. George III's opponents argued that he acted in an unconstitutional fashion, and Whig historians naturally believed them. It was, however, the assertion of royal will that was crucial. The real problem in the eyes of the politicians, whatever they alleged, was not George's unconstitutional tendencies, but the opposite: that, for the first time since William III, a monarch was determined to deploy to the full powers that could be seen as his; although, in terms of political practice, the novelty entailed by George's attitudes and policies seemed unconstitutional to critics. Except in May 1765, when George III climbed down, yielding to George Grenville's demand that James Stuart Mackenzie, Bute's brother, be dismissed as Lord Privy Seal for Scotland and lose his control of government management and policy in Scotland,[4] the King was prepared for confrontation, although he complained that it would ruin his health. He displayed a cool nerve, total conviction of rectitude and a bloody-minded determination to have his way that flowed from the assumption that he alone was taking a principled stand and that led others to regard him as peremptory.[6] Opponents were enraged, spiteful and helpless. The myth of despotism was their only recourse, although discontent over the actions of a young monarch was less politically destabilising than the belief that he had no right to rule because of the claims of another dynasty, as had been the case with the Jacobite challenge to George I and George II.

George III found that he was expected by many politicians to obey an unwelcome set of unwritten conventions that dictated his selection of ministers. At the outset of his reign, George encountered the argument of the Duke of Devonshire, a member of the inner cabinet inherited from George II, that he should retain George II's ministers:

> The Duke of Newcastle had united with him the principal nobility, the moneyed men and that interest which had brought about the [Glorious] Revolution, had set this Family [the Hanoverian dynasty] on the throne, and supported them in it, and were not only the most considerable party but the true solid strength that might be depended on for the support of government ... they were infallibly the people that the King must trust to for the effectual support of his government.[6]

George III, George IV and William IV had other views, and, in rejecting

Old Corps dominance, George III was far from alone. The Earl of Bath, an experienced politician (until 1742 William Pulteney), reflected in June 1762:

> I fear he will have a very troublesome reign; those who have lately turned out, or resigned as they call it, in my opinion were suffered to stay in too long, and get too great a power in Parliament but if we have a little good fortune abroad, and obtain a good peace, and show that we are determined to pursue steadily right and popular measures at home and above all that the King appears to be resolute and steadfast, I think it may still do, and numbers may be persuaded to stick by a young King rather than an old minister. We were very lately, I think, going into an aristocracy or what is worse a King governed by one set of men, and his people by nothing but corruption.[7]

Bath was correct to identify chance factors: Bute proved a broken reed. There was also a more structural tension over the issue of party: George III thought party factious, but the Duke of Richmond wrote of Lord North in 1771,

> I had a great objection to him, and that is that he is a single man ... That as such I thought he ought not to be the minister of this country, for that as such a man did not depend upon the opinion of the world for his consequence but merely upon the King's pleasure, he could not follow his own opinions or those of the nation, and must be in too literal a sense the *servant* of the crown.[8]

Thirty-one years earlier, Chesterfield had told the House of Lords that 'Kings are generally for consulting with such as are of their own choosing, and these are often such as have no dignity, privilege or right by their birth'.[9] His comment captured the sense of the King as the powerful but unpredictable factor in the political system. This was underlined by the vigour of George III's partisanship. Once he had found a minister whom he regarded as trustworthy, the King frequently urged Lord North to vigour:

> engaged in many difficulties, and an opposition to government formed of men that if they could succeed would restrain no one of the absurd ideas they have sported, I think it the duty nay personal honour of those in public stations must prompt them with zeal to make every effort to assist me, who have unreservedly supported them.[10]

The constitutional ambiguity of the issue raised by Devonshire also captured a tension within the British establishment, as the crown's traditional position, as the proactive arbiter of aristocratic factions, was reshaped in the new politics of the period. This was a dynamic process: whereas, for example, George III's resistance to Catholic Emancipation had been successful, George IV, despite bitter hostility, had to accept it. This disparity reflected different political circumstances, but also a shift in the position of the monarchy, as well as the contrasting character of the two monarchs.

Another shift was captured by the grant of aristocratic status. Whereas there had been sixty-six peerage creations under George I and seventy-four under George II, there were 197 by George III between 1760 and 1800, especially after 1784.[11] In part, this higher rate of creation reflected a shift from a more Germanic attitude under the first two Georges, with a relatively restrictive concern with lineage among candidates for the peerage, to an emphasis on service under George III, although the end of Tory proscription expanded the number of families the King was willing to reward, and his personal good relations with many of the landed elite were also important. The needs of the government, in the shape of inexpensive rewards in return for political support, also played a more prominent role under George III; the way in which this could threaten both royal and aristocratic assumptions was captured in 1832 in the crisis about the peerage creations threatened in order to pass the Reform Bill.

Despite George III's growing popularity from the 1783–84 crisis on, long-term trends lessened the active role of the monarch. The growth of business and the increased scope of government lessened the ability of one man, whether monarch or minister, to master the situation; this helped encourage the development of the cabinet. The ministries of Pitt the Younger (1783–1801, 1804–6) and Lord Liverpool (1812–27) were especially important in this process; and the longevity of Liverpool's ministry helped shape George IV's kingship. From the 1790s, the discussions and decisions of the inner core of ministers, the cabinet council, became more formal. Collective responsibility and loyalty to the leading minister increased, and this strengthened the cabinet's ties with that minister and increased his power with reference to the monarch: cabinet unanimity was a potential weapon against the crown. When it could be obtained, most obviously with the mass resignations of 1746 in protest against George II's support for Carteret , such unanimity was effective. Conversely, a lack of cabinet unity could strengthen the King's position with respect to the cabinet, as with the clash between George III and Pitt over Catholic Emancipation in 1801. Thanks, in part, to growing cabinet cohesion, George IV muttered against his ministries and ministers but was not strong enough to overthrow them: Liverpool was strongly supported by his cabinet. The sense of a monarch under instruction was captured by a letter of 1820:

> The King will be prepared to hold a Council to receive the Recorder's report, on either Thursday or Friday, as may best suit public business but, of which day, I request your Lordship may apprise me, for H.M.'s information.[12]

George pointed out to the Lord Chancellor that he seldom sent him a patronage request, and in 1828 had to bow to pressure to appoint as a KC Thomas Denman, who had spoken for the Queen against the Bill of Pains and Penalties, implicitly comparing George to Nero.[13] The show of royal favour was still important. Reporting on dinner with George IV at Ramsgate on 24 September 1821, Liverpool noted, 'His manner to *me* not *over*cordial but not sufficiently otherwise to attract any observation, upon the whole I should not complain'.[14]

Personal factors were very important to this shift. These included the breakdown of George III's health in 1788 and the consequent Regency Crisis of 1788–89, the subsequent slackening of his grip, and his later illnesses; the impact of Pitt's longevity in office; and the lack of interest in business displayed by George IV. As a consequence, greater cabinet cohesion and influence, and a consistent united cabinet control of policymaking, were more a feature from the 1790s on than of the 1780s; and this was not reversed when George IV or William IV came to the throne. Neither had the ambition for change their father had shown when he came to the throne in 1760. He had done so as a young man fired up with ideas. It is instructive to consider the situation had George III been succeeded, as George II had been, by a dynamic youngster determined to change politics. Instead, George III was the first young man to succeed to the throne since Edward VI (born in 1537), whose brief reign (1547–53) had been dominated by his ministers; the nearest not thus dominated was Henry VIII, born in 1491, who came to the throne in 1509. Although Victoria came to the throne at a younger age, no subsequent King was to do so.

A young Hanoverian monarch in the early nineteenth century determined to change politics might well have been a conservative unwilling to accept change. In 1819 George IV, as Prince Regent, thanked the Manchester authorities for their conduct at Peterloo – a panic charge by the Yeomanry, ordered on by the over-excitable magistrates, on an enormous crowd gathered to support demands for parliamentary reform. This was an unsympathetic action that failed to engage with the lack of judgement shown by the magistrates. In this period, however, the cause of counter-revolution was in the hands of the government, not under royal direction. As George was to discover over Catholic Emancipation in 1828–29, in the face of a determined ministry and with no strong alternatives, royal options were limited.

Crucially, William IV did not provide leadership for the opponents of reform in the early 1830s, and did not push the point when Peel failed in 1835. Another monarch might have taken a different view, or conversely could have been a keen supporter of stronger government committed to the cause of administrative reform and modernisation. Instead, although all very different, the succession of the illness of the last years of George III, the sensuality of George IV, the caution of William IV about reaction, the methodical constitutionalism of Victoria, the sensualism redux in the case of Edward VII, and, less successfully, Edward VIII, and a strong sense of duty on the part of George V, George VI, and Elizabeth II, was such that the continued role of monarchy in politics and government became far less proactive.

A lack of interest in reaction was generally linked to a clear royal commitment to order. George I was opposed to the 'Blacks' – Jacobites who attacked game in forests belonging to Whig landlords. George II expressed the fear in 1748 that the Dutch 'spirit of sedition' would spread to England',[15] George III associated disorder with moral failings, and George IV became committed to the established system of power with some of the energy he had earlier devoted to self-gratification. William IV feared crisis.

The role of individuals was seen in culture as well as politics. There was a major contrast between, on the one hand, Frederick, Prince of Wales, and George IV and, on the other, George II. Painted in 1733 by

Philip Mercier, playing music with his sisters Anne and Caroline, while another sister, Amelia, listens with a volume of Milton in her lap, Frederick was a significant supporter of music, gardens and literature, an important backer of Rococo art in England, and a discerning patron who, for example, enriched the royal collection of silverware with many fine pieces and patronised the leading sporting painter John Wootton. Through the patronage of Bute, Frederick's widow, Augusta, employed the architect Sir William Chambers (1726–96), who had studied in both Italy and Paris and travelled to China, to adorn the gardens of her house at Kew. In 1757–62, in the grounds, he built a number of structures in oriental and classical styles that had a great impact. Chambers, the author of *Designs of Chinese Buildings* (1757) and *Dissertation on Oriental Gardening* (1772), also taught architectural drawing to the future George III, who made him Comptroller of His Majesty's Works.[16]

George I was a more active patron of the arts than George II or William IV were to be, but he did not compare with William III, who had demolished earlier work and built essentially new palaces at Hampton Court and Kensington, both carefully integrated with their gardens. Indeed, for William III, Sir Christopher Wren remodelled Hampton Court with scant concern for the Tudor fabric. Nor did George II and George III compare in their building with continental contemporaries such as Elizabeth I and Catherine II of Russia. Sir John Vanbrugh (1664–1726) built new palaces for the Duke of Marlborough and the Earl of Carlisle, not for George I; the ideas he produced for Kensington Palace were thought too grandiose. British culture in the period is particularly noted for its gardens, but although George I was keen on re-landscaping the grounds of Kensington Palace, and both Charles Bridgeman and William Kent worked on the project, the royal family did not play a central role in the development of the distinctive British landscape. George II was an active patron of the German enamellist C. F. Zincke, but this form was scarcely central to British culture.

Aside from architecture and gardens, the history of theatre and music during this period revealed the declining significance of royal patronage. Handel's livelihood depended on the commercial success of his works on the London stage. Mozart, in 1764, and Haydn in 1791 and 1794, came to London in search of the same success. The major forces in artistic patronage were the landed elite and the middling orders, not the

monarchy. 'Taste' came from outside the royal court, although George IV
would have liked to spend enough to challenge the situation, while
Frederick, Prince of Wales's sponsorship of the Rococo was important.
It was indicative of the cultural importance of the public stage that
George Lillo's *The London Merchant* (1731) made his name as a
playwright, while the court masque he wrote in 1733 for the marriage of
Anne, the Princess Royal, with William IV of Orange was unperformed
because of the postponement of the marriage and made no impact.

Despite the grandeur sought by George IV, and the scale and style of
the royal court, the Hanoverians presided over an embourgeoisment of
British culture. *The London Merchant,* which represented a major change
in tragedy in that it was written in a prose idiom and given a bourgeois
setting and values, was a moral counterpart to William Hogarth's satires
and the novels of Samuel Richardson and later Jane Austen. If morality
was increasingly prescribed and indulgence proscribed in many works
– Richardson's first novel *Pamela* (1740) being a very popular work on
the prudence of virtue and the virtue of prudence – this represented
not so much a bourgeois reaction against aristocratic and royal culture
as a shift in sensibility that was common to both. For every decadent
aristocrat depicted on the stage in the second half of the eighteenth
century there were several royal or aristocratic heroes.

This cultural shift created problems for the monarchy, specifically
about how far the behaviour of the royal family should conform to what
was anticipated. Under George III, the absence of grand projects, accompanied by the continued established routine of court festivals and
the embellishment of palaces, which ensured that portraits were painted
and furniture and porcelain purchased, was an important ingredient in
the shift from 'grand' culture to 'domestic culture', which was more
accessible to the middling orders. George also took pains to cultivate
popularity. Thus, his visit with Queen Charlotte to the Earl of Coventry's
seat at Croome in 1788 was far from private. Arriving, he was received
'amidst the acclamations of some thousands of all ranks', and walked
for over two hours in the grounds 'gratifying their own and the curiosity
of the numerous spectators, whose plaudits they received with pleasure,
and returned by repeated salutes', while,

> After dinner, the royal guest, desirous of satisfying as much as in their
> power, that wish they had excited, appeared at the windows, where they

continued for some time, expressing by their looks and gestures the happiness they experienced in the evident and almost incessant marks of loyalty and affection shown them, by thousands of their surrounding subjects; in fact, the joy of the sovereign, his family, and his people, seemed totally reciprocal.[17]

The impact of such events was increased by their coverage in the press, which brought further publicity to reports of royal gentility and popularity, and also encouraged a sense of normative behaviour. Thus, the article above included the remark that the King was delighted 'with the respectful and becoming demeanour of those of inferior rank'. The following year,

> the Royal Party arrived at Longleat. On Tuesday at least twenty thousand persons were assembled to see them. With much condescension the King, Queen, and Princesses moved slowly on in an open carriage, so that every one present beheld them, and I believe nineteen out of the twenty were most highly gratified.[18]

Similarly, George's condescension in showing himself during his visit to Axminster in 1789 was applauded in the press. His interest in manufacturing was displayed by his visit to the carpet factory there.

This situation was challenged by George III's sons. The one description that did not pertain to the Prince Regent was domestic. He was not alone among his brothers in violating assumptions about appropriate royal behaviour and decorum that had become increasingly conventional not only because of the influence of Evangelicalism, but also due to the model established by George III. This caused tensions in the royal family, which were accentuated by the limited marital choices allowed royal princes and princesses. Aside from George III's anger with his children, Queen Charlotte was also a firm pursuer of restraint. In 1815 she expressed her concern about the marriage of Ernest, Duke of Cumberland, to his twice-widowed cousin Frederica because of imputations about the latter's character. There was reference to her 'anxious desire to preserve society upon the respectable footing which it had ever been the King's and her own study to maintain'. Charlotte refused, until the end of her life, to receive Frederica, despite the embarrassment caused to a government under pressure from Frederick William III of Prussia (Frederica had been married to a Prussian Prince).[19] The need to set a moral example even caused tension between the Princes themselves. In 1800–1, in the presence of his elder brothers, the future William IV used the House of Lords as a setting for a series of attacks on adultery, not the most tactful of courses.

More than personalities were also at issue in the political position of monarchs. There was a more general shift in political culture within the West. The rise of the public sphere was linked to a more utilitarian image of monarchy. Across Europe, the notion of honour and *gloire*, generally presented in the seventeenth century in personal and dynastic terms, was now increasingly seen in terms of the nation and country. This limited the relevance of dynasties as foci of identity and units, instead encouraging royal families to seek a stronger identification with nation and country. There were other important changes in monarchy. After about 1750, European monarchs were more prepared to risk abandoning traditional norms, a shift due to a different ideology of kingship, and a response to the particular need to improve government capability after the War of the Austrian Succession (1740–48). A lessened emphasis on the sacral aspect of kingship encouraged a stress on the monarch as the first servant of the state. This was an aspect both of a spread of reform Catholicism owing much to Jansenism and of a more general process of the social and cultural transformation of established hierarchies. This stress, which was related to the downgrading of dynasties in favour of the monarchs themselves, ensured that the position and views of cadet and collateral branches of the royal family became less important, as indeed was that of reversionary interests.

On the Continent, although significantly generally not in Britain, monarchs wore military uniform, demonstrating their role as servants of the state.[20] In France, monarchy was seen less and less in the eighteenth century as rooted in the Divine Right of Kings (an ideology which precluded much criticism of the crown). Increasingly, it was seen in secular 'contractual' terms. This left it more exposed to criticism. In Britain, an emphasis on the King as servant of the state also led to a stress on the other servants, which diminished the practical and symbolic role of the monarch. Much larger sums were raised for the monumental tributes to Fox and Pitt than for that to George III. Although there were earlier plans for a monument, the statue to the former King, was not unveiled until 1836, in part because of an injunction against its erection at the junction of Pall Mall and Cockspur Street, on the grounds that it would be a 'nuisance'.[21] The emphasis on Nelson and Wellington as heroes of the struggle against France was instructive, and the sense of greatness passing seen with Wellington's funeral in 1851 contrasted markedly with those of the three Kings who had died after the conclusion of the Napoleonic Wars. Similarly, Hawke and Wolfe had been the heroes of the Seven Years War.

If the character of particular monarchs and the nature of individual monarchies varied greatly, the importance of the system was clear. In the Thirteen Colonies in North America, France, Haiti, and Latin America, violent political changes from 1775 led to monarchies of some type or another, most dramatically to the imperial monarchy of Napoleon. This serves as a reminder of the difficulty of creating new political systems that did not revert to monarchy, which appeared the obvious form of government to most commentators, certainly for large states. In newly independent America, the major new political departure in the English-speaking world, it was initially difficult to establish political conventions. George Washington's willingness to give up power, and not to seek a presidency for life, was important to the creation of the particular American combination of responsible stability and elected legitimacy: there was to be no military dictatorship, no Bonapartism in the USA; or, to underline the danger of ignoring earlier parallels in the English-speaking world, no equivalent to the Cromwellian Protectorate. Had Washington, in the winter of 1782–83, put himself at the head of the officers at Newburgh who considered intimidating Congress into granting concessions over pensions, or at the head of the troops in June 1783 who briefly held Congress hostage, then a very different legacy would have probably been left. Given the combination of inherited assumptions, these, however, were highly unlikely choices, just as George III was not going to use the troops sent into London to suppress the Gordon Riots in 1780 to expand royal power. George took a close interest in the suppression of the riots and pressed for firm action – 'for I am convinced till the magistrates have ordered some military execution on the rioters this town will not be restored to order' – but that was all.

In Poland, the attempt in the early 1790s to create a constitutional monarchy that owed much to the British model,[22] was cut short by

Russian intervention, while in France the Revolution began as an attempt
to centre French constitutional monarchy on a representative element,
an attempt that in part failed because of Louis XVI's unwillingness to
support it. This failure, and the eventual move to Napoleonic imperial-
ism, did not mean, however, that constitutional monarchy was unviable;
simply that, as was also to be shown in the newly-independent Latin
American states which were *de jure* or *de facto* monarchies, that it was
difficult to operate successfully. The two most conspicuous examples of
the success of this system were those in the English-speaking world: the
legitimist monarchy of Britain and the elected, non-hereditary monarchy
represented by the American presidency. The former adjusted in the
later Hanoverian period not only in response to the changing political
culture but also to the classic problem of hereditary monarchy: its ability
to solve the problem of the succession but at the cost of abandoning
the option of merit offered by elective monarchy; whether formal, as
with the eighteenth-century Polish monarchy, the Holy Roman Empire,
and the Papacy, or not explicitly monarchical, as with the American
presidency.

   This adjustment was not without its difficulties. In effect, the Hanoverians abandoned the two ambitions seen in the first three reigns: the
attempts to secure advantages for Hanover (George I and George II)
and to revive monarchy in Britain (George III). Then in opposition,
Robert Walpole had warned about the dangers of royal ambition
when, in December 1718, attacking the government's plans to repeal the
Occasional Conformity and Schism Acts, he compared George I with
James II and VII:

> run parallels between King James and King George, declaring at the same
> time that, although they were not justly drawn, the Jacobites would per-
> suade the people they were; they had been told (said he) that King James
> recalled the Penal Laws and Tests, will they not be told King George recalls
> the security of the Church? They have been told King James set up a high
> commission court, will they not be told his present Majesty is now upon
> appointing commissioners for a royal visitation? ... he said he had one
> comfort still and that was although His Majesty had been led into such
> ill measures they were not hereditary in the royal family for that he had
> a son who not only voted against the Bill but entered his protest.[23]

From this perspective, the opposition's success in thwarting ministerial plans in 1719 and the reconstitution of the government in 1720 were instrumental in securing the stability of the Hanoverian regime by helping it avoid unpopular policies. In short the limitations, real or potential, posed by the parliamentary character of parliamentary monarchy in practice strengthened the position of the monarch, as indeed they were intended to do.

More generally, the Hanoverian monarchs became reactive. George I and George II had prefigured this by accepting ministers they did not want; but the major compromises were made by George IV and, less unwillingly, William IV, who, in some respects, was a modern figure prefiguring George V (1910–36), and was very much modern in comparison with George I. In 1867, in his influential *The English Constitution*, Walter Bagehot was to distinguish the 'efficient' parts of the constitution – the House of Commons and the cabinet – from what he termed the 'dignified' parts, namely the monarchy and the House of Lords. This was a misunderstanding, because both then retained considerable power, but one that captured the shift from a century and, even more, a century and a half earlier, when such a claim would have seemed bizarre.

An understanding of limits may not sound much of a triumph, but it is fundamental to any political system. Constitutional ambiguity could have developed into constant acrimony. Instead, by exercising restraint, Hanoverian monarchs created a business-like monarchy intent on security and continuation, not on the accumulation of power and absolute control. The understanding of limits also helped ensure that the Hanoverians did not suffer the fate of the Stuarts or the French Bourbons. The pubs named after William IV or his brother Frederick – the Duke of York of most of the pubs of that name – were not matched by others named after the Stuarts or, abroad, after continental monarchs. Where restraint failed was in North America, but the failure to manage the aspirations of the colonists, or even to respond to the problem of imperial management, was as much a failure of ministry and Parliament as of George III. This was not, however, the case with Catholic Emancipation, and the earlier failure to introduce this measure, which owed most to George III, helped compromise the appeal of parliamentary union in Ireland. George III also unsuccessfully opposed the banning of the slave trade, and William IV that of slavery. William's personal conservatism was reflected in his opposition to a knighthood for Captain Frederick

Marryat, the popular author of adventure stories, who had won a CB
for distinguished conduct as a naval officer in Burma in 1824–25:

> in consequence of Captain Marryat having written a book suggesting 'the
> Abolition of Impressment in the Naval Service' [1822], His Majesty cannot
> entertain his application for the honour of knighthood. It is impossible
> that any naval officer, possessing common sense, should not feel that the
> existence of the naval superiority of this country, its efficiency, and
> the possibility of defeating by early efforts any attempt made by foreign
> powers to reduce it, must depend upon the maintenance of the system of
> impressment. It must be equally obvious that the promulgation and pub-
> lication of proposals for abolishing a practice which rests on such a principle
> must be prejudicial and embarrassing to the king's government, and His
> Majesty therefore does not consider that he should be justified in distin-
> guishing by any mark of favor an officer who has so committed himself.[24]

Mention of failure, however, focuses attention on success, particularly
the avoidance of revolution in Britain. There was no comparison between George III's visit to Worcester in 1788 and the previous royal visit,
that by James II and VII in 1687, when there had been a fuss because
the mayor and aldermen had refused to follow the King into a Catholic
chapel to attend service, while the bishop was angry because, while
visiting his palace, the King had asked a Catholic priest to give the
mealtime blessing. Against such a background, the opposition James
encountered in 1688 was scarcely a surprise. George III was more
emollient and his policies more in keeping with public assumptions.

The avoidance of revolution became a new prominent issue when the
1820s and 1830s brought a series of revolutions across Europe. Successful
risings in Spain and Portugal in 1820 led to counter-revolutions in 1823,
but full-scale civil wars broke out over the royal successions in Portugal
in 1828 and in Spain in 1833. The First Carlist War (1833–40) in Spain
provides an instructive contrast to the ability of the British monarchy
to handle the interests of its members. Don Carlos resisted the bequest
of the Spanish throne to his niece Isabel by her father Ferdinand VII.
Opposition to a female monarch was combined with hostility to the
constitutional reforms, backed by Isabel's supporters, and more generally
to liberalism. There was nothing similar in Britain when Victoria came
to the throne in 1837. The Carlists were defeated, but that was not the
end to the disorder of those years; for, in 1836, there was a successful

liberal revolution in Spain; as there also was in Portugal. In 1820–21 there had also been liberal uprisings in Naples and Piedmont, both crushed with Austrian assistance. The Decembrist conspiracy in Russia in 1825 failed but in 1830 Charles X was overthrown in France, while William I of the Netherlands also lost Brussels to a popular rising. Belgium became independent after the subsequent war.

In contrast, the disturbances in Britain, while serious, especially those at Merthyr Tydfil in 1831, did not amount to anything comparable. Neither George IV nor William IV were faced by scenes similar to those in Paris in 1830 (and 1848); or, for that matter, to the Gordon Riots, although their brother Ernest, Duke of Cumberland, who was pelted for his opposition to the Reform Bill, pressed in 1831 for the establishment of a national guard.[25] The situation in Hanover was more serious. Aside from a student revolt in Göttingen in 1818, there was serious unrest in 1830–31, which led to the occupation of Göttingen by troops. The Duke of Cambridge, as Governor General, responded by recommending reforms, including greater openness in government. William IV agreed.

On the European scale, the Prince Regent might not have been an impressive rival to Napoleon, but Charles IV of Spain (1788–1808) was far worse. The Emperor Francis I of Austria (1792–1835) was more industrious than George IV, but he was also stubborn and fell out with the leading royal general, Archduke Charles. Like George IV, Frederick William II of Prussia (1786–97) was a follower of the politics of the boudoir, but he was also interested in mystical religion and his tergiversations made consistent policy-making difficult. The same was true of Paul I of Russia (1796–1801), who was assassinated. The difficulties of the dynastic system were also revealed within the Napoleonic family: Jerome, King of Westphalia (1807–13), and Joseph, King of Naples (1806–8) and of Spain (1808–14) and Louis, King of Holland (1806–10) lacked the ability or determination of their meteoric brother.

Adaptation to change is far from easy. The Hanoverians managed it, both individually and as a group. At times, as with George II's anger, George III's threats about abdication, and George IV's despair about having to yield to Catholic Emancipation, this process was far from comfortable; but it was achieved, and the monarchy in 1837 was in a more secure state than it had been in 1714.

Forty-five years later, in 1882, London audiences could listen to praise for the achievements of George III's reign that brilliantly distinguished constitutional position from national achievement. W. S. Gilbert's lyrics in *Iolanthe* made fun of the House of Lords. The same argument could have been employed about the monarchy, but, instead, the sentiments expressed linked the Crown with success:

> The House of Peers, throughout the war,
> Did nothing in particular,
> And did it very well:
> Yet Britain set the world ablaze
> In good King George's glorious days!

# Notes

## Notes to Preface

1. Madame van Muyden (ed.), *A Foreign View of England in the Reigns of George I and George II: The Letters of Monsieur César de Saussure to his Family* (1902), p. 265.
2. This was probably James Johnston, a former envoy to Prussia who often attended court and with whom George sometimes dined, and his new and much younger third wife, Lucy. On Johnston, E. Cruickshanks, S. Handley and D. W. Hayton (eds), *The House of Commons, 1690–1715* (5 vols, Cambridge, 2002), IV, pp. 513–16.
3. Friedrich Wilhelm von der Schulenburg to Friedrich Wilhelm von Görtz, 12 February 1717, Darmstadt, 153/6, fol. 14.

## Notes to Chapter 1: The House of Hanover

1. Edinburgh, National Library of Scotland, MS 16630, fol. 124.
2. M. Buschkühl, *Great Britain and the Holy See, 1746–1870* (Blackrock, Co. Dublin, 1982), pp. 25–398; G. Scott, *Gothic Rage Undone: English Monks in the Age of Enlightenment* (Downside, 1992), pp. 217–18.
3. Gosforth, Northumberland, CRO ZAL 98 13/2.
4. Bod, MS Don. c. 107 fol. 18.
5. Bedford CRO, HW 87/125.
6. A. Robinson, 'Identifying the Beast: Samuel Horsley and the Problem of Papal Antichrist', *Journal of Ecclesiastical History*, 43 (1992), p. 607.
7. J. Barrell, *Imagining the King's Death: Figurative Treason, Fantasies of Regicide, 1793–1796* (Oxford, 2000).
8. S. Poole, *The Politics of Regicide in England, 1760–1850: Troublesome Subjects* (Manchester, 2000), p. 212.
9. L. Steffen, *Defining a British State: Treason and National Identity, 1608–1820* (Basingstoke, 2001).
10. Peter Powney to Henry Addington, 23 September 1790, 152M/C 1790/OZ 32.
11. R. Glover, *Peninsular Preparation: The Reform of the British Army, 1795–1809* (Cambridge, 1963).

12. P. Mackesy, *War without Victory: The Downfall of Pitt, 1799–1802* (Oxford, 1984), pp. 153–54.

13. M. Raeff, *The Well-Ordered Police State: Social and Institutional Change through the Law in the Germanies and Russia, 1600–1800* (1983).

14. *Berrow's Weekly Journal*, 21 August 1788; T. Gray (ed.), *East Devon. The Travellers' Tales* (Exeter, 2000), pp. xii–xvi.

15. BL. Add. MS 33001, fol. 34 (undated, but in 1765 papers).

16. BL. Add. MS 33001, fol. 38.

17. BL. Add. MS 35417, fol. 92.

18. George III signature of appointment of – Gregory, 27 October 1760, *Autograph Letters and Historical Documents, Maggs Catalogue* no. 1345 (2003), item 85.

19. Arundell to Richard, 3rd Earl of Burlington, 14 April 1726, BL, Althorp MS, B3.

20. William, 2nd Earl of Shelburne, Secretary of State for the Southern Department, to Augustus, 3rd Duke of Grafton, First Lord of the Treasury, 11 June 1768, BL. Deposit 9516, Bowood papers, vol. 15, fol. 15.

21. Ossorio to Charles Emmanuel III, 17 January 1747, AST, LM. Ing. 53: For an emphasis on George II's need to know, Thomas, Duke of Newcastle, Secretary of State for the Southern Department, to Earl Waldergrave, envoy in Paris, 5 February (os) 1734, BL, Add. MS 32784, fol. 43.

22. Mornington to William Pole, 31 October 1797, BL, Add. MS 37924, fol. 10.

23. George III to Lord Grenville, the Foreign Secretary, 30 March, George III to William Pitt the Younger, 30 March 1791, BL, Add. MS 58856, fol. 26, Aspinall, *George III*, I, p. 526.

24. J. Bullion, 'George III on Empire', *William and Mary Quarterly*, 51 (1994), pp. 305–10.

25. Sheffield, Archives, Wentworth Woodhouse papers, R1–692, 694.

26. E. Gregg, *Queen Anne* (2nd edn, New Haven, 2001), p. 148.

27. F. Prochaska, *Royal Bounty: The Making of a Welfare Monarchy?* (New Haven, 1995).

## Notes to Chapter 2: Britain and Hanover

1. Cobbett, XX, columns 1019–20.

2. See J. M. Black, 'Hanover and British Foreign Policy, 1714–60', *English Historical Review* (forthcoming).

3. RA, Cumberland papers, 4/203–4, 201.

4. Sherlock to Edward Weston, 25 May (os) 1746, Farmington, Connecticut, Lewis Walpole Library, Weston papers, vol. 3.

5. Villiers to Robert Trevor, 20 December 1739, Aylesbury CRO, Trevor papers, vol. 20; I am most grateful for the advice of Peter Wilson.

6. R. N. Middleton, 'French Policy and Prussia after the Peace of Aix-la-Chapelle, 1749–1753' (unpublished PhD. thesis, Columbia, 1968), pp. 170, 174; La Touche, French envoy in Prussia, to Saint Contest, French Foreign Minister, 5 May 1753, AE, CP, Prusse 171 fols 239–41.

7. Haslang to the Bavarian and Palatine Foreign Ministers, Counts Preysing and Wachtendonck, 7 September 1762, Munich, London 239.

8. The best introduction is V. Press, 'Kurhannover im System des alten Reiches, 1692–1803', in A. Birke and K. Kluxen (eds), *England und Hannover* (Munich, 1986), pp. 53–79. See also U. Richter-Uhlig, *Hof und Politik unter den Bedingungen der Personalunion zwischen Hannover und England* (Hanover, 1992).

9. PRO, SP 98/44, fol. 526.

10. R. Hatton, *George I* (1978), p. 3.

11. Newcastle to Holdernesse, 5 January (os) 1750, PRO, SP 84/454.

12. Newcastle to Sir Charles Hanbury-Williams, 5 February (os) 1751, Newcastle to Holdernesse, 5 January (os) 1750, PRO, SP 88/71, 84/454 fol. 61.

13. Amelot to Bussy, 5 January, Valory to Bussy, 13 January 1742, PRO, SP 80/46, 107/52; *Polit. Corr.*, IV, p. 324.

14. R. Drögereit, 'Das Testament König Georgs I und die Frage der Personalunion zwischen England und Hannover', *Niedersächsisches Jahrbuch für Landesgeschichte*, 14 (1937), pp. 94–199.

15. Treaty, BL, Add. MS 32753, Wolfenbüttel, Staatsarchiv 1 Alt. 22 Nr 534; Peter, Lord King, 'Notes on Domestic and Foreign Affairs during the Last Years of the Reign of George I and the Early Part of the Reign of George II', in appendix to P. King, *Life of John Locke* (2 vols, 1830), II, pp. 50–54.

16. For support in 1737 and 1741 among British ministers for a division, A. W. Ward, *Great Britain and Hanover: some aspects of the personal union* (Oxford, 1899), pp. 64–5.

17. I. B. Campbell, 'The International Legal Relations between Great Britain and Hanover, 1714–1837' (unpublished Ph.D. thesis, Cambridge, 1966), pp. 41–45.

18. Newcastle to Hardwicke, and reply, both 21 November 1759, BL, Add. MS 32899, fols 6–7, 13–14.

19. J. Richard, *A Tour*, pp. 185–7; A. Thomson, *Letters of a Traveller*, p. 163; J. Moore, *A View of Society and Manners in France, Switzerland and*

*Germany* (2 vols, 1779), II, p. 91. For Hanoverian influence in the foundation of the two regius chairs of modern history, John Andrews, *Letters to a Young Gentleman on his Setting out for France* (1784), p. 364. See also M. O. B. Mangourit, *Travels in Hanover, 1803 and 1804* (1806).

20. Elizabeth Montagu to Mrs Carter, late December 1763, R. Blunt (ed.), *Mrs Montagu, 'Queen of the Blues'* (2 vols, 1923), I, p. 82.

21. Rouillé to Marshal Noailles, 21 July 1755, AE, CP, Ang. 439 fol. 266.

22. M. V. Leggiere, *Napoleon and Berlin: The Franco-Prussian War in North Germany, 1813* (Norman, Oklahoma, 2002), p. 9.

23. R. Muir, *Britain and the Defeat of Napoleon, 1807–1815* (New Haven, 1996), p. 254.

## Notes to Chapter 3: Father and Son

1. Lord Mahon, *History of England from the Peace of Utrecht 1713–83* (5th edn, 7 vols, 1858), II, p. xxxii.

2. George II to Newcastle, 21 May [1755], BL, Add. 32684, fol. 84.

3. Newcastle to [Henry Pelham], 29 September (os) 1719, BL, Add. MS 32686, fol. 54; Craggs to Stanhope, 3 November 1719, PRO, SP 44/269A.

4. George I to Charles VI, 2 December 1719, New York, Public Library, Hardwicke papers, vol. 54.

5. Schulenburg to Görtz, 30 November 1717, Darmstadt F23, fol. 132; Charles, 8th Lord Cathcart to 'My dear Lord', 8 March (os) 1718, HL, Loudoun papers, 7927.

6. The absence of a published study of the court's political role under George II has led to it being underrated. There is much of value in two unpublished theses, David Flaten's 'King George II and the Politicians: The Struggle for Political Power' (Fordham, 1999) and Hannah Smith's 'Georgian Monarchical Culture in England, 1714–60' (Cambridge, 2001). For recent work on the political role of courts, J. Duindam, *Vienna and Versailles: The Courts of Europe's Dynastic Rivals, 1550–1780* (Cambridge, 2003), pp. 223–97.

7. Earl of Ilchester (ed.), *Letters to Henry Fox ... With a Few Addressed to his Brother Stephen* (1915), p. 53.

8. Newcastle to Charles, 2nd Marquess of Rockingham, 1757, misdated 1751, WW, R1–5.

9. R. Middleton, *The Bells of Victory: The Pitt-Newcastle Ministry and the Conduct of the Seven Years' War, 1757–1762* (Cambridge, 1985), pp. 139–42.

10. Pulteney to Jonathan Swift, 2 December (os) 1736, BL, Add. MS 4806, fol. 178.

11. L. Melville, *Lady Suffolk and her Circle* (1824); John, Lord Hervey, *Some Materials towards Memoirs of the Reign of King George II*, edited by R. R. Sedgwick (3 vols, continuous pagination, 1931).

12. 'Mémoire sur l'état présent de la Grande Bretagne', AE, CP, Ang. 364, fols 397–98. See J. M. Black, 'Schöpflin in Britain', in B. Vogler and J. Voss (eds), *Strasbourg, Schoepflin et l'Europe au XVIIIe siècle* (Bonn, 1996), pp. 243–52.

13. L. J. Colley, *In Defiance of Oligarchy: The Tory Party, 1714–60* (Cambridge, 1982).

14. AE, CP, Ang. 259, fol. 39. See also, for 1721, BL, Add. 47029, fol. 66.

15. P. King, *Life of John Locke* (2 vols, 1830), II, pp. 49–50.

16. J. M. Black, 'Parliament and the Political and Diplomatic Crisis of 1717–18', *Parliamentary History*, 3 (1984), pp. 90–92.

17. George II to Newcastle, 4 June 1757, BL, Add. 32684 fol. 100.

18. M. Peters, 'Pitt as a Foil to Bute: The Public Debate over Ministerial Responsibility and the Powers of the Crown', in K. Schweizer (ed.), *Lord Bute: Essays in Re-Interpretation* (Leicester, 1988), p. 111.

19. Mirepoix, memorandum, November 1751, AE, MD Ang. 51, fol. 151.

20. Fox to William, 4th Duke of Devonshire, 11 December 1755, HP.

21. Churchill College, Cambridge, Erle-Drax MS 2/12.

22. Anon. to anon., 1742, BL, Add. MS 379334, fol. 32.

23. Townshend to Walpole, 15 November, 10 December 1723, PRO, SP 43/5.

24. Horatio Walpole to Malton, 10 October (os) 1738, WW, M3.

25. Newcastle to Holdernesse, 11 July 1755, BL, Add. MS 32857, fol. 54.

26. George II to Newcastle, 26 May 1749, BL, Add. MS 32684, fol. 74.

27. Newcastle to Hardwicke, 2 August 1752, BL, Add. MS 35412, fol. 205.

28. Newcastle to Hardwicke, 3 January 1758, BL, Add. MS 35417, fol. 171.

29. J. Beattie, *The English Court in the Reign of George I* (Cambridge, 1967).

30. *St. James's Post*, 8 January (os), *Original Weekly Journal*, 11 January (os), *Post Boy*, 11 January (os) 1718.

31. *Original Weekly Journal*, 22 February (os) 1718.

32. J. Niemeyer, *Die Revue bei Bemerode* (Beckum, 1985).

33. R. M. Hatton, *The Anglo-Hanoverian Connection, 1714–1760* (1982), p. 12.

34. C. Podmore, *The Moravian Church in England, 1728–1760* (Oxford, 1998).

35. G. C. Gibbs, review of R. Hatton, *George I*, in *Welsh History Review*, 10 (1980), p. 250.

36. S. Taylor, 'Queen Caroline and the Church of England', in S. Taylor, R. Connors and C. Jones (eds), *Hanoverian Britain and Empire: Essays in Memory of Philip Lawson* (Woodbridge, 1998), pp. 82–101.

37. Haslang to Count Preysing, 7 January 1757, Munich, London, vol. 233.

## Notes to Chapter 4: George I

1. Newcastle to Horatio Walpole, 21 May 1724, BL, Add. MS 9152, fol. 3.
2. J. H. and M. Shennan, 'The Protestant Succession, April 1713 – September 1715', in R. Hatton and J. S. Bromley (eds), *William III and Louis XIV: Essays 1680–1720 by and for Mark A. Thomson* (Liverpool, 1968), pp. 252–70; E. Gregg, *The Protestant Succession in International Politics, 1710–1716* (New York, 1986).
3. Schulenburg to Görtz, 19 November 1717, Darmstadt F23, fol. 126.
4. Lady Paulet to Lady Cowper, 4 August (os) 1716, Hertford, Hertfordshire CRO, Panshanger MS D/EP F204, fol. 16.
5. Schulenburg to Görtz, 4 March 1718, Darmstadt F23, fol. 194.
6. Bonet to Frederick William I of Prussia, 15 March 1718, Berlin, Geheimes Staatsarchiv, Preussischer Kulturbesitz, Rep. 11, vol. 41.
7. Dano-Hanoverian Treaty, BL, Add. MS 32755, fols 563–78.
8. George I to Philip, Duke of Orléans, 22 December 1719, New York, Public Library, Hardwicke papers, vol. 54.
9. Schulenburg to Görtz, 18 January 1718, Darmstadt F23, fol. 159.
10. BL, Add. MS 32686, fol. 175.
11. BL, Add. MS 37361, fol. 31.
12. BL, Add. MS 32686, fol. 269.
13. London, University Library, MS 93, fol. 9.
14. Anon, *A Letter from an English Traveler at Rome, to his Father of the 6th of May, 1721* [1721, no place given], pp. 11–14. See also *An Historical Account of the Advantages that have accru'd to England, By the Succession in the Illustrious House of Hanover* (1722).
15. Schulenburg to Görtz, 19 November 1717, Darmstadt F23, fol. 125.
16. Schulenburg to Görtz, 23 November 1717, Darmstadt F23, fol. 128.
17. Papers relating to the disagreement in the Stanhope collection, Maidstone, Kent Archive Office, U 1590 O 151. See also BL, Add. MS 61492, fols 201–2, PRO, SP 35/10, fol. 144.
18. Pentenrider to Königsegg, 14 December 1717, HHStA GK, 42, fol. 29.
19. Sunderland to Newcastle, 1 October (os) 1717, BL, Add. MS 32686, fol. 108.
20. BL, Add. MS 47028, fol. 223.
21. Schulenburg to Görtz, 25, 28 January 1718, Darmstadt F23, fols 114–15, 170; Craggs to Stair, 21 July (os) 1718, NAS, GD 135/41/13B.
22. Schulenburg to Görtz, 11 January 1718, Darmstadt F23, fol. 155.
23. Schulenburg to Görtz, 10, 14 December 1717, Darmstadt F23, fols 141–3; Cathcart to [Hugh, 3rd Earl of Loudoun?], 18 January (os) 1718, HL, LO. 7958; BL, Add. MS 17677 ZZZ, fols 15–20, 61492, fols 203–6.

24. Robethon to Stair, 30 December 1717, NAS, GD. 135/141/12; Schulenburg to Görtz, 4 January 1718, Darmstadt F23, fol. 149; Lord Perceval to Charles Dering, – January (os), 4 March (os) 1718, BL, Add. MS 47028, fols 221–21, 226; Stair to Craggs, 2 April 1718, BL, Stowe MS 246, fol. 78.

25. Bonet to Frederick William I, 25 January 1718, in response to his of 11 January 1718, Berlin, Rep. 11 vol. 41.

26. Schulenburg to Görtz, 28 December 1717, Darmstadt F23, fol. 146.

27. Newcastle to Stanhope, 14 October (os) 1719, BL, Add. MS 32686, fol. 151.

28. Stanhope to Newcastle, 27 October (os) 1719, BL, Add. MS 32686, fol. 156.

29. C. Jones, '"Venice Preserv'd; or A Plot Discovered": The Political and Social Context of the Peerage Bill of 1719', in Jones (ed.), *A Pillar of the Constitution: The House of Lords in British Politics, 1640–1784* (1989), p. 111.

30. Cadogan to [Sir Francis Dashwood?], 5 December 1719, Bod, MS. D. D. Dashwood (Bucks) B7/1/1b.

31. See p. 178.

32. Craggs to Stair, 11 May (os) 1718, NAS, GD 135/141/13B.

33. Stanhope to Newcastle, 27 October (os) 1719, BL, Add. MS 32686, fol. 156.

34. Newcastle to -, 29 November (os) 1719, BL, Add. MS 32686, fol. 88.

35. J. Carswell, *The South Sea Bubble* (2nd edn, Stroud, 1993). For the argument that the Bubble has been seriously misunderstood, J. Hoppit, 'The Myth of the South Sea Bubble', *Transactions of the Royal Historical Society*, 6th series, 12 (2002), pp. 141–65.

36. RA, Stuart Papers 49/77, 50/62.

37. Carteret to Newcastle, 27 August (os) 1721, BL, Add. MS 32686, fol. 193.

38. Hutcheson to William, 1st Earl Cowper, 21 March (os) 1722, Hertford CRO, Panshanger Mss. D/EP F 55.

39. Schaub to Görtz, 26 December 1719, Darmstadt F23; Madame van Muyden (ed.), *A Foreign View of England in the Reigns of George I and George II: The Letters of Monsieur César de Saussure to his Family* (1902), pp. 60, 229, 233.

40. PRO, SP 35/24/75, 35/6/66; *Pickering and Chatto List*, no. 40, September 1984, item 109.

41. Carteret to Newcastle, 9 September (os) 1721, BL, Add. MS 32686, fol. 197.

42. Those are the figures given by Carswell. A memorandum of 1720 concerning stock transactions by the directors, gives £10,000, £10,000 and £5000 each as the figures, New Haven, Beinecke Library, Osborn papers, Townshend Box 1. For money to Sophia Charlotte, Townshend to Walpole, 15 November 1723, PRO, SP 43/5, fol. 253.

43. Townshend to Walpole, 17 September 1723, PRO, SP 43/5, fol. 17.

44. C. S. Cowper (ed.), *Diary of Mary Countess Cowper, Lady of the Bedchamber to the Princess of Wales, 1714–1720* (1864), p. 4.

45. N. Smith, *The Royal Image and the English People* (Aldershot, 2001), p. 136.
46. Renard, agent in Amsterdam, to James Dayrolle, Resident at The Hague, 13 August 1732, Dayrolle to Tilson, 16, 19, 23 August 1732, PRO, SP 84/319; Charles Delafaye to James, 1st Earl Waldegrave, envoy in Paris, 14 August (os) 1732, Chewton House, Chewton Mendip, papers of James, 1st Earl Waldegrave.
47. See PRO, State Papers Regencies.
48. Newcastle to Robinson, 12 January (os) 1727, BL, Add. MS 32749, fol. 34.
49. As a result, there is a large portrait of George (from the studio of Kneller) on the right-hand side of the library's entrance hall (as you enter), while the King always has a place of honour in the university's commemoration of benefactors' choral service every October.
50. D. Burrows, 'Handel and Hanover', in P. Williams (ed.), *Bach, Handel, Scarlatti: Tercentenary Essays* (Cambridge, 1985).
51. BL, Add. MS 63093.

## Notes to Chapter 5: George II

1. Newcastle to Hardwicke, 14 October 1756, recounting a conversation with George II on why Newcastle felt he must appoint William Pitt the Elder a Secretary of State, and make him leader of the House of Commons, BL, Add. MS 35416, fol. 100.
2. M. Bertram, *Georg II. König und Kurfürst* (Göttingen, 2003), pp. 35–39.
3. Newcastle to Townshend, 28 June (os) 1723, Duke to Duchess of Portland, 15 October (os) 1723, BL, Add. MS 32686, BL, Egerton MS 1711; Broglie, French ambassador, to Morville, French Foreign Minister, 30 November 1724, 2 June 1727, AE, CP, Ang. 349, 359; Le Coq, Saxon envoy in London, to Marquis de Fleury, Saxon minister, 3 May 1726, Dresden, Hauptstaatsarchiv, Geheimes Kabinett, Gesandtschaften 2674; W. Coxe, *Memoirs of the Life and Administration of Robert Walpole* (3 vols, 1798), I, pp. 193–94, 271, 283; J. H. Plumb, *Sir Robert Walpole: The King's Minister* (1960), p. 163.
4. RA, Stuart Papers 108/79, 107/41.
5. HMC, *Onslow*, pp. 516–17.
6. Peter, Lord King, 'Notes on Domestic and Foreign Affairs during the Last Years of the Reign of George I and the Early Part of the Reign of George II', in appendix to P. King, *Life of John Locke* (2 vols, 1830), II, p. 46.
7. Harriet Pitt to her mother, Harriet, 27 June (os) 1727, BL, Add. MS 69285.
8. Le Coq to Augustus II, 22 July 1727, Dresden, 2676, 18a.
9. Le Coq to Augustus II, 22 July 1727, Dresden, 2676, 18a; R. R. Sedgwick (ed.), *The House of Commons, 1715–1754* (2 vols, 1970), I, pp. 34, 37.

10. Fleury to George II, 2, 11 July, Robinson, Secretary of Embassy in Paris, to St. Saphorin, 14 July 1727, PRO, SP 100/7, 80/61; James Hamilton to James III, 14 July (os), Atterbury to James, 20 August 1727, RA, Stuart Papers, 108/73, 109/87; *Craftsman*, 18 July (os) 1730.

11. Le Coq to Augustus II, 22 July 1727, Dresden, 2676, 18a; Coxe, *Walpole*, I, p. 286, II, pp. 519–20; *Hervey*, p. 46; HMC, *Manuscripts of the Earl of Egmont: Diary of the Earl of Egmont* (3 vols, 1920–23), II, pp. 156–7.

12. Horatio to Robert Walpole, 18 August 1727, Bloomington, Indiana, Lilly Library, Walpole papers.

13. Newcastle to Lord Blandford, 24 July (os) 1727, BL, Add. MS 32993.

14. Mussenden to Carteret Leathes, 20 June (os) 1727, Ipswich, East Suffolk RO, Leathes papers HA 403/1/10; Le Coq to Augustus, 22 July, 12, 26 August, 23 September 1727, Dresden, 2676, 18a; Broglie to Chauvelin, French Foreign Minister, 4 August 1727, AE, CP, Ang. 361; newsletters, 11 July, 30 September, 7 November, 16 December 1727, Osnabrück 299; D'Aix to Victor Amadeus II, 11 August, 15 December 1727, AST, LM, Ing. 35; L'Hermitage, Dutch agent in London, to States General, 7 November 1727, BL, Add. MS 17677 KKK, fol. 9; Tenth article of Carteret's instructions, 23 October (os) 1727, PRO, SP 63/389.

15. King, *John Locke*, II , pp. 47–48; D'Aix to Victor Amadeus II, 29 September 1727, AST, LM. Ing. 35; Le Coq to Augustus, 23 September 1727, Dresden, 2676, 18a.

16. Count Philip Kinsky, Austrian envoy, to Prince Eugene, 25 September 1728, HHStA, Grosse Korrespondenz, 95b.

17. R. Middleton, 'The Duke of Newcastle and the Conduct of Patronage during the Seven Years War, 1757–1762', *British Journal for Eighteenth-Century Studies*, 12 (1989), pp. 178–79.

18. Marquis de Vogüé (ed.), *Mémoires de maréchal de Villars* (6 vols, Paris, 1884–1904), V, p. 96; Le Coq to Augustus, 22 July 1727, Dresden, 2676, 18a.

19. Le Coq to Augustus, 19, 26 August 1727, Dresden, 2676, 18a.

20. Townshend to Waldegrave, 2 July (os) 1727, PRO, SP 80/62.

21. Du Bourgay, envoy in London, to Townshend, 9 August 1727, PRO, SP 90/22; Le Coq to Augustus, 25 July 1727, Dresden, 2676, 18a; Hanoverian Council to George, 5 August 1727, Hanover, Cal. Brief. 11, EI 274 M.

22. Townshend to Du Bourgay, 14 July (os), 19 September (os) 1727, PRO, SP 90/22; Newcastle to Horatio Walpole, 16 October (os) 1727, BL, Add. MS 32752.

23. Delafaye to Horatio Walpole, 8 August (os) 1727, PRO, SP 78/187; M. Hughes, 'The Imperial Supreme Judicial Authority under the Emperor

Charles VI and the Crises in Mecklenburg and East Frisia' (unpublished
Ph.D. thesis, London, 1969), p. 366; draft instructions for Horatio Walpole,
– 1727, PRO, SP 78/187, fols 1–7.

24. Le Coq report, 12 December 1727, Dresden, 2676, 18a, fols 412–13.
25. Townshend to William Finch, 12 December (os) 1727, PRO, SP 84/294.
26. Marquis Scaramuccia Visconti, an Austrian diplomat in London, to the
    Austrian Chancellor, Count Sinzendorf, 13 January 1728, HHStA, EK. 65;
    Count Berkentin, Danish envoy in Vienna, to -, 17 March 1728, PRO, SP
    80/326.
27. George's undated comment on letter from Newcastle of 31 October (os)
    1728, PRO, SP 36/8.
28. Townshend to George II, 1 October (os) 1729, PRO, SP 103/110.
29. Coxe, *Walpole*, I, p. 335.
30. Sydney to Philip, 2nd Earl Hardwicke, undated, New Haven, Connecticut,
    Beinecke Library, Osborn Files, Sydney.
31. Horatio Walpole to Stephen Poyntz, 21 January (os) 1730, Coxe, *Walpole*,
    II, p. 667.
32. J. M. Black, *The Collapse of the Anglo-French Alliance, 1727–1731* (Gloucester,
    1987), pp. 156–57.
33. Reichenbach to Friedrich Wilhelm von Grumbkow, Prussian minister, 24,
    28 March 1730, Hull, University Library, DDHO 3/3.
34. NAS, GD 150/3474/21.
35. C. S. Cowper (ed.), *The Diary of Mary, Countess Cowper, 1714–1720* (1864),
    p. 164.
36. BL, Add. MS 47033, fol. 62.
37. Robert to Horatio Walpole, 6 August (os) 1736, BL, Add. MS 63749,
    fol. 253.
38. Newcastle to Earl of Carlisle, 7 November (os) 1727, Castle Howard J8/1/817;
    Walpole to William, 3rd Duke of Devonshire, 4 December 1737, Chats-
    worth, Devonshire MS, 1st series, box 2, 114.9.
39. Sir James Lowther to John Spedding, 18 November (os) 1740, Carlisle,
    Cumbria CRO, D/Lons./W.
40. Zamboni to Haslang, 5 January 1742, Munich, London 370.
41. *The Lives of Dr Edward Pocock, Dr Zacharay Pearce, Dr Thomas Newton
    and the Rev. Philip Shelton* (2 vols, 1816), II, pp. 49, 69–70.
42. Earl of Cholmondely to Walpole, 5 November (os) 1744, BL, Add. MS
    63749A, fol. 339.
43. Sandon Hall, Harrowby papers, 21 R. 144.
44. C. Duffy, *The '45* (2003). All dates in this and the previous paragraph are
    old style.

45. M. Whitelock, *The Peace Offering. An Essay shewing the cession of Hanover to be the only probable means for extinguishing the present rebellion* (1746).

46. Digby to Hanbury-Williams, 10 November 1756, Farmington, Connecticut, Lewis Walpole Library, Hanbury-Williams papers, vol. 63, fol. 49.

47. Devonshire to Cumberland, 5 May 1757, J. C. D. Clark, *The Dynamics of Change: The Crisis of the 1750s and English Party Systems* (Cambridge, 1982), p. 374.

48. Nottingham University Library, Clumber papers (hereafter NeC), no. 3158; Duchess of Newcastle to her father, Francis, 2nd Earl of Godolphin, 15 June 1757, Northampton, CRO F(M)G 808.

49. *Hervey*, particularly pp. 261, 750–52.

50. George Tilson to Robert Trevor, 7 August 1736, Aylesbury, Buckinghamshire CRO, Trevor papers, vol. 4, no. 20.

51. Ryder diary, 2 December 1753, Sandon Hall, Harrowby papers; Newcastle to Pelham, 25 October 1750, BL, Add. MS 35411, fol. 189.

52. *Egmont*, I, p. 228.

53. New Haven, Beinecke Library, Osborn Shelves, Stair Letters, no. 22.

54. Horatio Walpole to Edward Weston, 3 July 1739, Farmington, Lewis Walpole Library, Weston papers, vol. 12.

55. Newcastle to Münchhausen, 10 October 1757, Hanover, Des. 91, G. A. Münchhausen I Nr 36, fol. 7.

56. Haslang to Count Preysing, 7 January 1757, Munich, London 233.

57. Mirepoix, 'Portrait de la Cour d'Angleterre', – November 1751, AE, Mémoires et Documents Ang. 51, fols 154–61; Newcastle to Hardwicke, 6 September 1751, BL, Add. MS 35412, fol. 3.

58. Holdernesse to Newcastle, 29 June 1755, BL, Add. MS 32856, fol. 380.

59. Frederick William I to Börck, Prussian envoy in London, 19 January 1736, BL, Add. MS 33007 fol. 28.

60. Bishop of Oxford to Hardwicke, enclosing Frederick's answer, 7 January (os) 1742, BL, Add. MS 35587, fols 2–5.

61. Mirepoix to Puysieulx, French Foreign Minister, 3 January 1750, AE, CP, Ang. 428, fol. 7.

62. Horace Walpole, *Memoirs of King George II*, edited by J. Brooke (3 vols, New Haven, 1985), I, p. 91.

63. Holdernesse to Andrew Mitchell, envoy in Berlin, 14 May 1756, PRO, SP 90/65.

64. Duchess of Newcastle to Earl of Lincoln, 23 May 1758, NeC 3154.

65. History of Parliament Trust, London, transcripts of the papers of James Harris, 13 May 1767.

66. Mirepoix to St Contest, French Foreign Minister, 10 January 1754, AE, CP, Ang. 437, fol. 21.

67. Perron, Sardinian envoy, to Charles Emmanuel III, 13 December 1753, AST, LM. Ing. 57; Fox to the 4th Duke of Devonshire, 27 March 1756, HP.; Viry, Sardinian envoy, to Charles Emmanuel III, 2 August, 6 September 1757, 13 June 1758, AST, LM. Ing. 62–63; Hardenberg, 21 November 1758, Marburg 257.

68. Frederick II to Michell, Prussian envoy in London, 6 March 1753, *Polit. Corresp.* IX, p. 363.

69. Lady Anson to Marchioness Grey, 12 October 1751, Bedford, CRO, Lucas papers, L 30/9/3/31.

70. Frederick to Michell, 10 September 1754, *Polit. Corresp*, X, p. 422; Fox to Devonshire, 5 February 1756, HP.

71. Viry to Charles Emmanuel III, 8 September 1755, AST. LM. Ing. 59.

72. Mirepoix to Rouillé, French Foreign Minister, 22 March, 7 June 1755, AE, CP, Ang. 438, fol. 305, 439, fol. 169.

73. Newcastle to Hardwicke, 19 October 1758, BL, Add. MS 35418, fol. 45.

74. Newcastle to Hardwicke, 15 October 1759, BL, Add. MS 32897, fol. 87.

75. Pitt to Newcastle, 28 January 1758, BL, Add. MS 35417, fols 187–88.

76. Newcastle to Hardwicke, 30 June 1759, BL, Add. MS 35418, fol. 188.

77. Newcastle to -, 28 October 1760, BL, Add. MS 32913, fol. 399; Carteret to Lady Sophia, 30 October 1760, Bod, MS. Lyell. empt. 35; Elizabeth Montagu to George, Lord Lyttelton, 31 October, Sarah Stanley to Elizabeth Montagu, 7 December 1760, HL, Montagu papers 1404, 5084.

78. Holdernesse to Mitchell, 11 May 1756, PRO, SP 90/65.

79. Paris, Bibliothèque Nationale, novelles acquisitions français 10716, fol. 12.

80. J. B. Owen, 'George II Reconsidered', in A. Whiteman, J. S. Bromley and P. G. M. Dickson (eds), *Statesmen, Scholars and Merchants: Essays in Eighteenth-Century History* (Oxford, 1973), pp. 113–34; J. Black, 'George II Reconsidered: A Consideration of George's Influence in the Conduct of Foreign Policy in the First Years of his reign', *Mitteilungen des Österreichischen Staatsarchivs*, 35 (1982), pp. 35–56; A. Newman, *The World Turned Inside Out: New Views on George II* (Leicester, 1988); J.Black, '"George II and All That Stuff": On the value of the Neglected', *Albion*, 35 (2004).

## Notes to Chapter 6: George III

1. George III to John Robinson, 2 August 1772, BL, Add. MS 37833, fol. 1.

2. J. Bullion, 'The Prince's Mentor: A New Perspective on the Friendship between George III and Lord Bute during the 1750s', *Albion*, 21 (1989),

pp. 34–55, and 'The Origins and Significance of Gossip about Princess Augusta and Lord Bute, 1755–1756', in P. B. Craddock and C. H. Hay (eds), *Studies in Eighteenth-Century Culture* (East Lansing, Michigan, 1991), pp. 245–65.

3. Tilson to Delafaye, 11 December 1723, PRO, SP 43/5, fol. 339.

4. P. D. G. Thomas, '"Thoughts on the British Constitution" by George III in 1760', *Bulletin of the Institute of Historical Research*, 60 (1987), pp. 361–63, and *George III: King and Politicians 1760–1770* (Manchester, 2002), p. 3.

5. Bute to Legge, no date but late 1759, Manchester, John Rylands Library, Eng. MS 668. More generally, J. L. McKelvey, *George III and Bute: The Leicester House Years* (Durham, North Carolina, 1973).

6. Mount Stuart, papers of 3rd Earl of Bute. See also R. R. Sedgwick (ed.), *Letters from George III to Lord Bute, 1756–1766* (1939), p. 11.

7. George III, draft, BL, Add. MS 32684, fol. 121.

8. George III to Münchhausen, 23 June 1749, in German, enclosing note, in English to George II of same date, BL, Add. MS 32684, fol. 80.

9. Haslang, Wittelsbach envoy in London, to Zeedhuitz, Palatine foreign minister, 30 June 1769, Munich, London 247.

10. Chesterfield to Richard Chenevix, Bishop of Waterford, 12 September 1761, Bloomington, Indiana, Lilly Library, Chesterfield MS, Chesterfield-Chenevix correspondence volume.

11. G. S. Rousseau, '"This Grand and Sacred Solemnity": Of Coronations, Republics, and Poetry', *British Journal for Eighteenth-Century Studies*, 5 (1982), pp. 9–12.

12. AE, CP, Ang. 450, fol. 337.

13. P. D. Brown and K. W. Schweizer (eds), *The Devonshire Diary: William Cavendish, Fourth Duke of Devonshire, Memoranda on State of Affairs* (1982), p. 43.

14. J. Bullion, '"George, Be a King!": The Relationship between Princess Augusta and George III', in S. Taylor, R. Connors and C. Jones (eds), *Hanoverian Britain and Empire* (Woodbridge, 1998), pp. 177–97.

15. Sedgwick (ed.), *Letters from George III*, p. 233.

16. D. Jarrett, 'The Regency Crisis of 1765', *English Historical Review*, 85 (1970), pp. 282–315.

17. F. O'Gorman, 'The Myth of Lord Bute's Secret Influence', in K. W. Schweizer (ed.), *Lord Bute. Essays in Re-interpretation* (Leicester, 1988), pp. 57–81.

18. George, Lord Lyttelton to Elizabeth Montagu, 14 October 1761, HL, Montagu papers, no. 1297.

19. I. R. Christie, 'The Changing Nature of Parliamentary Politics, 1742–1789', in J. Black (ed.), *British Politics and Society from Walpole to Pitt, 1742–1789* (1990), p. 114.

20. Reynolds to Grantham, 20 July 1773, Bedford, Bedfordshire CRO, Lucas papers 30/14/326/2.

21. Stanley to Lady Spencer, 29 June 1773, BL, Add. MS 75688.

22. George III to North, 5 October 1778, RA, GEO/3089.

23. M. Kilburn, 'Royalty and Public in Britain, 1714–1789' (unpublished D.Phil. thesis, Oxford, 1997), p. 132.

24. Queen Charlotte's diary, 16, 17 September 1789, RA, GEO/Add. 43/1.

25. George III to North, 7, 29 January 1770, RA, GEO/934, 939.

26. George III to North, 13 November 1770, RA, GEO/1024.

27. George III to North, 20, 28 February 1770, RA, GEO/946, 948.

28. George III to Robinson, 7 October 1774, BL, Add. MS 70990.

29. George III to Robinson, 8 October 1774, BL, Add. MS 37833, fol. 4.

30. Robinson to George III, 11 October 1775, BL, Add. MS 37833, fol. 17.

31. Robinson to George III, 2 November 1775, BL, Add. MS 37833, fol. 18.

32. Robinson to George III, 25 June 1776, BL, Add. MS 37833, fol. 20.

33. George III to Robinson, 14 September 1776, BL, Add. MS 37833, fol. 28.

34. George III to Robinson, 22 September 1780, BL, Add. MS 70990.

35. BL, Egerton MS 982, fol. 12.

36. Sir John Fortescue, *The Correspondence of King George the Third* (6 vols, 1928), III, p. 153.

37. Fortescue, *George the Third*, III, pp. 265–72.

38. Fortescue, *George the Third*, III, p. 406.

39. George III to North, 28 November, 6 December 1770, RA, GEO/1037, 1040.

40. George III to North, 13 October, 14 November 1778, RA, GEO/3094, 3116.

41. Fortescue, *George the Third*, IV, p. 54–88.

42. Fortescue, *George the Third*, IV, pp. 139–40.

43. George III to John Robinson, Joint-Secretary to the Treasury, 6 September 1780, BL, Add. MS 70990, fol. 8.

44. P. Mansel, *Prince of Europe: The Life of Charles-Joseph de Ligne* (2003), p. 105.

45. George III to Pitt, 23 December 1783, PRO, 30/8/103, fol. 14.

46. George III to Pitt, 13 January 1784, PRO, 30/8/103, fol. 30.

47. V. Green, *The History and Antiquities of the City and Suburbs of Worcester* (2 vols, 1796), I, p. 297.

48. George III to Pitt, 11 December 1787, Cambridge, University Library, Department of Manuscripts, vol. 6958 no. 437.

49. I. Macalpine and R. Hunter, *George III and the Mad Business* (1969) and,

more clearly, in J. Röhl, M. Warren, and D. Hunt, *Purple Secret: Genes, 'Madness' and the Royal Houses of Europe* (2nd edn, 1999).

50. George III to North, 30 November, 2 December 1778, RA, GEO/3129–30.
51. Hiley to Henry Addington, 15 November 1788, 152 M/C 1788/F36.
52. Henry to Anthony Addington, 8 February 1789, 152 M/C 1789/F9; J. W. Derry, *The Regency Crisis and the Whigs, 1788–9* (Cambridge, 1963); J. Brooke, *King George III* (1972), pp. 302–41; T. C. W. Blanning and C. Haase, 'Kurhannover, der Kaiser und die Regency Crisis von 1788/89', *Blätter für Landesgeschichte*, 113 (1979), pp. 432–49, and 'George III, Hanover and the Regency Crisis', in J. Black (ed.), *Knights Errant*, pp. 135–50; Black, *British Foreign Policy in an Age of Revolutions*, p. 199; George III to ?, 5 April 1789, *McDowell and Stern Catalogue* no. 27, p. 5.
53. Ralph Payne to Malmesbury, 1, 9 October 1789, Winchester, Hampshire RO, Malmesbury papers, vol. 162. John Brooke, however, refers to 'complete' recovery and subsequent 'good health', pp. 343, 374, and see Henry to Anthony Addington, 7 December 1789, 152 M/C 1789/F7.
54. Queen Charlotte's diary, 15 September 1789, RA, GEO/Add 43/1.
55. Auckland to Lord Grenville, Foreign Secretary, 26 November 1792, BL, Add. MS 58920, fol. 178.
56. George III to -, 8 October 1791, *Maggs Catalogue* 1292, p. 49, item no. 79.
57. George III to Grenville, 9 February 1793, BL, Add. MS 58857, fol. 87.
58. *Maggs Catalogue* 1345, item no. 86.
59. Queen Charlotte's diary, 5, 16, 26 September, 24 October, 7 November 1794, RA, GEO/Add. 43/3.
60. Grenville to Wellesley, 20 February 1801, BL, Add. MS 70927, fol. 80.
61. North to George III and reply, both 21 December 1778, RA, GEO/3160–1.
62. L. G. Mitchell, *Charles James Fox* (Oxford, 1992), p. 194.
63. George III to Richard Grenville, 29 August 1786, BL, Add. MS 70956.
64. L. J. Colley, 'The Apotheosis of George III: Loyalty, Royalty and the British Nation, 1760–1820', *Past and Present*, 102 (1984), pp. 94–129, and *Britons: Forging the Nation, 1707–1837* (New Haven, 1992), pp. 206–30.
65. Reynolds to Lord Grantham, 20 July 1773, Bedford, Bedfordshire CRO, Lucas papers 30/14/326/2; O. Hedley, *Queen Charlotte* (1975).
66. K. Sloan (ed.), *Enlightenment. Discovering the World in the Eighteenth Century* (2003), especially, pp. 38–44, 122, 127–29, 152–60.
67. J. B. Sidgwick, *William Herschel: Explorer of the Heavens* (1953).
68. H. Hoock, *The King's Artists: The Royal Academy of Arts and the Politics of British Culture, 1760–1840* (Oxford, 2003), pp. 28–29; J. Roberts, *Views of Windsor: Watercolours by Thomas and Paul Sandby* (1995); Roberts (ed.), *George III and Queen Charlotte. Patronage, Collecting and Court Taste* (2004).

69. W. Weber, *The Rise of Musical Classics in England* (Oxford, 1992), pp. 223–42.

70. Green, *Worcester*, I, 296–300.

71. D. Watkin, *The Architect King. George III and the Culture of the Enlightenment* (2004).

72. H. B. Carter, *His Majesty's Spanish Flock: Sir Joseph Banks and the Merinos of George III of England* (Sydney, 1964).

73. London report in *Berrow's Worcester Journal*, 30 October 1788.

74. *Berrow's Worcester Journal*, 27 November 1788.

75. M. Morris, 'The Royal Family and Family Values in Late Eighteenth-Century Britain', *Journal of Family History*, 21 (1996), pp. 519–32, and *The British Monarchy and the French Revolution* (New Haven, 1998).

76. G. Cornwallis-West, *The Life and Letters of Admiral Cornwallis* (1927), p. 30.

77. George III to Richard Grenville, 29 December 1780, BL, Add. MS 70956.

78. George III to Frederick, Duke of York, 29 December 1780, RA, GEO/16222.

79. J. Simon (ed.), *Handel: A Celebration of his Life and Times, 1685–1759* (1985), p. 251.

80. George III to North, 20 April 1770, RA, GEO/969.

81. George III to Lord Thurlow, Lord Chancellor, 23 November 1791, *Maggs Catalogue* 1173 (1994), p. 34, item no. 76.

82. Green, *Worcester* I, 297.

83. BL, Add. MS 34887, fol. 155.

84. Queen Charlotte's diary, 25 January 1794, RA, GEO/Add. 43/3.

85. George III to his sister, Augusta, Duchess of Brunswick, 6 October 1806, RA, GEO/12452.

## Notes to Chapter 7: George IV

1. V. Carretta, *George III and the Satirists from Hogarth to Byron* (Athens, Georgia, 1990); D. Donald, *The Age of Caricature: Satirical Prints in the Reign of George III* (New Haven, 1996).

2. Addington to Earl Talbot, 13 February 1820, 152M/C 1820/OH 67; E. Holt, *The Public and Domestic Life of His Most Gracious Majesty George the Third* (2 vols, 1820).

3. *The Martial Face: the Military Portrait in Britain, 1760–1800* (catalogue and exhibition at Brown University, 1991), p. 87.

4. A. Leslie, *Mrs Fitzherbert* (1960).

5. A. Plowden, *Caroline and Charlotte: The Regent's Wife and Daughter 1795–1821* (1989); F. Fraser, *The Unruly Queen: The Life of Queen Caroline* (1996).

6. W. Cobbett, *A History of the Regency and Reign of George IV* (1830), p.425.
7. Addington to Wellington, 21 March, Anon. to Addington, undated, Marquess of Salisbury to Addington, 12 September, Addington to Sir Benjamin Bloomfield, 19 September, Addington to George IV, 21, 22, 25, 26, 28 September 1820, 152M/C 1820/OH 68, 76, 80, 82–87.
8. Kenyon to Addington, 6 July, 8 August 1820, 152M/C 1820/OR 37, 46.
9. Testimonies, undated, 152M/C 1820/OR 53.
10. Sheffield to Addington, 20 November 1820, 152M/C 1820/OR 66.
11. Castlereagh to Addington, 5 December 1820, 152M/C 1820/OR 81.
12. E. A. Smith, *A Queen on Trial: The Affair of Queen Caroline* (Stroud, 1993).
13. Caroline to Addington, 11 July, and reply, 13 July, Caroline to George IV, 17 July, and reply, 20 July 1821, 152M/C 1821/OR 3, 5, 13, 15.
14. Bishop of Hereford to Addington, 25 July 1821, 152M/C 1821/OR 21.
15. Henry Hobhouse, Under Secretary in the Home Department, to Addington, 6 August 1821, 152M/C 1821/OR 25.
16. Liverpool to George IV, 8 August, Liverpool to Addington, 8 August, Addington to Liverpool, 9 August, Hobhouse to Addington, 12 August, Addington to Liverpool, 15 August 1821, 152M/C 1821/OR 31–32, 34, 38, 51.
17. Addington to Liverpool, 11, 27 August 1821, 152M/C 1821/OR 37, 72.
18. Addington to Liverpool, 11 August 1821, 152M/C 1821/OR 37.
19. Addington to Liverpool, 29 August 1821, 152M/C 1821/OR 73.
20. Clancarty to Addington, 1 October 1821, 152M/C 1821/OR 80.
21. Londonderry to Addington, 10 October 1821, 152M/C 1821/OR 82.
22. Londonderry to Addington, 16 October, Sir William Knighton to Londonderry, 16 October 1821, 152M/C 1821/OR 85–86.
23. Londonderry to Addington, 21, 24 October 1821, 152M/C 1821/OR 89, 90 (quote).
24. H. Temperley, *The Foreign Policy of Canning, 1822–27* (1925), pp. 242, 250–51.
25. G. Finley, *Turner and George the Fourth in Edinburgh 1822* (1981); J. Prebble, *The King's Jaunt: George IV in Scotland, August 1822* (1989).
26. *Maggs Catalogue*, 1345, no. 88.
27. Addington to Earl Talbot, 3, 13 February 1820, 152M/C 1820/OI 8, OH 67.
28. Liverpool to Addington, 28 July 1820, 152M/C 1820/OR 44.
29. Catalogues of exhibitions at the Queen's Gallery, Buckingham House: *Carlton House: The Past Glories of George IV's Palace* and *George IV and the Arts of France.* For George's patronage of Nash, D. J. Olsen, *Town Planning in London: The Eighteenth and Nineteenth Centuries* (New Haven, 1982).
30. 152M/C 1821/OR 71.
31. P. Mansel, *The Court of France, 1789–1830* (Cambridge, 1988).

32. E. A. Smith, *George IV* (1999). For a much harsher view, S. Parissien, *George IV: The Grand Entertainment* (2001), especially pp. 381–83.

33. Wellington to Knighton, 29 May 1827, draft, Southampton, University Library, Wellington papers. Knighton's papers were destroyed by his widow.

34. 'My dear boy ...' in some accounts.

## Notes to Chapter 8: William IV

1. On the King, see P. Ziegler, *King William IV* (1971); T. Pocock, *Sailor King: The Life of King William IV* (1991).

2. M. Lincoln, *Representing the Royal Navy: British Sea Power, 1750–1815* (Aldershot, 2002), p. 59.

3. George III to Sir Samuel Hood, 13 June 1779, BL, RP 2283; George III to Colonel Richard Grenville, 6 February 1781, BL, Add. MS 70956.

4. George III to Grenville, 1, 15 July 1783, George III to Prince William, 13 February 1784, BL, Add. MS 70956, 2382.

5. N. A. M. Rodger, *The Admiralty* (Lavenham, 1979), p. 95.

6. William IV to Sir James Graham, 1st Lord of the Admiralty, 21 January, 1 February, 16 March 1834, BL, Add. MS 79595–96.

7. N. Gash, *Pillars of Government and Other Essays on State and Policy, c. 1770–c. 1880* (1986), p. 106.

8. P. Ziegler, *Melbourne* (1976), p. 17.

9. Earl Grey (ed.), *The Correspondence of the late Earl Grey with His Majesty King William IV and with Sir Henry Taylor* (2 vols, 1867), II, pp. 351, 364.

10. N. Gash, *Reaction and Reconstruction in English Politics, 1832–1852* (Oxford, 1965), pp. 20–21.

11. Wellington to Lord Lyndhurst, 15 October 1836, Cardiff, Glamorgan Record Office, DLY/19/151.

12. J. Ingamells, *A Dictionary of British and Irish Travellers in Italy, 1701–1800* (New Haven, 1997), p. 260.

13. J. C. G. Röhl, M. Warren and D. Hunt, *Purple Secret. Genes, 'Madness' and the Royal Houses of Europe* (2nd edn, 1999), pp. 121–22.

14. C. Tomalin, *Mrs Jordan's Profession* (1994).

15. T. L. Hunt, *Defining John Bull: Political Caricature and National Identity in Late Georgian England* (Aldershot, 2003), pp. 263–64.

16. Ernest to Lord Lyndhurst, the Lord Chamcellor, 6 October 1845, Cardiff, Glamorgan Record Office, DLY/16/23.

17. E.g. re navy, William IV to Sir James Graham, 6 May 1833, and re diplomacy, William to Graham, 11 August 1833, BL, Add. MS 79596.

*Notes to Chapter 9: Hanover*

1. Townshend to Waldegrave, 16 February (os) 1729, PRO, SP 80/64.
2. Londonderry to Addington, 21 October 1821, 152M/C 1821/OR 89.
3. Townshend to Robert Walpole, 5 December 1723, PRO, SP 43/5 fols 312–13.
4. *Old England*, 12 November (os) 1752.
5. Gansinot, Wittelsbach envoy in The Hague, to Count Ferdinand Plettenberg, chief minister of the Elector of Cologne, 28 April 1722, Münster, Staatsarchiv, Dep. Nordkirchen, Nachtr. B. 259 fols 123–4; Destouches to Dubois, 11, 21 May 1722, AE, CP, Ang. sup. 7 fol. 36, 341 fol. 87; James 'III and VIII' to George, Lord Lansdowne, 13 Ap. 1722, RA. Stuart Papers 59/5.
6. Benjamin Kennicott to Thomas Bray, no date, Exeter College, Oxford, Bray papers.
7. Bod, MS Don. c. 106, fol. 134.
8. H.-J. Finke, 'The Hanoverian Junta, 1714–1719' (unpublished Ph.D.thesis, University of Michigan, 1970).
9. Harrington to Robert Trevor, envoy at The Hague, 19, 23 January (os) 1739, PRO, SP 84/378 fols 71, 95.
10. Newcastle to Waldegrave, 27 February (os) 1728, George to Townshend, no date, BL, Add. MS 32754, 38507, fol. 232.
11. Copy of decree, PRO, SP 100/15; Hughes, *Imperial Supreme Judicial Authority*, pp. 380–81; Naumann, *Österreich, England und das Reich*, p. 140.
12. Townshend to Horatio Walpole, 31 July (os) 1728, Norwich, County Record Office, Bradfer-Lawrence Collection, Townshend State Papers and Letters.
13. Newcastle to the Plenipotentiaries, 15 July (os) 1728, PRO, SP 80/326.
14. Chesterfield to Townshend, 6 July 1728, PRO, SP 84/301.
15. D'Aix to Victor Amadeus II, 23 June 1729, AST, LM, Ing. 35; Chavigny to Chauvelin, 19 September 1729, AE, CP, Brunswick-Hanovre 47; Augustus II to Watsdorf, 12 October 1730, Dresden, 2676.
16. Townshend to Hotham, 16 April (os) 1730, PRO, SP 90/27; draft of instructions, BL, Add. 9147 fols 89–90.
17. *Craftsman*, 20 January (os), *York Courant*, 23 January (os) 1739.
18. Walpole to Trevor, 30 January (os) 1736, quote 24 October (os) 1738, Aylesbury, Buckinghamshire CRO, Trevor papers, vols 1, 15.
19. Robinson to Trevor, 20 May 1739, Farmington, Lewis Walpole Library, Weston papers, vol. 12.
20. Trevor to Poyntz, 21 December (os) 1729, BL, Add. 75450.
21. Newcastle to Gerlach Adolph von Münchhausen, 3 March (os) 1752, Hanover, Cal, Br 11, Nr, 2244 fol. 50; Newcastle to Pelham, 17 May, 26 July

1752, BL, Add. 35412, fols 91, 208; report from Justus Alt, Hesse-Cassel envoy, 7 August 1753, Marburg, Staatsarchiv, Bestand 4: Politische Akten nach Philipp d. Gr., Britain 254.

22. A detailed account of this intertwining is an important topic for future research, not least because the history of dynasties involves the history of all their branches.

23. Cobbett, XIII, pp. 562, 382–83.

24. Cobham to Newcastle, 9 December (os) 1743, BL, Add. 35587, fol. 205.

25. Hanbury Williams to Henry Fox, 17 June 1751, BL, Add. 51393, fol. 52.

26. On Britain, not Briton, see J. Brooke, *King George III* (1972), pp. 390–91. Brooke was not sure why the change came about, but as the colloquial pronunciation was Britun, so, in terms of sound, there would have been no distinction between the two spellings.

27. This began with S. Conrady, 'Die Wirksamkeit König Georgs III für die hannoverschen kurlande', *Niedersachsisches Jahrbuch für Landesgeschichte*, 39 (1969), pp. 150–91, and was greatly developed by T. C. W. Blanning in '"That Horrid Electorate" or "Ma Patrie Germanique"? George III, Hanover and the *Fürstenbund* of 1785', *Historical Journal*, 20 (1977), pp. 311–44. See most recently, chapter 2 'George III as a European Figure' in G. M. Ditchfield, *George III: An Essay in Monarchy* (2002), pp. 22–48.

28. Zeedhuitz to Haslang, Wittelsbach envoy in London, 11 June, 22 July, Haslang to Zeedhuitz, 30 June, 7 July, Munich, London 247.

29. Haslang to Beckers, Palatine Foreign Minister, 14 June, 19 August 1774, Beckers to Haslang, 10 December 1774, Ritter, envoy in Vienna, to Beckers, 27 April, 3, 24, 31 August, 7 September, 5, 26 October 1774, Munich, London 252, Wien 702; *Westminster Journal*, 3, 17 September, 1 October 1774.

30. Hugh Elliot to Keith, 11 August 1778, Joseph Yorke, envoy at The Hague, to Keith, 9 October 1778, Keith to Stormont, 4 December 1779, BL, Add. MS 35514, fol. 242, 35515, fol. 154, 35517, fol. 311.

31. Kaunitz to Kageneck, 9 March, 13 November 1784, HHStA, EK 129.

32. York to George III, 28 February 1785, Aspinall, *George III*, I, p. 178.

33. Draft in George's hand, RA, 6071. The dates at the top were written by former archivists; misfiled in accordance with one of these, 18 August 1785. In fact, an answer to Frederick II's memorandum of 19 February 1785 sent to York and forwarded by him to George on 28 February, Aspinall I, p. 178. This is the document mentioned by Blanning, '*Fürstenbund* of 1785', n. 71, though he suggests it was written by York.

34. Blanning, '*Fürstenbund* of 1785', pp. 321–26.

35. For example, *Daily Universal Register*, 2, 3, 5 January, 4, 15, 22, 26 July, 14 August, 1 September 1786.

36. Kageneck to Kaunitz, 18, 25 October 1785, Kaunitz to Reviczky, 27 July 1786, HHStA, EK 124, 129; K. Aretin, *Heiliges Römisches Reich, 1776–1806: Reichsverfassung und Staatssouveränität* (2 vols, Wiesbaden, 1967), I, p. 178.

37. J. W. Marcum, 'Vorontsov and Pitt: The Russian Assessment of a British Statesman, 1785–1792', *Rocky Mountain Social Science Journal*, 10 (1973), pp. 50–51; York to George III, 1, 8 June 1787, Aspinall, *George III*, I, p. 370; F. C. Wittichen, *Preussen und England in der europäischen Politik, 1785–1788* (Heidelberg, 1902), p. 117.

38. Joseph Ewart, envoy in Berlin, to George Aust, senior clerk at the Foreign Office, 14 October 1791, private collection of the author, MS 695.

39. P. Glanvill, *The King's Silver: George III's Service in Hanover and England* (leaflet provided by National Trust, Waddesdon Manor, 2003).

40. G. S. Ford, *Hanover and Prussia, 1795–1803: A Study in Neutrality* (New York, 1903).

41. B. Simms, 'Charles James Fox, the Crown and British Policy during the Hanoverian Crisis of 1806', *Historical Journal*, 38 (1995), pp. 567–96.

42. W. D. Gruner, 'England, Hannover und der Deutsche Bund, 1814–1837', in A. M. Birke and K. Kluxen (eds), *England und Hannover* (Munich, 1986), pp. 81–126.

43. M. Bertram, '"Der Mondminister" und "General Killjoy": Ein Machtkampf im Hintergrund der Ernennung des Herzogs Adolph Friedrich von Cambridge zum Generalgouverneur von Hanover (1813–1816)', *Niedersächsischers Jahrbuch für Geschichte*, 65 (1993), pp. 213–62.

44. C. Webster, *The Foreign Policy of Palmerston, 1830–1841* (2 vols, 1951), I, pp. 27–28.

45. William Hutt, *The Stade Duties Considered* (1839) and 'The Stade Duties Considered', *Edinburgh Review* (1842), pp. 359–75.

46. E. Schubert, 'Die Schlacht bei Langensalza', in R. Sabellek (ed.), *Hannovers Übergang vom Königreich zur preussischen Provinz: 1866* (Hanover, 1995), pp. 101–23.

47. P. H. H. Draeger, 'Great Britain and Hanover, 1830–66' (unpublished Ph.D. thesis, University of Cambridge, 1998), p. 416.

*Notes to Chapter 10: Achievement*

1. Chesterfield to Bute, 9 April 1761, Mount Stuart, Cardiff papers, 6/82.
2. See, most recently, J. Miller, *The Stuarts* (2004).
3. Perron to Charles Emmanuel III, 9 September 1751, AST, LM, Ing. 56.
4. Sir John Fortescue, *The Correspondence of King George the Third* (6 vols, 1928) I, pp. 114–15, 172–73.

5. Newcastle to John White, 4 June 1765, BL, Add. MS 33003, fol. 5.

6. P. D. Brown and K. W. Schweizer (eds), *The Devonshire Diary: William Cavendish, Fourth Duke of Devonshire, Memoranda on State of Affairs* (1982), pp. 54, 60.

7. Bath to Elizabeth Montagu, 15 June 1762, HL, Montagu papers, 4260.

8. Richmond to Rockingham, 22 January 1771, WW, RI–1352.

9. Cobbett, XI, p. 732.

10. George III to North, 10 November 1778, RA, GEO/3112.

11. J. C. Sainty, *Peerage Creations, 1649–1800* (1998); J. Cannon, *Aristocratic Century* (Cambridge, 1984).

12. Bloomfield to Addington, 28 November 1820, 152M/C 1820/OH 91.

13. George IV to Lord Chancellor Lyndhurst, 22 August 1827, Cardiff, Glamorgan Record Office, DLY/16/22. Denman case, DLY/13/1–9.

14. Liverpool to Addington, 25 September 1821, 152M/C 1821/OR 79.

15. Andrew Stone to Henry Pelham, 26 June 1748, NeC 596.

16. J. Roberts, 'Sir William Chambers and George III', in J. Harris and M. Snodin (eds), *Sir William Chambers: Architect to George III* (New Haven, 1996), pp. 41–54.

17. *Berrow's Worcester Journal*, 31 July 1788.

18. George Huntingford, master of the school at Warminster, to Addington, 17 September 1789, 152 M/C 1789/F12.

19. 152M/C 1815/OR 111–114.

20. P. Mansel, 'Monarchy, Uniform and the Rise of the Frac', *Past and Present*, 96 (1982), pp. 103–32.

21. N. Smith, *The Royal Image and the English People* (Aldershot, 2001), p. 170.

22. R. Butterwick, *Poland's Last King and English Culture: Stanislaw August Poniatowski, 1732–1798* (Oxford, 1998), pp. 317–18.

23. BL, Add. MS 47028, fol. 257.

24. William IV to Sir Graham, 1st Lord of the Admiralty, 30 August 1833, BL, Add. MS 79596.

25. J. Wardroper, *Wicked Ernest* (2002), p. 200.

# Selected Reading

All works published in London unless otherwise stated.

Arkell, R. L., *Caroline of Ansbach. George the Second's Queen* (1939).

Aspinall, A. (ed.), *The Letters of the Princess Charlotte, 1811–1817* (1949).

Aspinall, A. (ed.), *The Correspondence of George, Prince of Wales, 1770–1812* (8 vols, 1963–71).

Aspinall, A. (ed.), *The Later Correspondence of George III* (5 vols, 1966–70).

Aspinall, A. (ed.), *The Letters of King George IV, 1812–1830* (3 vols, Cambridge, 1938).

Ayling, S., *George the Third* (1972).

Baldwin, D., *The Chapel Royal. Ancient and Modern* (1990).

Barnes, D. G., *George III and William Pitt* (New York, 1965).

Barrell, J., *Imagining the King's Death: Figurative Treason. Fantasies of Regicide 1793–1796* (Oxford, 2000).

Beattie, J. W., *The English Court in the Reign of George I* (Cambridge, 1967).

Bertram, M., *Georg II: König und Kurfürst* (Göttingen, 2003).

Bertram, *Das Königreich Hannover: Kleine Geschichte eines vergangenen deutschen Staates* (Hanover, 2003).

Birke, A. M. and Kluxen, K. (eds), *England und Hannover* (Munich, 1986).

Brooke, J. (ed.), *Memoirs of the Reign of George II by Horace Walpole* (3 vols, New Haven, 1985).

Brooke, J., *King George the Third* (1972).

Brown, P. D., and Schweizer, K. W. (eds), *The Devonshire Diary, William Cavendish, Fourth Duke of Devonshire, Memoranda on State of Affairs* (1982).

Butterfield, H., *George III and the Historians* (1957).

Cannon, J. (ed.), *The Letters of Junius* (Oxford, 1978).

Carlton, C., *Royal Warriors: A Military History of the British Monarchy* (Harlow, 2003).

Carretta, V., *George III and the Satirists from Hogarth to Byron* (Athens, Georgia, 1990).

Clark, J. C. D., *English Society, 1688–1832* (Cambridge, 1985).

Clark, J. C. D. (ed.), *The Memoirs and Speeches of James, 2nd Earl Waldegrave, 1742–1763* (Cambridge, 1988).

Colvin, H. M. et al., *The History of the King's Works*, V, *1660–1782* (1976).

Cowper, M., *Diary of Mary Countess Cowper, Lady of the Bedchamber to the Princess of Wales, 1714–1720* (1864).

Crook, J. M. and Port, M. H., *The History of the King's Works*, VI, *1782–1851* (1973).

Dann, U., *Hanover and Great Britain, 1740–1760* (Leicester, 1991).

Davies, J. D. G., *A King in Toils* (1938).

De-la-Noy, M., *The King Who Never Was: The Story of Frederick, Prince of Wales* (1996).

Derry, J. W., *The Regency Crisis and the Whigs, 1788–9* (Cambridge, 1963).

Ditchfield, Grayson, *George III: An Essay in Monarchy* (2003).

Donald, D., *The Age of Caricature: Satirical Prints in the Reign of George III* (New Haven, 1996).

Donne, W. B. (ed.), *The Correspondence of King George the Third with Lord North* (2 vols, 1867).

Edwards, A., *Frederick Louis, Prince of Wales* (1947).

Fortescue, J. W. (ed.), *The Correspondence of King George the Third* (6 vols, 1927–28).

Fraser, F., *The Unruly Queen: The Life of Queen Caroline* (1996).

Fulford, R., *The Royal Dukes: The Father and Uncles of Queen Victoria, 1782–1851* (2nd edn, 1973).

Gregg, E., *Queen Anne* (1980).

Hartshorne, A., *Memoirs of a Royal Chaplain* (1905).

Hatton, R. M., *George I: Elector and King* (1978).

Hatton, R. M., *The Anglo-Hanoverian Connection, 1714–1760* (1982).

Hedley, O., *Queen Charlotte* (1975).

Hibbert, C., *George IV* (1988).

Hibbert, C., *George III: A Personal History* (1998).

Jarrett, D. (ed.), *Memoirs of the Reign of King George III by Horace Walpole* (4 vols, New Haven, 2000).

Konig, P., *The Hanoverian Kings and their Homeland* (1993).

Macalpine, I., and Hunter, R., *George III and the Mad-Business* (1969).

McKelvey, J. L., *George III and Bute: The Leicester House Years* (Durham, North Carolina, 1973).

Morris, M., *The British Monarchy and the French Revolution* (New Haven, 1998).

Newman, A., *The World Turned Inside Out: New Views on George II* (Leicester, 1988).

Oberschelp, R., *Politische Geschichte Niedersachsens, 1714–1803* (Hildesheim, 1983).

Orr, C. C. (ed.), *Queenship in Britain 1660–1837: Royal Patronage, Court Culture and Dynastic Politics* (Manchester, 2002).

Pares, R., *King George III and the Politicians* (Oxford, 1953).

Parissien, S., *George IV: The Grand Entertainment* (2001).

Plumb, J. H., *The First Four Georges* (1956).

Plumb, J. H. and Weldon, H., *Royal Heritage: The Story of Britain's Royal Builders* (1977).

Pocock, T., *Sailor King: The Life of King William IV* (1991).

Portzek, H., *Friedrich der Grosse und Hannover in ihrem gegenseitigen Urteil(Hildesheim, 1958)*.

Prochaska, F., *Royal Bounty: The Making of a Welfare Monachy* (New Haven, 1995).

Prochaska, F., *The Republic of Britain, 1760–2000* (2000).

Reitan, E. A., *George III: Tyrant or Constitutional Monarch?* (Boston, 1964).

Richter-Uhlig, U., *Hof und Politik unter den Bedingungen der Personalunion: Die Aufenthalte Georgs II in Hanover zwischen 1729 und 1741* (Hanover, 1992).

Schweizer, K. W. (ed.), *Lord Bute: Essays in Re-Interpretation* (Leicester, 1988).

Sedgwick, R. R. (ed.), *Memoirs of the Reign of George II, by John, Lord Hervey* (3 vols, 1931).

Sedgwick, R. R. (ed.), *The Letters from George III to Lord Bute, 1756–66* (1939).

Smith, E. A., *George IV* (1999).

Trench, C. C., *George II* (1973).

Walpole, H. *see* Brooke, J., and Jarrett, D.

Ward. A. W., *Great Britain and Hanover* (Oxford, 1899).

Wilkins, W. H., *Caroline the Illustrious: Queen Consort of George II* (1901).

Yorke, P. C., *The Life and Correspondence of Philip Yorke, Earl of Hardwicke* (3 vols, Cambridge, 1913).

Young, G., *Poor Fred: The People's Prince* (1937).

Ziegler, P., *King William IV* (1971).

# Index